ror

Office

Campaigning in the Gay Nineties

**Edited by
Kathleen DeBold**

GAY AND
LESBIAN **VICTORY FUND**

*A political resource directory of the
Gay and Lesbian Victory Fund
1012 14th Street NW, Suite 707
Washington, DC 20005.
(202)842-8679*

Editors' Note

A listing in *Out for Office* is not meant to be an endorsement by the Gay and Lesbian Victory Fund. Those who appear in this edition responded to our written request to be included. We apologize for any omissions in the listings and would appreciate corrections and updates to any entries. Please see page 287 for a listing form for future issues of *Out for Office* and other Victory Fund publications.

ISBN # 1-883665-01-9

Library of Congress Catalog Card Number: 93-80847

Published by the Gay and Lesbian Victory Fund, a nonprofit, nonpartisan Federal political action committee, 1012 14th Street NW, Suite 707, Washington, DC 20005 U.S.A. Manufactured in the United States of America.

There is a major difference between a friend and a gay person in office. It's not enough just to have friends represent us, no matter how good those friends may be. We must give people the chance to judge us by our own leaders, and our own legislators.

– Harvey Milk

Reprinted with permission from the Estate of Harvey Milk.

*This book is dedicated to the memory
of Harvey Milk, and to all openly gay and lesbian
elected officials past and present.
To them we offer our heartfelt thanks;
to those who follow, our support, our
commitment and our votes.*

Table of Contents

Acknowledgements

WE wish to thank all the campaign professionals, political clubs and elected and appointed officials who are listed in this book. Your support and contributions are instrumental in electing qualified openly gay and lesbian people to public office.

Victory Fund staff Charles Cox, Van Do, Colleen Donnelly, Rick Ellsasser and William Waybourn for their long hours of hard work and for their unwavering efforts to win gay and lesbian equal rights.

Members of the Victory Fund Board of Directors, past - Roberta Bennett, Nancy Clack, David Detrick, Tim McFeeley, Avi Rome, Hilary Rosen, Van Alan Sheets and John Thomas — and present: Scott Hitt, Joy Tomchin, Howard Menaker, Andrew E. Barrer, Terry Bean, Mary Celeste, Jane Dolkart, Chuck Forrester, Jeffrey G. Gibson, Lynn Greer, Khadija Haynes, Fred McCall-Perez, David Mixner, Sharon Mylrea, Annise Parker, John Ramos, Thomas Reed, Joseph Steffan, Thomas Stoddard, David von Storch and Stephen Wood for their commitment and support.

Dedicated interns Tom McLaughlin, Donna Ortega, Laura Belmonte, Neal Fehrenbach, and volunteers Deanna New, Barbara Johnson and Craig Spaulding for their energy, enthusiasm and hard work.

Members of the Gay and Lesbian Victory Fund donor network for putting their money where their convictions are.

Barbara Grier of the Naiad Press, Sasha Alyson of Alyson Publications, Deacon McCubbin of Lambda Rising Bookstore, Annise Parker and Pokey Anderson of Inklings Bookstore, Jane Troxell of LAMMAS Bookstore, John Graves and Dennis Lonergan at Eidolon Communications, Melinda Taggart, Peter Kovar, Kevin James, Mike Verveer, Chris Riddiough, James Carville, Larry Bagneris, Eleanor Cooper, Bob Fraas, Kevin Ivers, Rocco Claps, Julie Davis, Sue Hibbard, Lee Lynch, Dee Flanagan, Babo Janssen, Craig McDaniel, Hope Forstenzer, Mark Wallem, Rodrick Dial, Alex Clemons, Zoon

Nguyen, Melissa Barker, Roberts Batson, Tom Brown, Tanya Domi, Will Woodruff, Larry Pickens and Amy Gerver for your help and invaluable advice.

The Estate of Harvey Milk, Tom Leavitt at Arcadia Press, Mike Bento at Ogilvy, Adams and Rinehart, S. Studios, which designed our cover, Jim Cramer, Lenn Mooney and the others at Rose Printing, which printed *Out for Office*, and Andrea and Rocky at Huff Printing and Copying.

Mandy Carter, Eric Rosenthal and Brian Albert for their campaign button collections.

Special appreciation goes to the sponsors (George Harris and Jack Evans, Michael Smith, Howard J. Cavalero, Capitol City Brewing Company, Carl Rosendorf, David Franco, Fentress Ott), patrons (Edith Dee Cofrin, David Geffen, Edward Gould, Charles Holmes, Jonathon Sheffer, The Colin Higgins Foundation) and Underwriters (Ron Ansin, Terry Watanabe, Andrew E. Barrer, Henry van Ameringen, Miller Brewing Company) who made this book possible.

Finally, special thanks to our friends and collaborators at the Human Rights Campaign Fund, Parents, Friends and Families of Lesbians and Gays, the National Organization for Women, People for the American Way, the National Gay and Lesbian Task Force, the International Network of Lesbian and Gay Officials, Lambda Legal Defense and Education Fund, Pro-Net, and the Log Cabin Republicans – it's great to have you on our side.

Preface

R UNNING for office as an openly lesbian or gay candidate is one of the greatest things you can do for
your country, your community and your own self-respect.
As lesbian and gay leaders assume greater responsibilities at all
levels of government, our nation will be forced to confront and,
finally, to free itself from the grip of its last socially acceptable
prejudice. This can only happen if we invest ourselves fully in the
political process. Each of us who enters public life assumes the
burden and the privilege of serving as a representative of our community and as a model for those still struggling with their sexuality.

Openness about every aspect of your identity – including your
sexual identity – will make you a stronger candidate, a more effective officeholder and a happier human being. At the most mundane
level, it will free you from the fear of exposure and allow you to
concentrate on real issues. More profoundly, being "out" as a
candidate will give you the inner strength that can only come from
being true to yourself. That strength will enable you to project the
candor and integrity that inspire trust.

As one who has known political life on both sides of the closet
door, I know that this is not an easy thing to do. But whether you
win or lose, the rewards will more than justify the risk.

– U.S. Congressman Gerry Studds

Elected in Massachusetts in 1972, Gerry Studds is one of only two openly gay members of Congress. In 1992 Studds was elected chair of the House Merchant Marine and Fisheries Committee. He also serves as chairman of the Subcommittee on Fisheries and Wildlife Conservation and the Environment, and is a member of the Committee on Energy and Commerce. As a member of the Health Subcommittee, Studds has worked to redesign the nation's health care system. He is a staunch advocate for lesbian and gay civil rights, for greater federal leadership in the struggle against AIDS and for reproductive freedom. He is an original cosponsor of the federal Lesbian and Gay Civil Rights Bill, the Hate Crimes Statistics Act and the Americans with Disabilities Act, and is a longtime leader in the fight to lift the ban on lesbians and gays in the U.S. military.

Foreword

EACH year the Gay and Lesbian Victory Fund receives requests for assistance from hundreds of gay men and lesbians who are considering running for office, but who have no idea what campaigning as openly gay entails. Although there are hundreds of books on electoral politics and campaigning in general, not one addresses the unique challenge of running for office as openly gay. This lack of documentation gives people the incorrect impression that there are no resources available to help openly gay and lesbian candidates run winning campaigns.

In 1993, Nancy Clack, then chair of the Victory Fund board's political committee, organized our first effort to assemble and make available to candidates a list of campaign resources. To assemble the list, we sent press releases and listing forms to gay-friendly campaign professionals, gay and mainstream media, *Campaigns & Elections* magazine, local and national gay and lesbian political organizations and clubs, our recommended candidates and openly gay and lesbian officials asking them to pass the word on to potential listees. We followed up by phone to verify the information received. The resultant *Gay and Lesbian Victory Fund Political Resource Directory* (ISBN 1-883665-00-0) was published in April 1993, just in time for the March On Washington. One month and two reprints later, we were secure in our belief that there was an urgent need for this information, and began work on *Out for Office*.

Out for Office takes the political resource directory idea a step further. Our goals in producing it were

▼ to introduce the reader to the unique and challenging role of the openly lesbian/gay candidate;

▼ to link openly gay and lesbian candidates with the people and resources they need to run winning campaigns;

▼ to instruct and inspire newcomers to the political arena.

Rather than write another how-to book on campaigning, we wanted to produce a gay-oriented supplement to the more nuts-and-bolts approach available in a number of other books. And, we reasoned, who better to share that information than openly gay and lesbian officials and the people who help run their campaigns? So, we asked openly gay and lesbian elected officials and gay/gay-friendly campaign professionals to write on some aspect of running for office as openly gay. The response was overwhelming. Inspired by the prospect of helping other openly gay and lesbian candidates run for office, more than 20 openly gay and lesbian elected officials sent in articles, and others offered invaluable advice and agreed to be listed in this book.

The listings in this book are not meant to be inclusive, but as our network grows and as this book circulates throughout our community, we hope that more campaign professionals, political clubs and openly gay and lesbian elected and appointed officials will want to be included. If you, your firm, or your political club would like to be listed in our political database and in future editions of *Out for Office*, please fill out the form on page 299 and return it to the Victory Fund. If you would like more information on the Victory Fund or if you are considering running for office, please call us at (202)-VICTORY. Remember, this book is only a start, for the wealth of resources available to openly gay and lesbian candidates is as rich and diverse as our community, and as powerful as our desire to elect our own.

– Kathleen DeBold, Political Services Coordinator

Introduction

When it comes right down to it, the one fact that really counts is this: Gay men and lesbians are the most underrepresented group in electoral politics. Of the

▼ 100 U.S. Senators, none are **openly** gay or lesbian;

▼ 425 U.S. Congressmen, only two are **openly** gay;

▼ 7,461 members of state legislatures, only 12 are **openly** gay or lesbian;

▼ 497,155 elected officials currently serving in the United States,[1] only 70 are **openly** gay or lesbian.

That simply is not enough to represent the number of gay men and lesbians in this country; furthermore, with such a small and disperse legislative body representing the needs, rights and interests of so many of us, how can we ever expect to attain equal rights? Gay men and lesbians already in office who are not open about their sexual orientation must come out of the closet; those with the right talents and skills to run for office should do so as openly gay or lesbian; and the rest of us should support them with our time, our money, our encouragement and our votes. *If we don't support our own, who will be there for us?*

The events of the past year have proven to the rest of our community what Victory Fund members have known all along – that **the inclusion and empowerment of gay men and lesbians in the political process can only happen when we are represented by our own.** Time and time again we have invested our hopes and energy and money into electing "friends," only to discover later that our rights and our progress are indeed negotiable. These experiences have taught us that no matter how well meaning our friends and supporters are, no one has as strong an interest in our issues and rights as we do. **Openly gay and lesbian officials guarantee us a place at the table where decisions concerning our lives are made.** They sponsor anti-discrimination bills in state, local and federal legislatures, they block anti-gay referendums, they promote domestic partnership bills, they vote to decriminalize sodomy laws and to outlaw hate crimes, they appoint other openly gay people to public office, they serve as positive role models to middle-America and to gay and lesbian youth, they defend women's reproductive freedom and they work to provide funding and recognition for AIDS programs and other gay and lesbian health care issues.

As you read this book, I hope you will realize the many ways that **you** can make a difference in the political future of our community. Vote. Join your local political club. Work on a campaign. Run for office. The Victory Fund motto is "Financial Clout for Candidates We Can Count On," and we are working hard to mobilize our community in support of qualified openly gay men and women who won't back down when our rights – when *their* rights are at stake. I hope you will join us.

*— **William Waybourn**, Executive Director*

[1]Stanley and Niemi, *Vital Statistics on American Politics, Fourth Edition*

A Selected Chronology of Openly Gay and Lesbian Elected Officials

1961
Jose Sarria
Openly gay man runs for San Francisco (CA) Board of Supervisors and gets 5,600 votes.

1971
Frank Kameny
Second openly gay candidate to run for office in the history of the United States comes in fourth out of six candidates in first Congressional race in the District of Columbia.

1974
Elaine Noble
Elected to the Massachusetts House of Representatives.

1974
Kathy Kozachenko
Elected to the Ann Arbor (MI) City Council.

▼

1974
Allan Spear
Minnesota State Senator, elected in 1972, publicly acknowledges being gay. Elected senate president in 1993.

▼

1977

Harvey Milk

Elected San Francisco (CA) City Supervisor.

1977

Steve Camara

Elected to the Fall River (MA) School Committee Office.
Elected in 1981 to the Fall River City Council; reelected six
consecutive times since then.

1979

Harry Britt

Appointed to the San Francisco (CA) Board of Supervisors when
Harvey Milk was assassinated, and officially elected later that
same year; reelected in 1980, 1984 and 1988.

1980

Gene Ulrich

Elected mayor of Bunceton, Missouri. Reelected every election
cycle since.

1980

Karen Clark

Elected to the Minnesota House of Representatives. Reelected
every election cycle since.

1980

Tim Wolfred

Elected to the San Francisco (CA) Community College Board.

1980
William Chambers
Morristown (NJ) Town Clerk, first elected in 1978, publicly
acknowledges being gay; reelected in 1980 and unanimously
tenured in 1983.

1980
Abby Soven
First appointed to the Los Angeles (CA) Municipal Court in
1978, she is officially elected in 1980. Elected to the Los Angeles
Superior Court in 1982.

1980
Mel Boozer
African-American gay activist is nominated for Vice-President of
the United States at the Democratic National Convention in New
York City.

1981
Richard Gordon
Elected to the Criminal Justice Council of San Mateo County
(CA); elected chair in 1993. Elected to the San Mateo County
Board of Education in 1992.

1981
John Laird
Elected to the Santa Cruz (CA) City Council. Elected mayor of
the city in 1983; remained in office until end of term limit in
1990.

1982
Richard Wagner
Dane County (WI) Supervisor publicly acknowledges being gay
(elected in 1980). Elected chair in 1988 and 1990.

▼

1982
Robert Gentry
Elected to the Laguna Beach (CA) City Council; reelected in
1986 and 1990. Elected mayor of the city in 1983; reelected in
1988 and 1991.

1983
Gerry Studds
Elected to the U.S. House of Representatives from Massachusetts
in 1972, Studds is the first member of Congress to publicly
acknowledge being gay. He has been reelected five times since.

1983
David Scondras
Elected to the Boston (MA) City Council; reelected every election
cycle until 1993.

1983
Al Oertwig
Elected to the St. Paul (MN) Board of Education. Reelected in
1987.

1983
Bryan Coyle
Elected to the Minneapolis (MN) City Council. Served until his
death in 1992.

1984
Valerie Terrigno
Elected mayor of West Hollywood, CA.

1984

John Heilman

Elected to the West Hollywood (CA) City Council; reelected in 1986. Concurrently elected mayor of the city in 1985; reelected in 1990.

1985

Tim Mains

Elected to the Rochester (NY) City Council; reelected in 1989 and 1993.

1985

Tom Nolan

Elected to the Board of Supervisors for San Mateo County (CA). Held office until 1993.

1986

Tammy Baldwin

First open lesbian on the Dane County (WI) Board of Supervisors.

1987

Gary Miller

Elected to the Robla (CA) School Board; elected chair in 1988 and 1992.

1987

Barney Frank

Elected to the United States House of Representatives from Massachusetts in 1981, he publicly acknowledges his sexual orientation; reelected in 1988, 1990 and 1992.

1987

Joe Herzenberg

Elected to the Chapel Hill (NC) Town Council; reelected in 1991.

1987
Tom Brougham
Elected to the Peralta (Alameda County, CA) Community College
Board; reelected in 1992.

1988
Jerold Krieger
Governor Jerry Brown's first openly gay appointee to the Los
Angeles (CA) Superior Court in 1983; officially elected in 1988.

1988
John Fiore
Elected to the Wilton Manors (FL) City Council; reelected in
1992.

1988
Earl Bricker
Elected to the Dane County (WI) Board of Supervisors. Resigned
in 1990; reappointed in 1991.

1988
Judy Abdo
Elected to the Santa Monica (CA) City Council. Elected mayor of
the city in 1990.

1989
Keith St. John
Elected to the Albany (NY) Common Council; reelected in 1993.

1989
John Neese
Elected to the Shorewood Hills (WI) Board of Trustees; reelected
in 1991.

1989

Ricardo Gonzalez

Elected to the Madison (WI) Common Council; reelected in 1991 and 1993.

1989

Joseph Grabarz

Elected to the Connecticut House of Representatives; reelected in 1991.

1989

Ken Reeves

Elected to the Cambridge (MA) City Council; council elects him vice mayor in 1990 and 1991, mayor in 1992 and 1993.

1990

Ronald Squires

Elected to the Vermont State Legislature; reelected in 1992 and served until his death in 1993.

1990

Tom Ammiano

Elected to the San Francisco (CA) School Board.

1990

Donna Hitchens

Elected to the California Superior Court for the City of San Francisco.

1990

Kenneth Hahn

Elected Los Angeles (CA) City Assessor.

▼

1990
Dale McCormick
Elected to the Maine State Senate; reelected in 1992.

1990
Deborah Glick
Elected to the New York State Assembly.

1990
Roberta Achtenberg
Elected to the San Francisco (CA) Board of Supervisors.

1990
Carole Migden
Elected to the San Francisco (CA) Board of Supervisors.

1991
Mark Pocan
Elected to the Dane County (WI) Board of Supervisors; reelected
in 1992.

1991
Thomas Duane
Elected to the New York (NY) City Council; reelected in 1993.

1991
Irene Rabinowitz
Elected to the Provincetown (MA) Board of Selectmen; elected
chair in 1992.

1991

Jeff Horton

Elected to Los Angeles (CA) Board of Education.

1991

Antonio Pagan

Elected to the New York (NY) City Council; reelected in 1993.

1991

Joe Pais

Elected to the Key West (FL) City Commission.

1991

Sherry Harris

Elected to the Seattle (WA) City Council.

1992

Gail Shibley

Appointed to the Oregon House of Representatives in 1992;
officially elected later that same year.

1992

Glen Maxey

Elected to the Texas House of Representatives by special election
in 1991; won general election in 1992.

1992

Janice Wilson

Appointed judge of the District Court of Multnomah County (OR)
in 1991; officially elected in 1992.

1992
Liz Stefanics
Elected to the New Mexico State Assembly.

1992
Tammy Baldwin
Elected to the Wisconsin State Assembly.

1992
Cal Anderson
Elected to the Washington House of Representatives.

1992
Ken Yeager
Elected to the San Jose-Evergreen (CA) Community College
Board.

1992
Will Fitzpatrick
Elected to the Rhode Island State Senate.

1992
Susan Farnsworth
Elected to the Maine House of Representatives.

1992
Angie Fa
Elected to the San Francisco (CA) School Board.

1992
Tom Fleury
Elected to the Vermont State Assembly.

1993
Linda Leslie
Elected Village Trustee of Douglas (MI).

1993
Chris Wilson
Elected to the Oakland Park (FL) City Council.

1993
Bill Crews
Melbourne (IA) mayor comes out at the March on Washington.

1993
Shelley Gaylord
Elected to the Madison (WI) Municipal Court.

1993
Craig McDaniel
Elected to the Dallas (TX) City Council.

1993
Jackie Goldberg
Elected to the Los Angeles (LA) City Council.

1993
Christine Kehoe
Elected to the San Diego (CA) City Council.

1993
Marilyn Shafer
Elected to the Manhattan (NY) Civil Court.
▼

1993
Michael Nelson
Elected to the Carrboro (NC) Board of Aldermen.

1993
Wallace Swan
Elected to the Minneapolis (MN) Board of Estimate and Taxation.

1993
Tom Roberts
Elected to the Santa Barbara (CA) City Council.

1993
Susan Hyde
Elected to the Hartford (CT) City Council.

1993
Katherine Triantafillou
Elected to the Cambridge (MA) City Council.

1993
Bruce Williams
Elected to the Takoma Park (MD) City Council.

A Historical Perspective
Franklin Kameny

I N 1971, I ran for Congress in the District of Columbia as the second openly gay candidate for any public office anywhere in the world. At the time I believed I was the first, but I have since learned that Jose Sarria ran for the San Francisco Board of Supervisors in 1961. My groundbreaking campaign created an ongoing gay political effort that has continued to the present.

In order to place my campaign in a comprehensible context, a brief explanation of Washington's unique political and governmental situation might be helpful. The United States Constitution gives Congress total jurisdiction over the affairs of the District. Because of this, Washington has been, more or less, a colony of the United States Government. Our degree of self-governance has ranged from none whatsoever to a fair amount of Congressionally delegated local control (although always under Congressional oversight and active intervention). Washingtonians could not even vote for President until the Constitution was amended to authorize it in time for the 1964 election. Aside from the nonpartisan election of our own school board (which started in 1968), we voted for nothing else. Thus, there were no local politics in the District at all.

In late 1970, as a first halting step toward granting the city a degree of democratic self-governance, Congress granted us the right to elect a non-voting Delegate to the House of Representatives. This Congressmember would have no vote on the floor of the House, but would have all other powers of a Representative, including membership and vote in committees. Because this Congressional action took place too late for the normal November 1970 Congressional elections, a primary election was scheduled for January 1971, with a general election in late March.

The then small and formative local gay political movement initially participated in the primary by submitting questionnaires to each of the eight candidates. Finding that level of participation unsatisfactory, however, a number of us realized that this was a unique opportunity to bring our issues before the public and to argue our case. (Remember, this was an era in which the word *gay* as a synonym for homosexual and homosexuality was just becoming generally known, when public discussion of gay-related issues was almost nonexistent, when gays were as firmly and completely excluded from U.S. Civil Service employment as they still are from the military, when there was no real public grasp of our grievances, when we were all still "sick" and when the idea of gays as other than marginal people was not only novel but shocking.)

We decided that we should run a candidate of our own in the general election. At that time, I was one of the very few completely "out" gay leaders in the country, and the only one in Washington. I had founded the local gay movement a decade earlier, initiating national gay activism and militancy in the process. In mid-January 1971, we held a meeting at which I was asked to run as an openly gay candidate. I told the group that if they would gather the requisite number of signatures on the nominating petition, I would run. They did, and I did.

It was not easy. Not only had there been no previous political activity of any kind in Washington, there had been no previous gay political activity of this kind anywhere. While many of the things narrated here may seem obvious now, they had to be devised by us with nothing at all to go on and no one at all to consult with, either in the gay community or in the general community. We had no guidance of any kind, and no role models. We had to plan and build from the ground up and to invent ourselves out of nothing as a political force.

The number of signatures required (5,000) was dauntingly large. No one in the city had ever gathered nominating signatures before, so we had no idea how to do this effectively. We had until February 25 to get our signatures. As late as February 13, we still had less than 1,500. At that time, the Gay Activists Alliance (GAA) in New York was on the cutting edge of the gay movement, having replaced the fading Gay Liberation Front. GAA was making a name for itself through effective activism, although they eschewed the kind of participatory politics in which we were involved in Washington. My formative campaign staff went to New York and arranged to bus a sizeable number of GAA volunteers to Washington to help gather signatures. They arrived on a Friday evening, just three days before the final day for the filing of nominating petitions. On Saturday morning they were placed in pairs at pre-selected locations from one end of the city to the other, each with a backup location if the first one did not work out.

That evening, we had arranged a dance for our GAA guests at a local synagogue (public gay dances were a rare and novel phenomenon at that time and worthy of note in their own right). In the middle of the evening, to my joy, in walked my campaign manager, Paul Kuntzler, staggering under the weight of two huge rolls of nominating petitions. On Tuesday, we turned in 7,500 signatures, more than all but one of the other candidates. Our campaign was off and running!

All of the candidates were subject to challenge, and several who were challenged by the *Washington Post* were ultimately removed from the ballot because they had an insufficient number of valid nominating-petition signatures. The *Post* told me that I had so many signatures on my petition they were not even going to attempt a challenge. (This led to a rule of thumb that has served us well since, and that I always pass on to others: Aim to obtain at least one-and-a-half times the minimum required number of signatures on a nominating petition.)

Six candidates appeared on the ballot: a Democrat, a Republican, an Independent, a Socialist Worker Party candidate, a Black United Front candidate and me, as a second Independent. We gave thought to creating what we called the Personal Freedom Party. Although it was not formalized, it was actively pursued and appeared in our literature and on many of our posters, and served as a subordinate thread throughout the campaign.

Because it was unprecedented for open gays to run for political office, the campaign immediately became the focus of continuing publicity, both local and national. Almost all of it was good, although some of it was sensationalized. As a candidate formally placed on the ballot by the Board of Elections and Ethics, I was required to be included on an equal basis in all public debates and public forums, including radio and television appearances. This provided me with an invaluable opportunity to make my pitch for gay rights. I utilized it to the fullest.

We opened a "storefront" campaign headquarters in a building across from the District Building (our city hall).   High up on the front of our headquarters, directly facing the District Building, we hung a four-by-six foot one-word sign: the largest KAMENY ever written.   We secured a supply of "Kameny for Congress" posters, buttons and bumper stickers, which we distributed generously.

Our intention was to wage as credible a campaign as possible. This meant that I could not be merely a gay rights candidate, but that I also had to campaign on a full agenda addressing all the issues at hand in Washington.   Thus, the first realization that impressed itself upon me, as a rank political amateur, was the requirement that I had to become an "instant expert" on every aspect of government, and on every local and federal issue facing the District, from trash collection to the appointment and training of judges, from home rule to taxes and other fiscal matters, and on and on.   I prepared a series of position papers on all of the issues and found myself quite well prepared to debate them with the other candidates.

Because we mounted the campaign to bring our existence and the issues affecting us into public view, and because I wanted to be more than merely reactive to questions that might come along haphazardly, I structured my campaign on a two-track basis.   First, there were routine public appearances on radio and television and at various forums throughout the city.   There the issues were broad-ranging, depending on the pre-set structure and content of the particular debate.   Those appearances were almost always in the company of my five fellow candidates.   Gay issues were sometimes raised and I seized every opportunity to raise and address them.

The second track consisted of a series of campaign-created public events dealing specifically with gay-related issues.   We wrote a letter to President Nixon addressing issues such as the ban on the employment of gays in the U.S. Civil Service and the military. After providing advance notice to the media, we marched the half mile from my campaign headquarters to the gate of the White House and passed the letter in to the President.   We held a press conference in the newsroom of the Pentagon following meetings in the offices of the Secretary of the Army and other military officials. We raised the issue of police harassment of gays in Washington. We got "Kameny for Congress" mentioned in one of the scenes in the musical *Hair*, then playing at the National Theater next door to my campaign headquarters, and we counterpicketed a group of anti-pornography protesters objecting to *Hair*. We viewed the campaign, and the media exposure necessarily accompanying it, as a golden opportunity to bring our issues before the public, and we took the fullest possible advantage of it.

Although we had no real expectations of actually winning, I came in fourth out of the six candidates, and first after the three "big-name" candidates. The *Washington Post* ran a highly complimentary editorial about my campaign. In the ensuing years, it seems like I have met every single person who voted for me. And now, more than 20 years later, I still receive compliments for a well-run and memorable campaign.

My 1971 "Kameny for Congress" campaign had two sets of consequences, one local, the other national. Locally, gays were moved immediately into a central position in the nascent municipal political structure. Because there had been no local politics up to that time, there was no entrenched political establishment or machine. As a result of my campaign, gays were built into them from the beginning. Within a month after the election, the nonpartisan Gay Activists Alliance of Washington (now called the Gay and Lesbian Activists Alliance) formed out of the nucleus of my campaign and has remained central to Washington gay politics for more than twenty years. A few years later, we formed the Gertrude Stein Democratic Club, which is still viewed as one of the more influential partisan political organizations at the city level.

In the first year after the campaign, we were able to exercise enough influence to persuade our school board to enact a then unprecedented resolution banning anti-gay discrimination. Shortly thereafter, we successfully lobbied our Presidentially appointed city council to enact one of the earliest and most sweeping human rights laws in the country. We successfully pressured the police department to back off to a significant degree from their quarter-century-long, Congressionally instigated efforts to ferret out and arrest gays.

In 1975, the first year of our "home rule," I became the first open gay to receive a mayoral appointment (to the D.C. Commission on Human Rights). We set up the Mayoral Appointments Project, which fed into the mayor's office the names of openly gay candidates for all openings on city boards and commissions. In the ensuing years, Washington ended up with not only more openly gay appointed officials than any other city in the country, but with more than all the other cities put together. In that same year, in our first budget hearing under our newly granted home rule, we easily persuaded the city council to delete the line item providing funding for the vice squad, thus ending 25 years of police persecution of gays in Washington. A year later, the city council enacted into law a provision prohibiting consideration of homosexuality as a factor in child custody and visitation rights cases. A few years later, when the city council enacted legislation creating initiative, referendum, and recall in the District of Columbia, we were successful in including provisions in the law prohibiting initiatives and referenda directed at repealing the gay rights provision of our Human Rights Law. We thus achieved immunization against the type of initiatives and referenda advocated by Anita Bryant and recently used in places such as Oregon and Colorado.

Having achieved a considerable amount of political momentum and clout as a result of my campaign, we here in Washington have since played our political cards sophisticatedly. Most recently, at our behest and in enactment of a law that I drafted at the invitation of the councilmember who introduced it, the city council unanimously repealed the District's sodomy law for the second time (the first repeal was overturned by a Falwell-terrorized Congress in 1981; this time the repeal stuck).

After my groundbreaking campaign I looked forward to an immediate surge of openly gay candidates all over the country, but was disappointed at the resounding silence. Then after a kind of incubation period of about two years, Elaine Noble ran successfully as an open lesbian for the Massachusetts State House of Representatives. Allen Spear soon followed in the Minnesota Senate. Although there have been numerous others since then, I must confess there aren't as many gay candidacies as I would like to see, and certainly not nearly as many victories.

Although we have not yet moved beyond the stage where openly gay elected public officials are still considered noteworthy simply because they are gay, we are moving rapidly toward that day. Additionally, and of possibly even greater significance, by introducing gays into direct participatory electoral politics, these individual electoral campaigns have led to the formation of both actual and perceived gay voting blocs, which have been, and continue to be, enormously effective in achieving our goals.

My campaign was one of the most arduous and gruelling tasks that I have ever undertaken, second only to my frontline combat in World War II. It also remains one of the most memorable and gratifying episodes in my life. While I'm certain that in due course other gays would have run for electoral office if I had not done so, it remains deeply satisfying to me that I was able to lead the way in this respect. What is even more satisfying to see is the ever-increasing participation of gays in all aspects of the American political process — a process of which we are properly an integral part, but in which we have only recently begun to become effective players — and through that process, in all aspects of American society and culture.

------

*One of the foremost leaders in the American gay community, **Dr. Franklin Kameny** founded the Washington, D.C. chapter of the Mattachine Society in 1961. He first began working to lift the ban on gays in the military in 1962. In 1968, he coined the slogan "Gay is good." Three years later, Kameny ran for Congress from the District of Columbia as one of the first openly gay candidates in the United States. Kameny played instrumental roles in the 1973 decision by the American Psychiatric Association to stop classifying homosexuality as a mental illness and the 1975 removal of the ban on gays in the U.S. Civil Service. He has served as a founder and board member for the National Gay Task Force (now the National Gay and Lesbian Task Force), the Gay Rights National Lobby, the Gay Activists Alliance of Washington and the Gertrude Stein Democratic Club. At 68, Dr. Kameny continues to play an active role in gay politics at the local and national level, and in 1993, his 30-year effort to repeal the D.C. sodomy law came to fruition.*

What Do We Want?
More lesbians and gays in office!
When do we want it? Now!
Deborah Glick

T HE increase in the number of openly lesbian and gay elected representatives in the last five years has been astonishing, paralleling the increase in the political clout of our whole community. It is a testament to our strength and increased organizational and political effectiveness that our community is at a point at which we can enter the long-standing debates about electoral representation. We have demonstrated our enormous fundraising capacity, run winning campaigns and become a force to be reckoned with across a broad spectrum of issues and geographic areas. It is exciting that we are now in a position to discuss such sophisticated issues as whether or not to run against candidates who are not all bad – specifically candidates who are "gay friendly."

A necessary first step in discussing and coming to consensus on the issue of lesbian and gay representation is to define representation We must address the fact that, like most other communities, we are not all of one mind. Therefore we must decide: Do we support openly lesbian and gay candidates who are fiscally conservative, oppose abortion, or take other positions not held by the progressive majority of our movement? And how do we balance issues of representation of women, African-Americans, Latinos, Asians and other underrepresented groups?

Once we have determined some basic principles, we must then identify, encourage, train and work with leaders in our community and then support them in their bids for elected office. We must not seek candidates who are running solely because they are lesbian or gay, but ones who are running because they have roots in our community and have an ability to communicate articulately, generate excitement about issues and ideas, and rally support among others. We must seek energetic and thoughtful leaders. We must identify future leaders and develop their potential. And when we identify and work with candidates, we must then commit ourselves to doing all of the necessary tasks involved in ensuring that they run meaningful campaigns that raise important issues, educate and excite people, and, whenever possible, win.

Selecting and training candidates is part of the work we must do. Another part is identifying races – seats to seek and districts in which to run. Here we must consider a variety of variables. Should lesbians and gays run to fill many local seats (including the school boards), or should we pool our resources and target higher level offices – the House of Representatives, the Senate, governorships, etc.? Should lesbians and gays run only in districts with high numbers of known lesbians and gays? And should lesbians and gays run against candidates who are "gay friendly?"

The issue of "gay-friendly" elected officials is particularly relevant as we seek to run more and more lesbian and gay candidates who can actually win. More lesbians and gays live in urban centers like San Francisco, New York, Los Angeles, Seattle, and Atlanta, or in liberal/progressive communities like Ann Arbor, Northampton, and Madison. But these are not the only places where lesbians and gay men have been successful. In New York, both Albany and Rochester elected gay men to their city councils before New York City did. Part of the dilemma is that in more liberal communities, people already in office often mirror our positions on many issues. Current office holders may be viewed as leaders on some of the most important battle fronts – reproductive freedom, lesbian and gay civil rights, funding for AIDS, domestic partnership and bias-motivated violence.

If the community is already represented by a person who supports these positions, is there a compelling case for change? I would argue that there is, for a variety of reasons. First, the office holder may not be providing the best representation possible or may vote appropriately on issues but not act as a strong leader or advocate for them. In addition, we must keep the electoral process vibrant. No elected official has the right to hold a seat for as long as she or he wishes. Officeholders must seek reelection by residents of their districts. And the process of seeking reelection is a good one. It forces candidates to constantly reach out to their constituencies. If a candidate "writes off" the lesbian and gay community because an openly lesbian or gay candidate is running against them, that tells us something about that person.

In seats with longtime incumbents, there will be many people within the general community who have been waiting for an opportunity to run for office. In 1990, when I decided to run for the New York State Assembly, I began my race by challenging a 36-year incumbent. While he had been the prime sponsor of the lesbian and gay civil rights bill for 15-20 years, the bill was never actively pursued. His positions reflected the liberal nature of the district, but he was no longer a force for change. He decided mid-race to retire and a whole new group of candidates entered the field, most of whom were also liberal. A field will rarely be empty. But we cannot wait forever to empower ourselves.

It is very difficult to run against an incumbent. It is difficult to get your name out, difficult to raise money and difficult to win. However, lesbians and gays have a slight advantage. Many in our community have always been electoral. We have provided creative energy and troops for many campaigns. We have provided a strong base of financial support for a variety of gay-friendly candidates. It is now our challenge to tap these resources and channel this energy into the election of openly lesbian and gay candidates.

Similarly, we must use our knowledge and show our strength in the area of redistricting. To participate in the next redistricting process, we must begin now to lay the groundwork. All around the country, lesbian and gay activists have made a case for "gay winnable" seats. When New York City expanded its city council, the lesbian and gay community focused on a seat on the west side of Manhattan. By pointing to memberships in lesbian and gay organizations, subscription lists to gay publications and other mailing lists, as well as the location of gay shops and a lesbian and gay community center, a clear case was made for a population nucleus of gay men and lesbians within a geographic area.

We must gather the type of hard data that will be necessary to make the same case in numerous other parts of the country when we face the next redistricting effort at the turn of the century. Crafting Congressional seats with maximum "gay winnability" should be a priority for our community. It requires that we cultivate relationships in each of the state legislatures where redistricting decisions are made. A coordinated effort must commence immediately.

If we are to be involved electorally, we must ensure that politics and empowerment supersede sentimental impulses. We cannot rely on the kindness of others or become satisfied with anything less than the best possible representation or anyone less than a strong and dynamic leader. As we grow and gather strength, we must use this power in all of the ways that other segments of the population do. In electoral politics, this means running for office – running for as many seats as we see fit and in as many races as we feel appropriate.

Deborah Glick became the first openly gay or lesbian elected official in New York City when she won the Manhattan district seat in the state legislature in 1990. As an assemblymember she serves on the Committees for Governmental Operations, Governmental Employees, Children and Families, Social Services, and Environmental Conservation. She has worked hard to obtain legal status for domestic partners, to repeal adultery and sodomy statutes and to extend state law to ban discrimination based on sexual orientation. Prior to running for office, Glick was an active member with the New York City Chapter of the National Organization for Women, serving as coordinator for the NOW Reproductive Rights Committee. She remains involved in a variety of civil rights, women's rights and environmental organizations.

Running Against Our "Friends"
Carole Migden

SINCE the election of Harvey Milk to the San Francisco Board of Supervisors in 1977, lesbians and gay men have made striking gains in securing elected office throughout the United States. But, given our share of the electorate, our high level of political activism, and the need for a heightened response to the issues affecting our community, there simply are not enough lesbians and gay men serving in public office, even in progressive, pro-gay cities.

The reasons for this are many: the high cost of running for office, the unfair stereotype that lesbians, gays and bisexuals are "single-issue" candidates and the barriers erected by political machines to preserve their power. But in the final analysis, the problem is not that we cannot win office, but that we are often too afraid to run — against our "friends," if necessary.

In 1976, Harvey Milk first ran for the California State Assembly against Art Agnos, the candidate of San Francisco's Democratic Party establishment. Harvey insisted that it was not enough for lesbians and gay men to count on friendly liberal politicians to carry our issues — politicians who would claim that their voices would be most likely to be heard in decision-making bodies. He insisted that lesbians and gay men need to have sufficient pride to run for office ourselves.

Agnos went on to be a strongly pro-gay legislator and mayor. But the political machine of which he was a part has continued to block gay political self-empowerment, holding the line against such highly qualified lesbian and gay candidates for Congress and the State Assembly as Harry Britt, Roberta Achtenberg, John Duran and John Laird.

It is clear that, despite the strength and loyalty we have brought to the Democratic Party, we are still not dubbed by the power brokers to run for office. Time and time again — in California and throughout the country — the gay political community has been disappointed to have the power establishment run their own hand-picked candidates, people they feel they can "count on," against viable gay candidates in races that we could win. Responding to the pressure they receive from a homophobic society, straight party leaders become nervous at the thought of openly supporting us for office.

Many in the party still subscribe to the condescending and self-serving notion that only politicians have the experience and can claim the respect necessary to secure legislation on issues affecting lesbians and gay men. Pro-gay legislators have even suggested that we should leave them alone and run our candidates in districts with homophobic incumbents – districts where we could never win. Our "friends" just can't understand why we're not simply grateful for everything they've done for us.

There's no question that many straight elected officials have supported the lesbian and gay community on issues including civil rights and AIDS. Certainly, we appreciate their efforts. But let's be realistic: our strongest champions serve in districts where a strong record on gay rights and AIDS is required to stay in office.

For that political reality, the lesbian and gay community should not be so grateful that we do not assert ourselves in electoral politics. Our community must be willing to run against our straight friends to meet our goal of self-empowerment — just as African-Americans, Latinos, and other minorities often must challenge white allies to win self-representation.

The goal of electing lesbians and gay men to office is not simply to flex our muscles; we can be far more articulate and un-compromising in representing our issues than can non-gay elected officials. Beyond that, lesbians and gay men in office have shown that we are effective on every policy issue at all levels of govern-ment. Most importantly, the power we gain by electing ourselves to office is the power to break down homophobia and change public attitudes about lesbians and gay men.

As the number of lesbian and gay officials has grown, espe-cially recently with the leadership of the Gay and Lesbian Victory Fund, we have been able to provide a higher level of practical sup-port for lesbians and gay men considering races for public office. But the most important advice we can give is to simply have the courage to run. Power is never relinquished; it has to be taken.

An openly lesbian member of the San Francisco Board of Supervisors since 1990, Carole Migden has been active in both the Democratic National Committee and the California Democratic Party for more than a decade, serving as two-term chair of the Lesbian and Gay Caucus. During the 1992 Presidential campaign, Migden, as chair of the San Francisco Democratic Party, led one of the most successful Get-Out-the-Vote efforts in California's history, helping President Clinton win a landslide victory in that state. As chair of the State Party Platform Committee, Migden has brought inclusion of lesbians and gays on the civil rights bill, AIDS-related issues and health care to the top of the party's agenda. On the Board of Supervisors, Migden has been the leader on similar efforts and on the response to the far right's anti-gay initiatives in California. As supervisor Migden serves as chair of the powerful Budget Committee, where she is leading the effort to resolve the city's fiscal crisis.

Are You Ready to Run?

Cathy Allen

IT is often said that the public gets the kind of politicians it deserves. If that is the case, certainly the public deserves more openly gay and lesbian elected officials because that's what it's been getting. In the last four years, there has been a steady increase in the number of gay and lesbian candidates running for – and winning – elective office.

Lesbians and gay men are running for office from San Diego to Anchorage, from Austin to Boston. They are running for Congress, for state legislatures, for mayor, for judicial posts and for city councils in urban and rural America. We are living through one of the most significant historical periods of the gay movement – and electing gay officials will be one of the strongest statements of this decade.

The playing field of politics is changing, and it is likely to result in a geometric increase in the number of gays who will consider running for office. Traditionally, gays seeking office have been considered viable only if they came from districts perceived as having strong gay communities. Gay candidates had to be from the "politically correct" targeted community or they were considered unelectable.

This is no longer the case. Lesbian and gay candidates are running and winning in city, county and statewide races throughout the nation, and the question for any gay or lesbian potential candidate is *could you be one of them?*

As a prospective, first-time candidate you must take a realistic look at running for office. It is critical that you consider key baseline questions such as:

▼ Why do you want to run? What office is viable for you to seek?

▼ What makes you a credible candidate?

▼ Have your accomplishments made a difference for your constituents?

▼ Do you have an impressive resumé?

▼ What role will your sexual orientation play in the race?

▼ What is your message?

▼ Is running for office worth the risk both financially and personally?

▼ What constituencies can you count on for support?

▼ Do you have the time to put together a good campaign?

▼ Is this an open seat or do you have to take on an incumbent?

If you can get past the above questions, you are ready to proceed to the five general areas that will make or break an openly gay candidate: money, people, background, viability and the importance of being gay in the race.

Money

Personal... Most first-time candidates finance 15 percent of their campaign budget from their own bank accounts. What kind of money can you afford to put into your own campaign?

High donors... Do you have 200 people upon whom you can count to give at least $100? Who are they? Where might you find them?

Lesbian/gay supporters... How can you tap into the resources of the community? Are there gay candidates who have run in your area previous to now? Where have they gotten their money?

Organizational help... Which groups will help you raise money? Are there coalitions you can build with progressive organizations? Do you have lists (on disk) of members of politically important groups?

People

Volunteers... Do you know 20 people who will give at least five hours a week *starting now* to help you run? Have you donated a lot of personal volunteer time to political organizations so that you might expect some reciprocity in the future?

Finance Committee... Do you have a dozen acquaintances

who have raised money for other candidates or organizations and who would be willing to do the same for you? Do you have friends who have organized fundraisers in the past? Can you find party or local activists who will help you organize events?

Key Staff... Understanding that most first campaigns have few resources to hire campaign staffers, do you have three or four people willing to accept key responsibilities in your campaign for little or no pay? Do you have someone to help you with the press? How about a scheduler? What about a treasurer? Or a field/Get-Out-the-Vote organizer?

Endorsements... Which elected officials can you get to anchor your steering committee? Which community leaders will you be able to place on your letterhead? Do you have seniors, key women, leaders of color, business, religious and labor leaders who will give your candidacy credibility?

Background

Personal... Do you have the personality to be a candidate? Can you delegate responsibility? Can you convince others that you are worthy of their trust? Do you have a strong image? Are you willing to make changes in your style/appearance to sharpen your presence? Can you handle criticism without losing control? How much of your private life are you willing to share with the public at large? Is your partner willing to have a public role in this campaign?

Professional... Some campaigns require a full-time commitment from the candidate. Can you afford to give up your job for this campaign? Do you have another source of income to help you survive personally while you campaign politically? What happens if you lose? Can you get your old job back (or find a new one)? Even if you don't need to give up your job to run, do you have enough flexibility in your work schedule to allow you to meet campaign commitments? Do you have accrued leave you can use during the crucial final weeks of the campaign?

Closet... What's in yours? Have you ever been arrested? What kind of employment problems have you had? Have you been involved in projects that attracted scandal? A personal or business bankruptcy? Have you ever been involved with organizations that received a lot of press for radical actions and could now hurt your chances of capturing mainstream voters? Have you been caught in a public lie? Are there things in your past that could show up in print and destroy your chances of winning?

Viability

Who else is in the race?... Is there an incumbent? Have you done research on the other candidates who are seeking to run? Will these other candidates have more money, name recognition, traditional support from organizations or volunteers than you will have? What is your "niche" among the voters? Where can you expect to win support that these other candidates might not?

What about your constituents?... Who traditionally votes in your district? What is the voter profile (Democrat, Republican, conservative, liberal, etc.)? What foothold do right-wing groups such as the Christian Coalition have in your district? Is there a large gay community? Have there been civil rights issues that have gotten on the ballot through initiatives or referendum? How did they do?

What else is on the ballot?... What other issues or candidates will be on the same ballot as your prospective race? As these might bring out certain classes or numbers of voters, will you be on the majority side of these issues?

The impact of being gay on this race

The gay/lesbian community... What is your background in gay politics and gay issues? Will you have gay community support? Are there other gay leaders thinking of running who might expect you to wait until they have run? Has the gay community ever been successful in raising large amounts of money for a candidate in your area? Have you supported their causes in the past?

Mainstreaming... Do you have an agenda that parallels the general issue concerns of the constituents you seek to represent? Can your past gay community accomplishments be bridged to represent key concerns of the general public? Will the voters be able to see you as an advocate of their most important issues? How much of your agenda will you have to compromise to adopt a more mainstream agenda?

The Far Right... Have "stealth" candidates run and won

in your local races? Are there right wing political action committees that will put a lot of money into the race against you? Is there a
loud homophobic voice in your community that will continue to
point out that you are gay and, thus, make it more difficult for you
to control the issue agenda?

Talking about being gay... How will you talk about your
sexual orientation? How will you integrate a gay-positive agenda
within the context of other more mainstream issues? Will you acknowledge your partner at events? How will you get the press to
move beyond constantly identifying you as "the gay candidate?"

After you've asked yourself these tough questions, take the
same list and ask good friends, political acquaintances, and even
your worthy adversaries what they think of the answers you've given.
But don't make your decision based solely on what other people
think. (When Sherry Harris, now a Seattle City Councilmember,
ran for office as an out lesbian, she was discouraged from doing so
by 72 out of 74 of the people she spoke with in her decision-making
phase!) Although there are no absolute right or wrong answers to
any of these questions, you need to be honest in assessing "the big
picture" these answers present. Those problems that are likely to
disqualify a gay candidate are the same as those that would affect
any candidate. In most cases, it's the total effect of all the questions
that can skew the decision.

Give yourself a specific deadline to decide. Once you've
done a reasonable amount of intelligence gathering, you will have
your answer. If you have answered the questions and still can't
decide, maybe that is a decision clue in itself.

You will never have exact, clear evidence about whether or
not you should run. But the history books are now being rewritten
to include many other people who once thought they would never be
elected as an openly lesbian/gay candidate.

Do your homework. Get good advice. Be realistic. And
start early. There is certainly room for more names in the history
books.

Cathy Allen, current director of Campaign Connection, a Seattle-based political consulting firm which specializes in women, gay/lesbian and candidates of color, has managed and done consulting for more than 40 successful campaigns. Campaign Connection has served as consultant to more than a dozen gay/lesbian candidates, including Seattle City Councilmember Sherry Harris; San Mateo County Congressional Candidate Tom Nolan; Alaskans for Civil Rights, Joyce Murphy for Mayor (Anchorage); and is working with four openly gay prospective candidates for the 1994 campaign cycle. Allen has published many works on running for elective office, including the groundbreaking Political Campaigning: the National Women's Political Caucus' Guide to Winning in the '90s.

Selecting a Campaign Manager
Marilyn Gordon

A CCORDING to journalist and literary critic H.L. Mencken, *campaign* took on a whole new meaning in this country at the beginning of the nineteenth century. In the political sense, it was often preceded by *electioneering*, but eventually acquired its own status and spawned a host of related political Americanisms, including *campaign manager*. Mencken's classic text, *The American Language*, pinpoints 1882 as the time when a *campaign manager* was first linguistically recognized, thereafter becoming a part of the fabric of American politics.

There is little doubt that 100 or more years ago, managing a political campaign was just as challenging as it is today. Few would argue that a manager — then and now — needs to possess the right qualities to run a successful race on any scale. For instance, a campaign manager, constantly faced with a million details, needs to be organized. And because most campaigns depend on the help of volunteers, each one endowed with various capabilities and skills, a campaign manager should be able to motivate and interact with people on many levels. The ability to delegate and follow through with plans is essential. Last, but not least, knowing the right people — these days known as the "movers and shakers" — is a must. Influential people, in any day and age, mean votes and campaign funds to any candidate.

More than ever before, communication plays a key role in a successful campaign. Candidates need to be seen and heard by the voters through a variety of means — both electronic and print — and the campaign manager must have the ability to make these things happen. From arranging a media conference to a one-on-one interview, from composing a press release to drafting a constituents letter, the campaign manager must have the communications know-how to keep the candidate and his/her message in the public eye.

Up until now, what's been described is a jack(jill)-of-all-trades manager who is capable of wearing many hats — the type of campaign "generalist" that most candidates for political office would need to hire. The decision on who should manage a campaign and the staff necessary to carry out campaign plans would, however, depend largely on funds — how much money is available to hire and maintain operations for the campaign duration.

Most political campaigns haven't the need or the dollars available to support a large-scale campaign effort replete with manager, strategy consultants, public relations advisors, schedulers, demographers, writers, graphic artists, secretaries, etc. Most campaigns, in fact, are smaller in scope and would be best served by a competent generalist who can perform many of these tasks, delegate others to volunteers, and after other avenues are exhausted, buy the remainder of the campaign services.

The rule of thumb is to mount a campaign effort consistent with the type of race you're entering. In other words, a $50,000 campaign needs a talented generalist who can do it all. So how do you recognize that one-in-a-million generalist — the right campaign manager? Here are a few of the qualities you need to look for when making that crucial "make-it-or-break-it" decision.

The Three Rs: Record, Recommendations, Results. Not to say that rank beginners don't stand a chance as successful campaign managers, it just isn't as likely that *no* experience with political races would allow for success. Campaign veterans are those who have labored in many capacities, from volunteer to "insider." They know the process. They know the people. They know the ropes.

Talk with successful candidates to determine your short list of names. Then interview your choices extensively. Carefully note the results. Can this person raise funds? Can this person garner headlines for a candidate? Does this person know how to get the votes?

Stay away from the stranger in a stranger land. For a campaign manager to be effective, he or she must know the targeted community. What are the issues? Who are the power players? What kind of resources are available? By already knowing the "lay of the land," a campaign manager can be miles ahead of the game — and you don't pay for the learning curve.

Good people skills. A good campaign manager instills trust and confidence in others and has the ability to relate to everyone from the powerful contributor to the occasional volunteer. Mastering monetary support takes one set of skills, training volunteers to handle the challenge of phone-back calling is quite another. The good campaign manager knows how to get the most out of people and have them coming back for more.

Motivation and inspiration. Akin to good people skills, the ability to motivate workers and inspire voters is a gift. There's always something to be done for a campaign and rarely enough workers to tackle the tasks. A campaign manager with the ability to motivate workers and volunteers will get things done quickly and smoothly and inspire the kind of camaraderie necessary to build a united campaign effort that, in turn, translates to influencing the vote.

Money talks. The ability to raise money is absolutely essential. Campaigns on any scale are expensive propositions, so the campaign manager who can keep the effort afloat through powerful letter campaigns, special events, and targeted fundraisers should get your attention. Keeping the lights on, the phones ringing and your name in front of the public translates to votes.

If it's Tuesday, this must be city hall. It takes far more than rolodexes and daytimers to make a person organized. A good campaign manager has the ability to schedule your political days and nights, keep the office operating at high speed, pay the bills, maintain the volunteer schedule, work in a brief speech or two and remember to pick up the dry cleaning, all at the same time without ever missing a beat. Being truly organized may be something a good campaign manager is born with.

Someone who can take the heat. Everyone loves the spotlight these days, and often when well-meaning friends and family want to get involved in a campaign, the result can be more fireworks than good works. The campaign manager should be prepared to step into the situation, come between friends, family and the candidate if necessary, and say "no." In short, diffuse the situation and take the heat.

Honesty in politics? Yes, you can link *honesty* and *politics* in the same sentence. Likewise, you should be able to find a campaign manager who understands the ins and outs of the politics at hand and, at the same time, renders an honest opinion that you can respect and live with. Because the manager is typically in tune with the everyday reality of the campaign, he or she must have the ability to communicate candidly with the candidate about everything from finances and hot issues to hair color.

An understanding of the issues. A candidate and a campaign manager should be philosophically *simpatico*. And because a manager may often be asked to address an issue, explain the campaign platform, or even stand in for the candidate on occasion, a thorough understanding of the issues at hand is critical.

By the same token, a campaign manager must understand the law of numbers. In this country, you're elected by everyone, not just your own kind. Getting elected results from widespread support, that is, from the gay community, the Hispanic community, the African-American community, the disabled, women, the young and the old. Focus is the key. A campaign manager should have the ability to help focus your views and broaden your appeal.

It's all in who you know. There's a difference between *knowing* people and *knowing of* people. Your campaign manager must *know* the right people who can get involved and help you to get elected. In addition, *knowing* a reporter or two couldn't hurt. Headlines and ink help you meet more people, communicate your message, and win over more voters. In essence, a good campaign manager should widen your horizons.

Communicating through technology. With the advent of the personal computer and the desktop publishing revolution, there's no excuse for a lack of good communication. Your campaign manager should have more than a passing acquaintance with the word processing, database, and graphics technology that can make communicating with contributors, potential supporters, your constituents, the media and the world an effective and powerful tool. Finding a manager who can handle most communications in-house is a real plus and the equivalent of "found" money. Economically speaking, this is the way to go.

A strong, informed decision maker. During the life of a campaign, decisions will need to be made on every conceivable matter, some very quickly. The good campaign manager involves you directly in the critical decision-making and handles the rest without delay — then stands by those decisions even under duress.

An eye for the big picture, but a handle on the details. These are important qualities and often overlooked. Many people have one ability or the other, but rarely both. A good campaign manager needs to know when to "micro-manage" and when to adopt a broader approach. The most important thing to note is that this person has the ability to look at situations and issues from more than one perspective, but always with your best campaign interests at heart.

As Mencken noted in *The American Language*, the word *campaign* took on a whole new meaning in America nearly 200 years ago. With the right campaign manager at the helm, your own campaign will gain new meaning as well.

President of MG Associates, Marilyn Gordon has extensive experience in fundraising for political candidates and nonprofit organizations. She has also done public relations work for various law firms and corporations and has served as a legislative aid for children's and environmental issues for which she was named an LBJ Scholar at the recommendation of Speaker of the House Jim Wright.

Money = Message

Andrew E. Barrer

COMMUNICATING your message and getting positive name recognition can only be accomplished by raising enough money for the campaign. Mailings, literature drops, signs, bumper stickers, paid media and staff all require financing. Good ideas, a sound message, and a competent candidate are meaningless if the electorate doesn't know anything about you or your message because you can't afford to tell them.

You must be realistic about what is necessary to mount a successful campaign. Even before you decide to throw your hat into the ring, you must develop a sound budget of revenues and expenses. Budgeting expenses is the easy part. How much money will it take to get your message out to the voters? Find out what past campaigns for the office have cost, how the money was raised, how it was spent and when. Build on this information to estimate your own campaign's expense budget.

Budgeting revenue is more difficult. If you decide you need $75,000 to wage a campaign, you now have to figure out where the money will come from. Most of the campaign budgets I see are detailed with how the money will be spent, but not on how it will be raised. As you review each item on your expense budget, stop and ask yourself "Where am I going to get the money that I want to spend on this?" Your responses to this ever-repeated question will form your revenue budget. Remember, if you can't raise a realistic amount of money, you will have to rethink your candidacy.

The following basic fundraising tips are based on my experience in raising millions of dollars for numerous candidates over the past ten years:

1. Send every contributor a thank-you note within 72 hours of his/her donation. This is the number-one piece of advice I try to impress on every candidate. I cannot overemphasize the importance of sending thank-you notes to your contributors right away. Un-thanked contribu-

tors are lost votes and a lost opportunity to raise additional money from them and their friends.

2. Your budget should outline not only how you are going to spend the money, but also when, where and how the contributions will be raised.

3. Target likely donors and categorize them based on how much money you expect them to give.

4. Have diverse membership on your fundraising committee so you can reach the widest range of possible donors.

5. Set a dollar goal for what each member of your committee, including you yourself, should raise.

6. Make as many fundraising calls yourself as possible from a call list prepared by the campaign staff and committee.

7. Ask potential contributors for a specific amount; start a little high and work lower if they can't commit to the first amount.

8. You, not your staff, have to learn to do the "ask" and make the "close" on larger donations.

9. Don't be shy about asking someone twice or more for a donation.

10. Ask each contributor to give you at least three names of other people to approach.

11. Establish a system for following up when someone makes a pledge to contribute to your campaign.

12. Any mailings or literature drops should include an ask for money, even if it's only a subtle one.

13. Each mailing, event and list of major donors should have a fundraising goal attached to it.

And always remember, no one is going to give you money if you don't ask them to.

A member of the Board of Directors of the Gay and Lesbian Victory Fund, Andrew E. Barrer is a noted fundraiser for Democratic candidates, including United States Senator Russ Feingold of Wisconsin and Tammy Baldwin, the first openly lesbian member of the Wisconsin State Assembly. Barrer served as part of the Clinton/Gore Transition Team and as director of COALITION '93, the gay and lesbian community's presidential transition project that sought the appointment of openly gay men and lesbians to the Clinton administration. Barrer serves as Senior Advisor to the White House Office of AIDS policy.

The International Network of Lesbian and Gay Officials

Lance Ringel

RUNNING for office or seeking appointment as an openly lesbian or gay candidate is something that only a few people have experienced. That experience can be accompanied by the exhilaration that comes with being a pioneer, but also by a very real sense of isolation. To alleviate that sense (and to avoid reinventing the wheel whenever possible), it is important for candidates to connect with people who have been in similar situations. Making those connections possible – for candidates as well as for elected and appointed officials – is why the International Network of Lesbian and Gay Officials (INLGO) was created.

Every year since 1986, openly lesbian and gay elected and appointed officials and candidates have met the weekend before Thanksgiving at a conference that provides an opportunity for networking and renewal – a venue where they can compare and contrast their political and personal experiences, discuss shared concerns and problems, and give each other mutual support. For the lesbian or gay candidate, the conference provides a rare opportunity to meet and talk with people who have already faced the unique challenges of running "out."

A typical conference includes receptions and plenary sessions featuring nationally prominent speakers, as well as smaller workshops on a variety of topics like fundraising and media skills. Candidates and campaign workers, elected and appointed officials, and partners also have the opportunity to meet in their own caucuses. (Partners of officials have been integral to the conference workshop on survival skills for couples, designed specifically for officials and their partners.) Time is always provided to explore the host city and its lesbian/gay community, as well as to meet other conference participants in less structured settings.

INLGO is an inclusive organization. From the beginning, the conferences have attracted diverse participants: women and men; Republicans and Democrats; rural, suburban and urban residents; Americans of African, Asian, Latino and European descent; candidates for office and their campaign workers; and local, state and national officials, appointed and elected as well as activists working outside the government system. The attendees as well as the host cities for the conference have been geographically diverse, and every conference has also attracted participants from outside the United States.

INLGO was established not only to ensure that future conferences took place, but also to facilitate ongoing communication among current and aspiring openly lesbian and gay elected and appointed officials. To that end, the International Network is embarking on "Project 365," an electronic bulletin board that will allow candidates and officials to keep in touch with each other more easily between conferences.

For further information, write INLGO Secretary, 3801 26th Street East, Minneapolis, Minnesota 55406-1857 or call (312) 443-4201 or (612) 724-5581. All inquiries are welcome.

In October, 1991, Lance Ringel became the first open gay or lesbian to serve as a New York State Division of Human Rights (DHR) commissioner. At the DHR he served as assistant commissioner for program and policy, and shared in the supervision of the governor's Office of Lesbian and Gay Concerns (OLGC), the sole government-funded U.S. state office devoted exclusively to the needs of the lesbian and gay community. Prior to directing OLGC, Ringel oversaw enforcement of the Governor's executive order prohibiting sexual orientation discrimination by agencies of New York State.

Human Rights Campaign Fund
Eric Rosenthal

T HE Human Rights Campaign Fund is the nation's largest
lesbian and gay political organization, with almost 100,000
members across the country. We work at the federal level
to mobilize the power of the lesbian and gay community (and our
straight allies) to enact congressional legislation and executive branch
policies for our community. We lobby Congress and the administration, work to elect our friends and build a Federal Advocacy
Network of people around the United States to support these activities.

While we are not organized primarily to elect lesbian and gay
candidates to office (that is the job of the Gay and Lesbian Victory
Fund), we have spent considerable effort in doing so over the years.
Let me separate our work with lesbian and gay candidates into two
topics: candidates running for Congress and candidates running for
state or local office.

Congressional candidates
We interview hundreds of candidates for Congress during each
two-year election cycle and support about 200 of these, both Republicans and Democrats. Most of them, of course, are not openly gay
or lesbian. In determining whom to support, we evaluate each
candidate's positions on the issues on our agenda (federal lesbian
and gay civil rights, lifting the ban against gays in the military, anti-
lesbian and gay violence legislation, reproductive freedom, increased
funding for AIDS research, and health care reform) and analyze his
or her campaign. We look for candidates with good records, positions consistent with ours on the issues we follow and good campaigns. We support incumbents with strong records even if they
are challenged by candidates who also support our issues.

The process we use to evaluate a lesbian or gay candidate is essentially the same as that we use to evaluate any candidate. We seek candidates who are strong on our issues and have a chance to win. We prefer they not be running against an incumbent with a strong record on gay and lesbian issues, for instance, it would be difficult to support *anyone* against Senator Ted Kennedy (D-MA) or Senator Carol Moseley-Braun (D-IL).

Having seats at the table for our community is critical and for a lesbian or gay candidate meeting the above criteria, the Campaign Fund would make a major effort to elect him or her, well beyond that we would make for any other candidate. We would provide strategic advice, staff support, financial contributions, fundraising assistance (within the limits imposed by the Federal Election Campaign Act) and suggestions on hiring consultants and staff. Electing such a candidate would be a priority for the Campaign Fund.

State or local candidates

In the case of a candidate running for state or local office, the Campaign Fund would provide more modest assistance. For a viable candidate, we might be able to provide some fundraising assistance, depending on our membership base in his or her geographic area. We also would be able to provide strategic advice and access to Washington-based pollsters, media wizards and other political consultants. If the candidate is openly gay or lesbian, we most likely would see this type of race as one in which the Victory Fund would take the lead.

Procedure

Candidate interviews with a member of the Campaign Fund political department are required before endorsement decisions are made. The political department will also consult with members of the local lesbian and gay community and with the Victory Fund before making a decision in a race with a gay or lesbian candidate. There is no deadline to apply for support, but candidates should be certain to begin their campaigns early, probably at least a year before the election. Obviously, the earlier we were asked to become involved in a race, the greater the support the Campaign Fund would be able to provide.

To request support from the Human Rights Campaign Fund, contact the assistant political director at:

Human Rights Campaign Fund
1012 14th Street NW
Sixth Floor
Washington, D.C. 20005
202-628-4160 - voice
202-347-5323 - fax

We hope that over the next few years, strong lesbian and gay candidates emerge and run for office, especially for Congress, and that we can work together as a community to see that they are elected.

In 1985, after almost two decades in politics (during which he worked on many campaigns, including McCarthy, McGovern, Udall, Kennedy, Cranston and Carter for President, Shapp for (PA) Governor and Wilson Goode for [Philadelphia] Mayor), Eric Rosenthal joined the staff of the Human Rights Campaign Fund where he now serves as political director. Rosenthal developed the Campaign Fund's PAC and election-related programs, including presidential, congressional and ballot-measure campaigns. He is also an experienced congressional lobbyist on lesbian and gay issues, a past officer of the Gertrude Stein Democratic Club and was an active member of the Gay and Lesbian Activists Alliance.

The Log Cabin Federation
Richard Tafel

THE Log Cabin Federation (LCF) is a national, grassroots, gay and lesbian Republican federation of local and statewide clubs in over 20 states across the country. The local Log Cabin clubs are partisan Republican organizations that endorse candidates, organize volunteer efforts (Get-Out-the-Vote, phone banks, rallies, voter registration drives, candidate forums, etc.), funnel donor network funds and contribute directly to candidates through political action committees (PACs).

The local clubs are politically autonomous and set their own guidelines for endorsing and supporting candidates. Federation bylaws limit endorsements to GOP candidates in partisan races. Since the LCF is a growing organization, the size and scope of the clubs vary. Some clubs have hundreds of active members, some of whom are elected or appointed officials in city and state governments. Newer clubs look for campaigns to bolster their growth and exposure.

LCF divides the nation into seven regions, and a regional director is assigned to support the clubs in each region. If you are interested in finding out if there is a Log Cabin club in your area, contact the LCF national president, Abner Mason at (617) 266-7052. He can put interested persons in touch with their regional director.

Generally LCF's strongest endorsements have gone to candidates who demonstrate their support for gay and lesbian participation in the Republican Party. While a candidate's positions on gay and lesbian issues are always evaluated, issues such as crime, taxes, government spending and other traditional GOP issues have also played an important role, particularly in nonpartisan elections. Among the more notable recipients of Log Cabin endorsements have been Governor William Weld of Massachusetts (1990), Mayor Richard Riordan of Los Angeles (1993), Mayor Rudolph Giuliani of New York (1993), and Governor Christine Todd Whitman of New Jersey (1993).

Log Cabin does not make comparisons between a GOP candidate and the non-Republican opponent(s) when deciding on an endorsement in a partisan general election, particularly when the GOP candidate is openly hostile to the gay and lesbian community. Instead of endorsing the candidate of another party, we will, in most cases, issue a public "non-endorsement" of the Republican candidate. The best-known example of this was in Houston in 1992, when the LCF unanimously approved a non-endorsement of President George Bush.

Log Cabin Republicans (LCR), the Washington, DC-based information and advocacy arm of the LCF, has a full-time staff that focuses on compiling election data from around the country, as well as developing voter education guides and other instructional materials for those looking to get involved in campaigns and policy advocacy. For more information, call (202) 347-5307 or write LCR at 1012 14th Street, NW, Suite 703, Washington, DC 20005.

Richard L. Tafel is the national director of the Log Cabin Republicans. In 1987 he earned a Master of Divinity degree from Harvard Divinity School and was ordained in 1988 by the American Baptist Church. From August 1989 through November 1990, Tafel managed Republican Mike Duffy's race for state representative of Massachusetts from Boston. His blueprint for the Duffy campaign is currently taught as a case study at the Kennedy School of Government. In June 1992, Massachusetts Governor William Weld appointed Tafel as director of the Adolescent Health Program in the Massachusetts Department of Public Health. In this role, Tafel oversaw four million dollars in contracts for 32 state-funded adolescent health providers. In September 1993, Tafel left this position to launch Log Cabin Republicans

Gay and Lesbian Victory Fund

Christine Kehoe

THE Gay and Lesbian Victory Fund is a donor network of individuals committed to electing qualified openly gay and lesbian public officials. A nonconnected, nonpartisan, multi-candidate Federal political action committee, the Victory Fund supports candidates through training, in-kind contributions, referrals to campaign professionals and access to its donor network. It has no affiliation with any other organization and backs candidates for races at the city, county, state and Federal levels.

The election of Texas Governor Ann Richards provided the unlikely catalyst for the beginnings of the Gay and Lesbian Victory Fund. Her multi-millionaire opponent, Clayton Williams, raised $20 million, with at least $10 million in the form of a personal loan to his own campaign. Clearly outspent by her oilman foe, Richards raised $10.5 million to become the Lone Star State's chief executive officer. When you strip away the advantage provided to Williams by his own checkbook, Richards not only beat him at the ballot box, but she actually raised $500,000 more than he did. These contributions were directly related to EMILY's List, a donor network of dedicated contributors who had agreed in advance to support at least two national races with contributions of $100 or more. The acronym EMILY stands for "Early Money Is Like Yeast" – it makes the "dough" rise.

Within days of Richards' election, Dallas gay activist William Waybourn placed a call to former Human Rights Campaign Fund executive director Vic Basile. Waybourn believed that the lesbian and gay community and its candidates were missing out on the opportunity afforded women candidates by the strategy developed by EMILY's List. In December 1990, Basile and Waybourn met in Washington, DC, to formulate a strategy for developing a similar organization. The initial reaction of gay and lesbian activists to the Victory Fund idea was tremendous. Waybourn and Basile met again in New York in January 1991 to further outline a strategy for electing more openly gay and lesbian candidates to public office. Activists again reacted positively and encouraged them to found the Victory Fund. During the next several months, Waybourn and Basile sought financial commitments from major funders and asked activists selected for their fundraising and political prowess to serve on the founding board of directors. Portland activist and fundraiser Terry Bean; political guru David Mixner of Los Angeles; former professional athlete and business woman Lynn Greer of Columbus, Ohio; Los Angeles AIDS researcher and physician Dr. Scott Hitt; West Coast attorney and activist Roberta Bennett; Dallas Gay and Lesbian Alliance Executive Director John Thomas; recording industry executive Hilary Rosen; and Human Rights Campaign Fund Executive Director Tim McFeeley were among those who committed to raise $10,000 each and to serve on the board. These funds would be used to sustain the operation of the Victory Fund until a sufficient number of members could be attained.

On May 1, 1991, the Gay and Lesbian Victory Fund was formally created as a multi-candidate Federal political action committee – that is, as a donor network like EMILY's List but responsive to a different community. Waybourn was hired as Executive Director and Basile signed on as a consultant. In the fall of 1991, Seattle City Council candidate Sherry Harris became the first candidate recommended to the Victory Fund donor network, then consisting of 181 members. The overriding question at that time was whether or not lesbians and gay men living in other regions of the country would contribute money to the campaign of a woman running for office in the Northwest. The answer was an overwhelming "yes." A total of 41 members responded to the first candidate mailing with over $4,000. Harris used the money to help pay for a brochure entitled "With All Due Respect," which was sent directly to Seattle voters. Additional contributions kept rolling in from the network and, including City of Seattle matching funds for each check up to $50, eventually totalled over $14,000. With Victory Fund help, Harris beat a 24-year incumbent and became the nation's first openly lesbian African-American city councilmember.

In 1993, the Victory Fund supported me in my successful race to become San Diego's first openly lesbian city councilmember and it has helped elect many other "firsts" for our community including the first openly gay and lesbian state representatives in Oregon (Gail Shibley), Texas (Glen Maxey) and Wisconsin (Tammy Baldwin), and the first openly gay and lesbian city councilmembers in Seattle (Sherry Harris), Los Angeles (Jackie Goldberg), Santa Barbara (Tom Roberts), Dallas (Craig McDaniel) and Carrboro, North Carolina (Mike Nelson). The Victory Fund also played an important role in the 1992 re-election of Massachusetts Congressman Gerry Studds. During the 1993 election cycle alone, the Victory Fund helped elect eight candidates, including New York City Civil Court Judge Marilyn Shafer; Madison Municipal Judge Shelley Gaylord; and Minneapolis Board of Estimate and Taxation member Wally Swan.

The Victory Fund represents the most innovative and powerful process available for our movement to mobilize and empower our own. Because of its unique structure, the Victory Fund enables small donors to have a major impact on races. Early contributions of sufficient quantities to viable candidates transform qualified openly gay candidates from "fringe" status to "frontrunners." Individuals join the Victory Fund donor network for $100 or more and pledge to contribute $100 or more to at least two recommended candidates during a 12-month period. Members receive profiles of recommended candidates and decide which ones to support, and when. They make their checks payable to the candidate's campaign, but send them to the Victory Fund, where they are combined with contributions from other members and sent to the campaign as a massive show of community support. In order to be considered for Victory Fund recommendation, a candidate must:

▼ be openly gay or lesbian;

▼ endorse the Federal Gay/Lesbian Civil Rights Bill and similar state and local anti-discrimination laws and legislation;

▼ advocate progressive public policies and campaign positions relevant to AIDS research, education and treatment, gay and lesbian health and wellness, and women's reproductive freedom;

▼ demonstrate electoral viability.

To determine viability, the candidate must complete an exhaustive screening process and provide detailed responses to the following questions:

1. What do demographics and past voting behavior say about your ability to win? (Explain in detail and include poll data, if available.)

2. What is your campaign plan? What is your strategy for winning?

3. What demographic groups will you target?

4. What is your theme or message? What issues will you emphasize?

5. What are your greatest strengths *and* weaknesses as a candidate?

6. Have you ever run for office or worked on a campaign? Give details.

7. Have you ever held elected or appointed office? Please list offices and dates.

8. Who is (are) your opponent(s)? If you are an incumbent, explain in detail how your re-election is threatened and how you plan to overcome that threat.[1] Are there likely to be other viable openly gay/lesbian candidates in this race?[2] If your opponent is an incumbent, how is she/he vulnerable? If there is no incumbent, who are the other candidates and how are they vulnerable?

9. What is your campaign structure? What staff do you plan to hire?

10. Who is your campaign manager? What is his/her campaign experience?

11. What consultants have you/will you hire for media, polling, field operations and fundraising?

12. What is your itemized budget for both the primary and general elections? Include detailed expense and income budgets.

13. What is your fundraising plan?

14. How much money have you raised in past campaigns? How much have you raised to date? How much cash do you have on hand?

15. What are the individual and corporate spending limits for this race? What are the maximum individual and corporate campaign contributions allowed?

16. What endorsements have you received or do you expect

---

[1] The Victory Fund does not recommend incumbents unless they are seriously threatened.

[2] The Victory Fund will not recommend one viable openly gay/lesbian candidate over another.

to receive? What endorsements has (have) your opponent(s) received?

17. What is the date of the primary election? The general election?

The Victory Fund helps candidates and potential candidates in many other ways. The Victory Fund Leadership Development seminars organize regional and national workshops for candidates and campaign managers to give them an edge on the competition. The Victory Fund political resource database links qualified candidates (and potential candidates) with gay and lesbian officials, gay and lesbian political clubs and gay-friendly campaign professionals who can help them run winning campaigns.

Since it's inception in May of 1991, the Gay and Lesbian Victory Fund has grown to more than 4,000 members who have contributed more than a half million dollars directly to recommended candidates. These dedicated individuals and the openly gay and lesbian officials they help to elect are moving our community closer to its goal of true political empowerment. They embody both the spirit and the reality of the Victory Fund's motto: *Financial Clout for Candidates We Can Count On.*

Christine Kehoe was elected to the San Diego City Council in November 1993. Prior to her election, Kehoe served as a community development specialist for the City of San Diego and was responsible for project administration and development for neighborhood commercial areas and citywide public improvement projects. In her years as a city council aide, she directed legislation on small business, transportation, land use and planning issues. Recognized as a leader in the gay and lesbian community, she was one of the early directors of the AIDS Assistance Fund and served as editor of the award-winning San Diego Gayzette. *During her tenure as co-chair of the San Diego Gay and Lesbian Pride Celebration, the organization grew from a debt of $20,000 to its current annual operating budget of $125,000.*

Campaign Finance Disclosure:
Avoiding the Land Mines
Ken Gross

BECAUSE gay and lesbian candidates undergo even more public scrutiny than other candidates, it is especially important that you pay strict attention to campaign finance disclosure laws before you decide to run. Always keep in mind that the financing of your campaign, even that done while you were merely "testing the waters," must be disclosed after you decide to run. In fact, many jurisdictions require disclosure of personal income and financial holdings when you file for candidacy.

When considering the preparation of personal and campaign financial disclosure statements, do not approach the task looking for loopholes in the law or creative interpretations in the disclosure requirements. Some of the most politically destructive scandals regarding the disclosure of financial information did not involve violations of law, but interpretations that were considered too close to the line. Such problems sunk the Vice-Presidential campaign of Geraldine Ferraro, even though after years of investigation the Department of Justice and the Federal Election Commission found no violation of law.

The following guideposts will assist you in avoiding campaign finance disclosure land mines, but there is no substitute for obtaining qualified legal advice and assistance, both on the mechanics of the law and on the political implications of disclosure.

The Reporting Agency

▼ Reporting requirements and schedules vary from state to state, so before you start your campaign, determine exactly what the reporting obligations are.

▼ Find out when you must file a Statement of Candidacy and whether it is possible to "test the waters" before filing a Statement.

▼ When you file your Statement of Candidacy, you will get

some basic information and reporting forms from the state elections commission or the Secretary of State's office. Go to the office where you will be filing the reports. These offices have a wealth of information available to assist you. Pick up extra copies of the state or local rules that govern elections. Look at other candidates' reports.

▼ Find out the name and telephone number of the agency staff person responsible for reviewing your reports for accuracy. Be attentive to inquiries or informational notices they may send you or your campaign.

▼ Do not be afraid to call the agency to ask questions. It is much easier to get the answer beforehand than it is to go back and correct a problem.

▼ Generally, if it is impossible to gather all the necessary information to file a complete campaign finance report, it is usually better to file an incomplete report in a timely fashion (with a notation on the report indicating that the additional information is on request and the report will be amended upon its receipt), than to file a late report.

▼ Review all reports carefully. Although campaign finance reports are usually prepared, signed and filed by your campaign treasurer, you will be held accountable by your constituents and the press for any discrepancies or errors in these reports.

Accounting

▼ Maintain control over your campaign finances. Make sure there is a system for approving every expenditure and obtaining receipts for all disbursements.

▼ If your campaign can afford to hire a professional to assist in the preparation of the reports, do so. Otherwise, take the time to find a good campaign employee who will be around for the long haul. Continuity makes a world of difference.

▼ While there are several computer software packages on the market to assist in accurately reporting financial activities, you do not necessarily have to use one of these. Any computer program with spreadsheet capabilities will be a big help. If you use one of these, keep your records with as many fields as possible for easier and more efficient sorting.

Contributor Information

▼ Keeping contributor information on a computer program with sorting abilities will help you to spot your fundraising strengths and weaknesses and will greatly facilitate compliance with campaign finance laws.

▼ If you do not have all the information about a contributor that the reporting agency requires, write back to the contributor as soon as possible and request the missing information. Keep in mind that states vary on what information must be included in the report, and federal regulations specify the timing and wording of such requests. If the report becomes due before the information is available, type "Requested" (instead of leaving a blank space) wherever information is missing, and attach copies of the request letters to your report. This will let the agency, the press and the public know that you are attempting to obtain the information. When the contributor supplies the information, either amend your report or file supplemental statements.

▼ Set up a screening process to determine whether a contribution is illegal or one that you do not want to take because association with the contributor could cause political embarrassment. If you return the check before it is deposited, in federal elections and in most states, you do not have to report the receipt and return of the check. Once the check is deposited, however, you must show the receipt and the refund. Therefore, it is far more desirable to return checks before depositing. Most jurisdictions require that checks be deposited without delay (*i.e.*, within ten days of receipt) so the screening process must be done with dispatch.

▼ Even if you only need to disclose information about individuals who contributed more than a certain amount, try to get as much information as possible about all of your contributors.

▼ There is a wealth of information available on your opponent's campaign finance reports. Compare the contribution information that your opponent files with your own. Is your opponent receiving large amounts of money from a single industry or source? Is your opponent complying with both reporting and fundraising guidelines? Reviewing this information carefully will you help you determine your opponent's fundraising strengths and weaknesses. If your find that your opponent may have violated the law, he or she can be kept off balance if a publicized complaint is filed against their campaign. (Of course, be 100 percent certain that your reports are in order before embarking on such a strategy, as someone will certainly check into your disclosure record if such a charge is filed.)

Expenditure Information

▼ Expenditure information should also be kept on a computer program with sorting abilities. Make note of the expenditure type (*e.g.*, fundraising, media, administrative, etc.). This will save valuable time when preparing the reports.

▼ Sorting your expenditure list can provide valuable information. Are you spending a large percentage of your funds on a particular aspect of your campaign, such as advertising? Are you covering all voting districts evenly? The more fields in your database, the easier it will be to determine where your funds are going.

▼ Compare your own expenditure information with your opponent's. Where is your opponent purchasing mailing lists? How much has your opponent spent on print, radio and television advertising? Gather as much information about your opponent's expenditures as you do your own, so that you are as well versed as possible in his or her affairs.

Cash on Hand, Debts

▼ Keep as up-to-date as possible on your opponent's cash-on-hand situation, realizing that many candidates will, if it's within campaign finance disclosure laws, either declare or withhold funds which are brought in close to either side of a filing deadline. Do not assume that the filings represent absolute accuracy in your opponent's campaign finances.

▼ Compare debts with cash on hand for both you and your opponent. Will you have the funds for any last-minute expenditures? Will your opponent? To whom does your opponent owe large sums of money? To whom do you?

Compliance with the campaign finance and personal financial disclosure laws must be a major concern of your campaign. Expediting your campaign finance disclosure procedures efficiently and accurately will prevent your campaign from becoming mired in compliance issues that can sidetrack your campaign and mute its message. If your affairs are in order, it will not only make it more difficult for your opponent to find you at fault financially, but will also make you able to investigate and expose any mistake – intentional and otherwise — in his or hers without fear of a counter investigation.

An expert in the financial regulations and laws applying to political action committees, campaigns and businesses involved in the political process, **Ken Gross** is an advisor to the clients of Skadden, Arps, Slate, Meagher and Flom law firm. In addition to handling matters of campaign finance, Gross advises clients on various federal and state lobby registration laws and on ethics and conflict-of-interest laws, teaches law at George Washington University and serves as co-chair of the Practicing Law Institute's seminar on "Funding Federal Political Campaigns — PACs, Corporate Political Activities and Lobbying Law." From 1980 to 1986, Gross served as Associate General Counsel of the Federal Election Commission (FEC) for which he headed the Enforcement Division in the Office of General Counsel and supervised the legal staff that advises the FEC's audit division. He was also chair of the Political Campaign and Election Law Division of the Federal Bar Association, and has published many articles on campaign finance.

Getting Endorsements

Shelley Gaylord

W

HY should a candidate for public office care about getting endorsements? **First, endorsements give you a vehicle for talking to people about your qualifications and your message.** A request for an endorsement is a great way to persuade people that you're the right person for the office you seek. Some people actually expect to be asked for their endorsements and will be disappointed if you don't ask. Others will be flattered you thought of them. Many will give you an endorsement simply because you asked. The more seasoned political people will wait until the full slate is declared before lending their public support to you. In all cases, asking for endorsements gives you the opportunity to get your message out personally and to test out your message on different people and organizations. You have more time to persuade them in this way than with a TV or radio ad, and you can tailor your message precisely to meet your listeners' concerns.

Second, endorsements by well-known people and groups are instantaneous testimonies to your acceptability. Particularly when your race is one about which the broader voting public may not be aware, there will be very little attention paid to your campaign by the print and electronic media. And the less attention they provide for free, the more you need to generate and fund yourself. Impressive endorsements listed in various ads placed strategically for your voting audience may have as much impact as your message, which should also be included in the ads. Consider what you want these media ads to say about you. How much space and time can you afford to buy? Where and when will the ads be placed? What audience will likely see them? All these questions must be answered early in your campaign so you have a clear plan.

Third, endorsements that represent a wide spectrum of interests and attitudes convey fairness, competence and broad-based agreement on your candidacy. If your endorsements are from a variety of people and organizations, that tells the general public that you are not a single-issue candidate, one of the most common threats to a gay or lesbian candidacy. If the subtextual message of your campaign material listing your endorsements is: "If people who normally disagree can agree on this candidate, she/ he must be good!" then people who like to vote with the majority are going to feel comfortable supporting you because such a diverse group of people do so as well. Be careful, however, that you don't gather endorsements from people or groups who are too far apart or you'll risk losing endorsements by groups who don't want to be associated with one another, as well as presenting yourself as someone who isn't taking a stance on the issues and is instead trying to please everyone.

Fourth, endorsements lead to other forms of support. People are more likely to give you money if they think you can win. Organizations that endorse you may also be willing to give you their mailing lists or do mailings, literature drops, phone banking, advertisements of a slate they support or other favors for you. This means you get free benefits, votes and positive exposure that your opponent does not. Even if you lose the group endorsement, you may still persuade some of the members to support you and they will tell others.

Fifth, early and strong endorsements can scare off serious opponents. If you gain early endorsements from key influential people in your voting district, potential opponents may decide not to run because of your formidable show of support. Find out how early you can start campaigning given your local election rules. In many cases, you only have to be a properly declared candidate to start seeking endorsements.

Sixth, newspaper endorsements are politically powerful and they give you free advertising when the endorsement is announced. People always read the editorial page of the newspaper, particularly pending an election, and this kind of endorsement, accompanied as they often are by editorials with pithy reasons for the endorsement and a contrast between you and your opponents, has far-reaching effects as free and what some people think of as unbiased advertising for your candidacy. Newspaper endorsements can then be touted in other venues.

Now that you know why endorsements are so important to a successful campaign, how do you go about getting them? Endorsements are like money to your campaign – the earlier you get them the more effective they are – so begin researching all your possibilities as soon as, if not before, you announce your candidacy.

Gather endorsement lists from recently successful candidates in your campaign district. Find out who has run in the past with a platform similar to yours, then contact that person and ask for their list of endorsers. If you really are similar to this candidate, there's a good chance his/her endorsers will be eager to see you elected as well. This list will hopefully include individuals, groups, (labor unions of all kinds, women's groups, gay/lesbian/bisexual groups, police, firefighters, neighborhood associations, NAACP, student groups, etc.) newspapers, and television and radio stations that are influential in your race. Figure out who the influential people and groups are for the likely voters in your race, then spend hours *every* day calling potential endorsers and keep written records of all your calls and results. There's no real reason to stop calling people. Groups and newspapers should be contacted early by phone and mail. Send them literature of interest on your candidacy and specifically request an endorsement. Find out what the endorsement process is from each group or from others who have had recent success with it.

For all your endorsement interviews, do your homework. It is difficult to do your homework alone. You need to surround yourself with people who are up-to-date on the political scene and the influential players. Try out your message on your campaign team before taking it to any potential endorsers, focusing on the likely reaction of the intended audience. At this point you should figure out what you're going to say based on whether or not people are aware of your race, understand what the job is about, and know who you are and are familiar with your platform. Consider what the listener or listeners are interested in that is relevant to you and your race. Who else influences the listener – positively and negatively? What questions are likely to be asked by the individual or group? What responses are you going to give? Will your opponent be present while you speak to the group? What is the order of events? Do you prefer to speak last so you have the final word and can rebut your opponent's claims? Even for group endorsement processes, you may be able to call the people attending in advance of the meeting and spend time individually with them on the phone. (Find out first if they'll be offended by this! If not, you're simply giving the individual a fuller opportunity to ask you questions and become comfortable with you.) At many endorsement meetings you will only be given five minutes to talk, so advance discussion should help your chances of receiving the endorsement you seek. People like to talk to candidates; it makes them feel important because it conveys to them that you are interested in them personally and that you're willing to work hard to get their support.

Prepare both a long and short version of your message and target it to your audience. The short version is for people who are already inclined to support you. The longer version is: "Hi, I'm Shelley Gaylord and I'm running for municipal judge. The election is April 6th and I would like your support. Would you like to know what a municipal judge does and why you should support me?" Then give a two- to three-point explanation of the interesting parts of the job and your qualifications, highlighted by endorsements if you think they might matter to the person to whom you are speaking. Ask explicitly if you can use their name publicly as an endorser. If they're unsure, offer to send them some literature. If you are able to ask for money, do it right then. Do a follow-up mailing that day and get a return card confirming that you can use their name publicly as a supporter.

Finally, you have to believe in yourself and try to stay relaxed. Stressful questions will always arise and you should try to anticipate them. But not all questions have to be answered, or answered exactly as the questioner intended. Highlight your campaign message in your responses to questions. Also, think about what issues are hot right now. You should be able to answer the questions: "What distinguishes you from the other candidate(s)?" and "Why should I support you?" Also remember that any person you're talking to doesn't really care about how hard your day has been – he/she may already be a supporter of your opponent – so be professional. What you've said may be quoted later on.

*In April 1993, Madison Municipal Judge Shelley **Gaylord** became the first openly lesbian or gay person to be elected judge in Wisconsin. Prior to her election, Gaylord worked as a trial lawyer, serving the gay and lesbian community on a variety of issues, from domestic partner benefits to HIV and anti-discrimination cases, and in an effort to recognize the parental rights of gays and lesbians brought the only lesbian custody case to date before the Supreme Court. For her work on family law issues, Gaylord was appointed Family Law Chair of the Equal Justice Task Force, a statewide task force appointed to study gender bias in the legal system, by the Wisconsin Supreme Court. Gaylord also served as co-chair of the Dane County Bar Committee, on the Governor's Lesbian and Gay Task Force and as media coordinator for the 1989 GALVanize (Gay and Lesbian Visibility Alliance) March on Madison.*

Gays and Lesbians Winning

Beth Schapiro

POLLING is a key element of most successful campaigns. Strategic planning starts with polling. Polling data can provide a wealth of information on voter attitudes toward candidates, issues and institutions. Polling helps identify the themes and messages of the campaign, the targeted voters and specific messages for reaching those voters.

Polling is particularly important for gay and lesbian candidates because it can help uncover perceptions, attitudes and candidate expectations or voter expectations that might be rooted in the candidate's sexual orientation. Despite societal changes and the growing visibility of lesbians and gay men, voters generally perceive openly gay candidates through the lens of sexual orientation. A good campaign will be aware of those perceptions and will develop its strategic plan accordingly.

The campaign needs to understand the impact of the candidate's sexual orientation from the outset, so the initial focus groups and benchmark poll should test for this. If sexual orientation seems to be a major issue, the campaign may want to conduct additional focus groups with the demographic groups most likely to factor sexual orientation into their voting decisions.

Where do you incorporate sexual orientation into the polling research design? The basic research components and the quantity of research do not change significantly. You will still conduct a benchmark poll, and possibly focus groups, at the beginning of the campaign. You will still need follow-up and tracking polls during the campaign. You may still do focus groups to test themes and ads as the campaign unfolds. Where sexual orientation comes into play in research is in the content of questions asked in the focus groups and in the polls. When developing questions for the survey, be aware of some of the perceptions straight voters may have about homosexuality and gay candidates.

One set of perceptions revolves around attitudes toward homosexuality in general. The research should test for acceptance of homosexuality and the efforts to achieve equal treatment for gays and lesbians. Another set of perceptions relates to support for increasing the numbers of openly gay elected officials. Voters should be asked how important it is to them to elect more gays and lesbians to public office. Respondents should also be asked how likely they are to support an openly gay candidate. This can be tested in a self-contained question or as one of a list of characteristics that describe the candidates.

One way to uncover these distinctions is to use a split-sample methodology for some of the questions. Almost all of the questions asked every respondent should be identical. On a very small number of questions, half of the sample should be asked the question one way while the other half of the sample should be asked the question a different way. For instance, a common question involves a choice between two hypothetical candidates, Candidate A and Candidate B. The question might read "I am going to read brief descriptions of two candidates for city council." After reading the two descriptions, respondents are asked to choose the one they would pick if the election were held today. Respondents are then asked to explain the reason for their choice.

A description might read something like: "Candidate A is a business executive who has been president of the neighborhood civic association for the past six years. She is gay. Her supporters contend that her business experience is needed on the council and that her knowledge of neighborhood issues will help protect our neighborhoods. Her critics argue that the incumbent is effective and we should not sacrifice his 20 years of experience on the council." A similar description, including current office, strengths and weaknesses, is presented for Candidate B.

To test for the impact of sexual orientation, leave the "She is gay" or "He is straight" sentence in the descriptions read to half the sample. For the other half, do not insert a sentence concerning sexual orientation into either description. Do not change the descriptions in any other way. The follow-up question asking why the respondent made that choice also remains the same.

Compare the answers to the two different wordings of the question. There are two places to look to determine whether sexual orientation is an issue. First, examine the percentage of voters who choose each candidate in both samples, Look to see if support for gay Candidate A is higher than, lower than, or the same as for Candidate A with no reference to sexual orientation. If the numbers are higher or lower, then you can safely assume that homosexuality is an issue.

Second, analyze the answers to the follow-up question. Although some respondents may tell you openly that they will not support a candidate because she is a lesbian, others may give more subtle answers which also are based on the candidate's orientation. Review the follow-up responses carefully.

When analyzing the data, you want to look at it through three progressively smaller lenses. First, look at responses from the entire sample. Does sexual orientation seem to emerge as a consideration? If so, around what issues, characteristics or candidates?

Regardless of whether homosexuality surfaces anywhere within the entire sample, the second lens is that of broad demographic groups. Analyze each question by sex, race, age, religion, income, education, party affiliation, geographic location and any other variable that might differentiate among subsamples of the overall population. Look especially for differences between men and women because women generally are more tolerant and accepting of homosexuality.

The third and most discreet level of analysis is within subgroups of the broad demographic groups. Again you want to focus on women and men. Break each sex down into categories by age, income, and other variables that might be important to your race.

What you want to do is identify the specific groups of voters who are likely to be affected by the fact that the candidate is openly gay. Determine just what it is about sexual orientation that has an impact. The data analysis should enable you to understand who is likely to support an openly gay candidate and why. You also need to know where opposition is likely to come from. The more you know about specific demographic groups, the more precisely you can target. Data analysis should help you create overall campaign themes as well as show you how sexual orientation fits into your overall message.

Being openly gay will have an impact on the voters, but it is certainly not the only factor that voters look at. The candidate still must be credible and must have reasons to be supported in addition to being gay. Polling can help you understand the impact of sexual orientation and use it to your advantage. Now go out there and build a winning coalition and get elected to office!

Dr. Beth Schapiro holds an M.A. and a Ph.D. in political science from Emory University. Before establishing the consulting firm of Beth Schapiro and Associates, she served as Executive Director of Research Atlanta and as Senior Planner in the Georgia Governor's Office of Planning and Budget. She has taught courses at Emory University and the Georgia Institute of Technology and led numerous political and lobbying skills workshops, and is a member of the American Association for Public Opinion Research and the American Association of Political Consultants.

Targeting the Voters
Robert G. Meadow

E
VERYBODY uses the term "targeting" in political campaigns. Some consultants and candidates even think that "targeting"is a campaign strategy. It is not. Targeting is a method for implementing your strategy and conveying your message by choosing where campaign efforts are best made. Fundraising specialists target likely donors for special attention. A scheduler will target certain communities for a personal visit by the candidate. A direct mail specialist will target a brochure focused on Medicare cutbacks only to senior citizens while sending a pro-choice piece to Republican women under the age of 45. A field coordinator for an openly gay candidate will target an area where gay and lesbian candidates have performed well in previous elections for a Get-Out-the-Vote campaign. All of these activities are forms of targeting, and all are motivated by the same fundamental campaign reality: resources in a campaign are limited.

Most often, targeting decisions are made based on the need to gain 50 percent plus one vote on election day. How and where do we find the voters who can be persuaded from undecided to supporting our candidate? How and where do we find voters who can be converted from their support of the opposing candidate? How and where do we find voters who support our candidate, but who need reinforcing messages or who have to be brought out to the polls? What messages do we have to provide to these voters? These are the key elements of election targeting.

Why should I target?

Because resources in a campaign are limited, you must target to win. There are never enough volunteers to walk precincts or make phone calls. There is never enough time for the candidate to make all the personal appearances that are requested. And, of course, there is never enough money for voter contact through direct mail or electronic media. Targeting helps you concentrate your resources where they will do the most good.

Targeting is based on a very simple principle: all people are not the same, but some people are more alike than they are like other people. All of us belong to several groups – we are women or men, we are gay or lesbian or straight, we are in certain age brackets, we belong to different political parties and religious organizations, we have different professions, and so forth. As a result, our interests, concerns and priorities are not all the same. Because the electorate is diverse, the same message does not work for all voters. And even if the "message" is the same, the vehicle for delivering that message may vary because not all voters have the same media habits or use the same vocabulary to describe the issues.

In addition to the scarcity of resources, there is another important reason to target. Unlike candidates and consultants, voters do not live and breathe politics. To many voters, elections are a lot of clutter and noise. To cut through this, you must get the right message to the right voter. Voters need to know that candidates are responsive to them. Touching voters with a message that will move them, persuade them and reinforce their support is crucial. Senior citizens are more concerned about health and money; young adults are more concerned about jobs; young to middle-age voters who are parents of school-age children are concerned about education. The connection a candidate has to a voter depends on how the voter is touched. And more voters can be touched if the right message is targeted to the right person.

What types of targeting are there?

There are three types of targeting: aggregate, individual and hybrid.

Aggregate targeting, also known as geographic, historical or precinct targeting, seeks to identify regions and areas that have provided a core of support (or opposition), and, more importantly, where "switch" voters and ticket-splitters can be found. Aggregate targeting does not take into account individual voting characteristics, but only the voting patterns and demographics of the community as a whole. Aggregate targeting is best used where there is no individual-level data available through a political database or where there are no resources available to target voters individually.

The fundamental assumption of aggregate targeting is that there are "good" and "bad" neighborhoods for a given campaign. This can be based on past election performances of an identified community of interest or even on "gut" feelings. If, for example, candidates stressing "traditional family values" and "fundamentalism" have been successful in certain neighborhoods in the past, an openly gay or lesbian candidate is not likely to meet with success in those areas. Here's an example of aggregate targeting: In an attempt to reach gay and lesbian voters, a car with a loudspeaker announcing "Vote for Chris Kehoe" drives around a neighborhood that has a large gay and lesbian population. The whole community – gay and straight alike – gets the same message. Election-eve doorhanging parties, when doorhangers are indiscriminately placed in selected neighborhoods, are another form of aggregate targeting.

Individual targeting, on the other hand, requires that you have data on individual voters. It is the most widely used form of targeting because it replaces assumptions about voters (which are based on where the voter lives) with facts. For individual targeting to work, there must be an integration of a voter database and information on which messages work with which voters. Using this information, you can classify voters who meet the appropriate demographic profiles (as identified through research) as persuadable opponents, weak supporters and undecided voters to be targeted.

The first tool for doing individual targeting is a (preferably computerized) voter database. The database can be built from information provided by the clerk or registrar of voters, or purchased from a commercial vendor. Typically, the information carried by the registrar of voters includes a name, address, date of birth, date of registration and political precinct for each individual. It may also include other information such as political party, sex or race. Having this basic data enables some manipulation of messages to voters based not only on where they live, but on these factors and various combinations thereof. Thus, even without a sophisticated database, it still may be possible to target messages to such groups as Democratic voters under 65 who live near the prison, or Republican women over 55 who have been registered at the same address for 20 years.

The second major tool for individual targeting is public opinion research. If you know how to use it, the data from public opinion polls can identify which messages are the most persuasive for the electorate as a whole, and provide information on precisely which demographic subgroups of voters are moved by which messages. If you have a good pollster, he/she can provide a profile of each group of voters and help you target the right message to each one. The goal is to target the voters who can be persuaded by messages identified in the polling data.

Hybrid targeting, sometimes called geodemographic targeting, is a blend of aggregate and individual targeting. With this method, voters are targeted in those census tracts where a high number of voters who meet a demographic profile of supporters are known to reside. This method is particularly valuable where, because of poor voter and registrar of voter files, there is no demographic information on individual voters. It can also be used to supplement individual database targeting. The assumption for using census data is that people who live in the same neighborhood tend to share the same demographic characteristics. For example, poor people tend to live near other poor people; gay and lesbian voters are more likely to cluster in the central city areas than in the suburbs. Mapping this information onto political precincts, which is becoming easier because of the way census data is now being reported, allows the targeter to have an empirical indication of the demographic characteristics of the political precincts to replace his or her intuition. It is important to note, however, that census data tells us only about neighborhoods, not about each person in that neighborhood, so we may be making false assumptions about some individuals.

Finally, hybrid targeting can be most powerful when combined with a political database. Geodemographic clusters can be included in the voter file. Based on the polling data – which can be analyzed by cluster group — messages can then be tailored to the voter's cluster. In election districts that have many media markets with different geodemographic profiles, different political spots can be aired that are persuasive to voters of particular clusters.

Which type of targeting should you use? Because votes are cast by voters, not by precincts, it is best in most cases to target by individual, provided that you have a good database that enables messages to be targeted to voters with identified characteristics. The more information in the voter database, the more finely targeted your messages can be. But effective use of an individual database requires that there be a good public opinion poll conducted. Although it is possible to target messages through "gut" feelings, such messages are likely to be so broad and generic that full advantage will not be taken of the diverse interests of the electorate. Without a poll, there is also a substantial risk that the wrong messages will go to the wrong voters.

Although party discipline has broken down in recent decades, party identification is still the best predictor of how a person will vote in partisan elections. Thus, a rough look at voting history is a valuable first cut to determine whether any effort will pay off. After all, the most outstanding database won't help you if the number of voters who can be persuaded by effectively targeting your message to them is not enough to win the election.

What are the tactical applications of targeting?

Depending on the election district, the diversity of the electorate, the quality of the database and the cost of transmission, campaign messages can be either broadcast or narrowcast. If the same message works for most voters, a broadcast message through an imprecise vehicle such as television is warranted. More narrowcast messages can be sent using such methods as direct mailing.

Targeting can play a major role even in political television advertising. In multiple-media-market election districts, aggregate targeting will show where the broadcast money should be spent by indicating those media markets where the greatest percentage of ticket-splitters and switchers reside. Guided by polling results that determine precisely which programs or program types are viewed by the persuadable voters (or those who have to be reinforced), a good buyer can pinpoint those times and slots to target the broadcast message. But even if you buy media time when persuadable voters are most likely to be viewing, there is still a lack of precision inherent in the medium.

Targeting is essential for a direct mail program. Different mail pieces can be targeted to different groups. When voting groups with shared interests and concerns are large, brochures and self-mailers are best. When there is a well-developed voter database with supporters clearly identified, or when the voters' issue concerns have been identified by phone banks and precinct walking, personalized letters may be more appropriate. A direct mail program can target different voters for persuasion or reinforcement. Perhaps most importantly, if targeting is done well and there is good individual data, it may be possible to drop strong supporters or strong opponents from the mail program completely, allowing campaign resources to be deployed where they are most needed: persuading undecided voters, reinforcing weak supporters and converting voters leaning toward the opposing candidate.

Cable television lies between television and direct mail, offering some ability to target narrowly (gay and lesbian broadcasts, senior channel, news junkies, Spanish language, etc.). Radio, with some ability to find smaller audiences based on listener demographics, also lies somewhere in between television and direct mail in terms of casting your message narrowly or broadly. New technologies can also be harnessed with good targeting. You can target special messages to users of computer bulletin boards. Targeting of very likely voters through a database that contains good voting history records may reduce the voting universe so much that relatively expensive media, such as individual videotapes, can be sent to likely voting households. This gives you the possibility of sending different taped messages to voters with different interests as identified through the survey research. Targeting can also play a role in scheduling determining where candidate time is best spent.

Targeting the gay and lesbian community

The registrar of voters or county clerks generally maintains voter files with gender or date of birth, so grouping voters into age or gender groups is simple when developing a voter file for individual targeting. But gay and lesbian voters cannot be identified the same way that voters can be identified across age groups, or by ethnicity or sex. Census reports indicate which areas of a community have a large percentage of African-American or Hispanic residents, making it possible to apply geodemographic or hybrid targeting. But there is no census data identifying geographic areas in terms of which communities have an unusually high percentage of gay and lesbian residents. As a result, most candidates and consultants have relied on one of two methods to target gay and lesbian voters. First, for individual targeting, gay and lesbian candidates use "affinity lists" – those who have made previous campaign contributions to gay and lesbian candidates, members of gay and lesbian organizations, and so forth. Second, candidates use broad aggregate targeting to identify where gays and lesbians live, or where gay and lesbian candidates have performed well.

It is possible to use some of the methods of individual targeting to "guess" at which households contain gay and lesbian voters who do not appear on any "lists." For example, using the voter file, it is possible to "flag" households that have two residents, with different last names, of the same sex, who have birth dates within 18 years of one another. This would yield households that potentially have gay or lesbian couples by eliminating married couples, two brothers or sisters, or straight couples, and most father/child and mother/child combinations. The flagged voters could then be sent a targeted "gay/lesbian" message.

As is always the case with individual targeting, there are assumptions that have to be made that may be inaccurate for individual cases. It is important to note, therefore, that some straight men and women who have roommates of the same sex will be flagged in the voter file using the method just described. But if the targeted voters live in areas that are known to contain a high proportion of gay and lesbian voters, it may be assumed that the straight voters have opinions that are sympathetic to the gay community.

Who does the targeting?

Each type of targeting requires a different level of expertise. Aggregate targeting generally requires only an analysis of election returns, which can be calculated by a competent student volunteer and a computer. The campaign consultant or manager can take the results of the sorts and make decisions about where to make efforts.

For individual and hybrid targeting without a poll, a media or direct mail specialist will use his/her experience and "gut" feelings about how to target. When a poll is conducted, the pollster, electronic media and direct mail specialist will jointly be responsible for targeting.

How are messages and targeting linked?

Every campaign has — or should have — a message, and the message has to go to the right people. Although the campaign may have a single theme, such as "change" or "the economy," the way it is manifested may be different for each demographic group. The "economy" may mean jobs for young people, and safe pensions for older people. "Health care" may mean nursing home costs for seniors and health insurance for young people. Each group may need to have a different focus and a different vocabulary so that the campaign message is tailored to the unique needs of each targeted group.

In all cases, it is important to temper the results of a precinct sort or of a poll with sound political judgment that takes into account the unique characteristics of the district. There are also a number of other factors to consider, such as budget. Each piece of direct mail that is narrowly targeted costs more, because the print run is smaller per piece. Broadcast media may be cheaper in some markets, more expensive in others. There may be no need for dozens of combinations of direct mail in some circumstances when there is a single message, and at other times a broadcast television message just will not do. With targeting, your message eggs are not just in one basket.

What are the risks of targeting?

The first risk is that you will do it poorly. Because all targeting depends on our ability to generalize, if we make erroneous assumptions and generalize inappropriately the wrong message will go to the wrong people.

Trying to do aggregate targeting when district boundaries change is also problematic. Shifting political boundaries means that elections are not quite comparable, especially if precincts are merged and divided. Comparing election returns in this kind of environment is almost impossible.

One of the major criticisms of the principle of targeting is that it suggests that different things are said to different audiences. But no candidate worthy of office expresses inconsistent views to audiences by pandering to their concerns, telling one group of voters she is opposed to family leave, and another group she favors it.

Good candidates, however, know that voter interests vary, so one group of voters, such as women 25-40, may hear her position on day care, but another group of voters, such as men between 25 and 40, will hear her message on job creation.

There is also the risk that voters will feel their "privacy" is being violated when they receive highly targeted mail such as laser letters that address them by name. Or voters may consider themselves de-individualized and may resent being "lumped" with other voters who share their demographic characteristics and who are targeted with a "Jewish voter" letter or a "gay brochure" or a "women's mailer."

Finally, although on some issues, such as partnership benefits, AIDS funding or anti-discrimination laws based on sexual orientation, there may be strong gay and lesbian voting unity, on a range of other issues, sexual orientation may be irrelevant. Obviously, there are gay and lesbian Democrats and Republicans, gay and lesbian conservatives and liberals, and of course there may be issues on which gay men and lesbians may disagree with one another.

But overall, targeting (tempered by research and political judgment) is worth the risks. It enables the campaign to use resources effectively, touch voters with messages that move them and propel the campaign toward election day victory.

Robert Meadow, Ph.D., is the founder and president of Decision Research, a California-based company that provides public opinion research services and strategic advice to Democratic political candidates, governmental and nonprofit organizations and ballot proposition committees. He has served as consultant to many campaigns, including that of Jackie Goldberg, elected as the first openly lesbian Los Angeles City Councilmember, and Tom Nolan, who ran for Congress from California as openly gay. He has also held full-time faculty positions at several research universities and is now an adjunct professor at the Annenberg School for Communications at the University of Southern California. Meadow has published extensively in social science research and applied public opinion journals, and has authored four books on politics and political analysis.

Voter Contact Strategy

David Clarenbach

A S modern campaign techniques become more sophisticated and specialized, campaigns increasingly rely, for good reason, on polls and focus groups, media gurus and spin doctors, computers, telemarketing, targeting, and direct mail. Yet the basic premise of a candidate running for public office remains the same: the one who gets the most voters to pull his or her lever wins the election.

The days have long since passed when an office seeker could expect to win an election by standing on a soapbox in the village square. A successful voter contact strategy must use the most modern techniques to identify likely voters. But, as is too often the case, those of us who run for office can become overwhelmed with the glitzy aspects of the campaign and ignore the surefire strategy of direct voter contact. In any campaign where the voting jurisdiction is less than statewide, it is necessary for the candidate to engage in truly participatory politics. Nothing can replace the personal touch of voter contact and, as the centerpiece of a grass-roots strategy, the candidate must act to bring the campaign directly to the voter.

The Personal Sacrifice

Participatory politics require candidates to make personal sacrifices and take responsibility for doing some things for themselves. To carry out a successful voter contact strategy, the candidate must make the commitment to spend long hours pounding the pavement on a daily basis over many months of the campaign. The result of this effort is not only the many thousands of personal interactions with real voters that will likely provide the margin of victory in a close election, but also the building of a relationship between leader and constituency based on mutual trust, which is especially important for those running as openly gay or lesbian.

When to begin

Of all the aspects of running a winning campaign, the decision by the candidate to run is perhaps the most intimate and fundamental. In making the decision, it's important to look at what wins a campaign. A campaign is usually won or lost by a series of choices: choices by community leaders and volunteers to work for the campaign; decisions to take stands on some issues and to ignore others; selection of themes and principles on which the campaign will be based; identification of key and trusted managers; and contracting with pollsters, researchers, media advisors and other campaign specialists. All are important, yet all are secondary to the decision by the candidate to run an honest campaign as an openly gay or lesbian individual. And then comes the decision to put oneself on the line – at the voter's doorstep – to make sure the campaign is won.

This personal decision by the candidate must be made as early as possible, many months in advance of the election, or even the announcement of candidacy. To personally meet as many likely voters as will be necessary to win takes time, and lots of it. So, don't sell yourself short of time!

Planning, planning, planning

This strategy of direct voter contact begins with planning. Think of your own neighborhood and the hundreds of people who live there. Then multiply that by the numerous neighborhoods that make up your election district. Overwhelming? Yes. Impossible? NO!

Remember that in some areas less than half of all residents are registered to vote. If, for example, your neighborhood has 500 residents, perhaps as few as 250 are registered. In the average general election, a 50-percent turnout of registered voters is considered good, so now you've narrowed your focus to 125 individuals. Primary elections usually turn out even fewer. If you live in a 55-percent Democratic area (and you're running in the Democratic primary), your target list is 55 percent of 125 individuals, or 68.75 people. Okay, let's call it 69. Add to that the fact that most voting households have an average of two voters in it, and because households tend to have similar partisan voting patterns, that means you've narrowed your list of doors to as few as 34.

How long would it take, then, for the candidate to personally cover an entire neighborhood of 500 people door-to-door? My experience is about an hour and a half, if you use the Voter Contact Strategy System.

The system

Over the years, I have refined the Voter Contact Strategy System to a science. Most communities have lists of registered voters, identified by name, address, voting history, and frequently by party affiliation, age, gender, phone number, and other useful information. If you are running in a primary, the targeted voters are those of your party affiliation who regularly vote in primary elections. Use your computer geniuses (or, for noncomputerized registration systems, put your volunteers to work) to cull the voter files to identify your primary voters and print them out by street address.

Schedule four or five days a week, preferably during late afternoon and evening daylight hours, for the candidate to "do the doors." (Note to schedulers: None but the most psychotic of candidates will actually want to do the doors, and a few have been known to lie about doing them, so build in some fail-safe device to ensure compliance.) Prioritize the geographical voting units (wards or precincts) based on the strategy unique to your campaign. Where is the campaign the strongest, or where is the volatility index the highest? Avoid your weakest ward at almost every cost. As they say in Wisconsin, "Pick the cherries where the trees grow."

Put one person in charge of The System to make it happen and to provide the follow-through on each step. Put the wards to be visited on the candidate's schedule each week. The week before a ward is scheduled, send a letter or postcard, signed personally by the candidate, to each of the targeted households announcing that the candidate will be visiting the neighborhood in the near future (don't promise a specific date; see candidate reluctance disclaimer above, and always be prepared for other unforeseen scheduling changes). This not only alerts the community that the candidate is accessible, has a presence, and is actively soliciting their support, but provides an address correction return so, when "Door Day" arrives, the candidate doesn't waste time at a door if the targeted voter has moved.

D-Day every day

Each "Door Day," send a responsible volunteer with the candidate to do the recordkeeping (and to ensure candidate compliance!). Bring along buttons, window signs and contribution/volunteer cards to give to supporters who seem especially hot. In more disbursed neighborhoods or rural areas, have the volunteer drive the car, keep the notes, and work the map while the candidate runs to the door. In compact areas, the volunteer should accompany the candidate on foot. Don't forget to stop into businesses along the way to greet the employees and customers and to ask about putting up a sign.

The candidate's goal is to make a quick hit and move on – a few sentences of introduction should be sufficient. NEVER spend more than a minute or two at any one door, and never argue or engage in prolonged discussions. Think of each contact as the candidate's opportunity for a 30-second, in-person commercial. Every ten minutes you waste gabbing with one voter is three or four voters you will miss.

The candidate should hand the voters his/her basic literature and determine their willingness to support him/her ("May I count on your support on election day?"). The volunteer should make note of this crucial information, as well as name and spelling corrections, on the walking list of targeted voters. If no one is at home, leave your literature and a pre-signed note saying you're sorry to have missed them.

Every single voter must be rated during your visit. Ratings can be plus, minus, zero or one through five, based on their responsiveness. Make note of those who weren't home, questions to be followed up on by volunteers, and any special issue interests for future mailings and phone calls. Your rating of targeted voters will prove useful for issue mailings, financial solicitations, and the all-important Get-Out-the-Vote (GOTV) effort on election day.

If the candidate has hustle, and depending on the compactness of the neighborhood, he/she can hit up to 25 doors in an hour. If the candidate does doors four hours a day just four days per week, that's

1,600 doors — potentially 3,200 voters — every month. That alone will win a tight race for you!

Follow-up

Even though the candidate's day is done, the coordinator of the Voter Contact Strategy System must immediately follow-up on the contacts made each day. A thank-you letter, personally signed by the candidate, should be sent to each household, with separate texts available for those who are supportive, undecided, not at home and, perhaps, even those opposed (it's funny what changes people's minds). Insert a position paper on their favorite issue or an invitation to an upcoming neighborhood meeting or fundraiser. Always forward supportive names to the volunteer coordinator — "doing the doors" is a great way to recruit new people to work on the campaign. "Door Day" is a source of potential contributors, endorsers and lawn sign locations. And, it's the basis for GOTV activities on election day.

The guarantee

The System guarantees that the candidate directly touches the real lives of real people, from all walks of life and all parts of the district, on a regular basis.

The System is compatible with a more traditional grass-roots volunteer campaign based on ward captains and voter registration, in addition to the media, fundraising, and direct mail techniques of the modern campaign. It forces the candidate off the rubber-chicken circuit and away from an exclusive reliance on the political elite, television packaging and photo opportunities. And, it makes every politician stronger as a candidate and as an officeholder, more in touch with constituents and less vulnerable to gay/lesbian-bashing political attacks.

I have been elected to two terms on our County Board of Supervisors, served on our City Council, and have been a member of the Wisconsin State Assembly for 18 years — over two decades of public service, of which I am most proud. Throughout my tenure in office, I have refined this plan with every campaign. I can guarantee that it makes a weak candidate stronger, a marginal candidate viable, and a candidate on the edge a winner.

A political and public affairs consultant with the Clarenbach Consulting Group, David Clarenbach was a Democratic congressional candidate from Wisconsin's 2nd District in 1992. He began his political career in 1972 when he won his first term as county supervisor at the age of 18. He served on the Dane County Board of Supervisors from 1972-74, on the Madison Common Council in 1974 and on the Wisconsin State Assembly from 1975-1993, where he served as Speaker Pro Tem from 1983 to 1993. During his tenure as assemblyman, Clarenbach wrote the legislation that extended statewide anti-discrimination laws to include sexual orientation. He also authored Wisconsin's Hate Crimes Act, which was upheld unanimously by the U.S. Supreme Court, and a Bill of Rights for People with AIDS and HIV infection.

Coming Out on Every Doorstep

Gail Shibley

"The personal is political."

THAT phrase was used time and time again in the modern feminist movement to signal that women "got it." Women, and many men, used the phrase to express recognition of the political policies underlying what they had come to accept as everyday reality.

Since the 1970s, I'd not given much thought to that phrase, a nostalgic relic of a historic era. But it fits. It fits the battles that lesbians and gay men are fighting against discrimination and anti-gay legislation throughout the nation. It fits my fight to become Oregon's first openly gay elected state representative. And for all openly gay and lesbian candidates, it fits even better backwards: The political is personal.

Let me share with you some absurdly conflicting stereotypes:

"They are clannish/They are loners; They look like everybody else/They look absolutely different than everybody else; They are communists and anarchists/They are affluent capitalists; They love money/They despise worldly goods."

Sound familiar? Likely so. For these and other stereotypes have been used against gays and lesbians in Oregon and around the world. But that's not where they come from. They are, in fact, a paraphrase of Cornell University's Sander Gillman's comments in the opening scene of "The Longest Hatred," Oregon Public Broadcasting's show on anti-semitism. I borrow them here for three reasons:

First, all discrimination is unique to the targeted minority. The cost is specific; it cannot be quantified or equated. But the dynamics of the scapegoating and the illogic behind the phenomenon – and the pain it is intended to inflict – are the same. Thus, we shed light on one by illuminating another. National gay activist Phil Wilson captured this truth succinctly when he stated, "I've been called a 'nigger,' and I've been called a 'faggot' – and I know the difference: *nothing*."

Second, as with religious, cultural, and racial minorities, the stereotypical image of gays and lesbians is a protean one. It shifts. That is precisely what is so convenient about it. It isn't just that gays and lesbians are "x." Gays and lesbians are portrayed as everything you don't want yourself – or your family – to be. Gays and lesbians are painted as everything that threatens you, your sense of the way things are, and the way things ought to be. St. John Chrisastum, at the turn of the century, said of the Jews, "They are the common disgrace and the infection of the whole world." A thousand years later, in 1990, the Reverend Lou Sheldon said of gays and lesbians, "They live perverted, twisted lives that feed upon the unsuspecting and the innocent — like our children." In the 1940s, government "experts" argued that integrating blacks into the military would spread disease, erode the morals of soldiers, and undermine the effectiveness of the armed services. Sound familiar?

Third, it is exactly this kind of stereotypical image that the openly gay/lesbian candidate has to conquer. Gays and lesbians, like other groups throughout history, know what it is to be accursed; we know what it's like to be excluded; what it's like to be considered unworthy of respect; to be stigmatized as the "other." What could be more personal, or more political?

It is this sadly human phenomenon of scapegoating and stereotyping that was played out in Oregon's political stage in 1992. The Radical Right was trying to pass Ballot Measure 9; its target was gays and lesbians. Lest we forget, the question was whether or not to amend Oregon's constitution to require discrimination on the basis of one's status, one's sexual orientation. In the midst of this, I was running for office, in the unique position of being both an (appointed) incumbent and a first-time candidate. As an incumbent, I was the first and only openly gay legislator in our state's history – one of only a few in the history of state legislatures in our country.

Daily the media was filled with stories about the nefarious anti-gay initiative; debates, speeches, rallies and marches were held on both sides to garner support. Not surprisingly, the issues and emotions brought out by Measure 9 were on many minds during that time. Because of my unique position of sharing the ballot with the initiative, I felt it important for people to know where I stood and why. Thus, I came out to thousands of strangers – not once, twice or a mere dozen times, but on doorstep after doorstep, in neighborhood after neighborhood, week after week, month after month. Campaigning, for any candidate, is extremely stressful and fatiguing. As tiring as the rest of my political campaign was, however, it did not compare with the personal fatigue and, at times, fear of coming out person to person, face to face. People literally thumped me away from their doorsteps with bibles. At times I was physically frightened. I received harassing phone calls and hate mail at home. My house was egged, my car vandalized, my lawn signs targeted for destruction and theft. My partner and I slept with a crowbar by our bed. Below is one short, edited portion of a letter I received:

Dear Ms. Lesbo,
Having just read about your efforts in behalf of the queer community and pending legislation thereof, you may be interested in my bigoted opinions:
(He then listed several, among them:)
I run a major company, it is our policy not to consider any fags or dikes [sic] for employment, this will never change despite any legislation you may come up with.
I um not homophobic, I have no fear of your type, just contempt, you are a crime against nature.
As far as I am concerned AIDS is the best disease ever to come along. I personally get a lot of pleasure each time some [expletive deleted] faggot dies, hopefully all will follow.
In summation, you never will be more than the slimey pervert that you are now, forcing a law upon the rest of us will only act to stimulate more people to become active against you.
– The Committee to Keep Clackamas County Fag/Dike [sic] Free!

These experiences made me even more determined to get out and meet as many voters as I could. Although all candidates use personal contact to build name recognition and get their message out, for the openly gay or lesbian candidate, personal contact has the added dimension of educating the voters. Ignorance breeds fear, fear breeds resentment, resentment breeds hatred and hatred breeds discrimination – and violence. Personal contact is the best way to counteract this ignorance because it breaks down the stereotypes that form the barriers of mistrust, allowing voters to see the sameness instead of the imagined differences.

Although the candidate's time is limited and it is only possible to personally visit so many people, the impact that each visit has can be incredible. The story of your visit will quickly spread to friends, neighbors, colleagues. And the next time these people hear the words "gay" or "lesbian," instead of recalling the stereotype, they will remember your smile, your strong handshake and your willingness to listen to their concerns. A major victory, both personal and political.

Even though some consider it "preaching to the choir," openly gay candidates should not neglect their gay constituents. Gay and lesbian voters often need special attention themselves. With good reason, many in our community feel disenfranchised by the political process and betrayed by "friends" in office who didn't keep their promises. Your voter contact program can help fight two related enemies in the gay and lesbian community: complacency and apathy. Complacency results when people don't believe they need to get involved, when they don't perceive a threat as real, when they don't understand the connection between events happening outside their lives and events happening within their lives. Apathy results when people don't believe they make a difference when they do get involved. *Both* are deadly to our community, to our democracy and to our rights and responsibilities as citizens.

My campaign organization doubled as we continued the voter identification and Get-Out-the-Vote (GOTV) effort for the No-on-9 Committee, canvassing and phoning to identify supporters and opponents alike. We worked hard, and because we worked, it worked: my district opposed Measure 9 by more than 85 percent, and I won overwhelmingly against a well-funded opponent. In fact, I came close to garnering the most votes of any House candidate – including those with no opponent.

It was during my campaign that I realized the advantages of being an openly gay candidate. We are much better prepared than our straight counterparts for dealing with certain aspects of a political race. Like all gay citizens, we have already been the target of a vitriolic campaign of lies — what kind of negative campaigning could an opponent come up with to beat what we have to deal with in our everyday lives? After you've spent a lifetime justifying who you are to family, friends, employers, etc., explaining where you stand on political issues is a breeze. Openly gay and lesbian candidates already know what it's like to have our humanity up for a popular vote. We've done a lot of self-examination, and we know who we are and where we stand. We know what's important to us and we're willing to fight for it. And we are good fighters.

The campaign against Measure 9 was enormously costly in money, time and expertise – precious resources that were necessarily diverted from the many pressing, real problems facing our state. The human toll, however, was even more devastating. Personally, the combination of the Measure 9 fight and my own election campaign left me utterly fatigued, abjectly exhausted. I felt as though I'd run six marathons in two months. In a true manifestation of community, however, I soon learned I was far from alone. Gays and lesbians met in formal and informal support groups, meetings, and discussions. Some took on the added role of emotional counselor, helping others they knew from professional associations, social relationships and so on. The political became intensely personal. We made it through, and we will never be the same.

One of the shifting stereotypes often faced was (and is), "How can gays and lesbians be oppressed when there are so many of them in high places?" In reply, I am reminded of 1930s Austria, when Jews there included poets, playwrights, jurists, physicians, psychoanalysts like Sigmund Freud and composers like Schoenberg and Mahler. But even as they prospered in their individual professions, European anti-semitism was rampant. The rest is history.

Thus the question is not, "How can there be oppression when there are so many in high places?" but rather, "How can strides be made in the face of such oppression?" The remarkable thing is, there *have* been strides. Today, in national politics, there are numerous gays and lesbians in high-ranking positions in the Clinton Administration. And now I'm no longer Oregon's *only* openly gay state representative. Our state again made history with the appointment to the legislature of the first openly gay man, Portland attorney George Eighmey. And State Representative Cynthia Wooten recently "came out," making her our third openly gay/lesbian state legislator.

Here in Portland, we are also making strides. In a double-edged sword of progress and pain, a 1989 law requires law enforcement personnel to track hate crimes based on a person's real or perceived sexual orientation. Enactment of that law was progress; the pain comes with the resultant knowledge that this category of hate crime is increasing at two, three and four times the rate of crimes based on other factors. Furthermore, Oregon leads the nation in teen suicides, and national studies show that gay and lesbian teens are four to six times more likely to attempt suicide, and more are "successful" in their attempts.

During my time in Salem, fellow legislators have told me privately about gay family members or close friends they have; they have shared the pain they witness as their loved ones suffer humiliation and degradation. Legislative and committee staff furtively seek me out to thank me for speaking out on behalf of equal rights for gays and lesbians. Two particularly poignant moments came shortly after testifying for a bill codifying equal protection for gays and lesbians – first in 1991 and again in 1993. Various staffers sought me out each time, with appreciative glances and words, vicariously grateful for my having the courage to go public.

I look forward to the day when employees — at our state's capitol and around Oregon — are not afraid to be open about who they are. I look forward to the day when they are valued for their unique, professional contribution to their workplace. That will not happen until Oregon guarantees basic protection from discrimination for all its citizens, including gays and lesbians. Such legislation has been introduced in the Oregon Legislature every session for the past twenty years. Still, there is no statewide protection from discrimination against gays and lesbians in housing, employment or public accommodations. Winning that legislation is both a political and a personal goal.

Last January, though the election was long over, I learned I was far from recovered. In a Legislative Caucus meeting, the discussion understandably turned to Measure 9 and the political lessons learned. I literally could not stomach such dispassionate discourse about a subject so personal; I had to leave the room. To this day, I have not yet learned how to distance my personal life, my family's life or my friends' lives from the harsh political reality we faced in 1992, and we continue to face today.

I hope I never do.

Gail Shibley was appointed mid-term to the Oregon House of Representatives in 1991. In 1992, she was officially elected as the state's first openly lesbian state representative. As a state legislator, Shibley has served on the Housing and Urban Development Committee and on the Intergovernmental Affairs Committee, and was appointed to the Children's Care Team, the Joint Legislative Audit Committee, the Government Mandates Task Force, the Revenue and School Finance Committee — and its Subcommittee on Income Taxation — and to the Special Committee on Children and Families. As a representative, Shibley has sponsored three bills — among the twenty-odd she has sponsored overall — which promote civil rights for lesbians and gays in Oregon: one banning employment discrimination on the basis of sexual orientation; one calling on Congress to repeal the ban on gays and lesbians in the military; and one to ban discrimination in housing and public accommodations, deny tax deductions to discriminatory organizations and thwart the Oregon Citizen Alliance's attempt to enact discriminatory city and county ordinances.

Campaign Research
Agustin Paculdar

G OOD research provides the foundation for developing and getting out your message. Research gives you the information for press releases, direct mail, position papers, debates and speeches. Moreover, carefully planned use of opposition research allows you to drive a forceful free press strategy.

This article covers the basic guidelines in researching your opponent. As you read the chapter, keep in mind two points:

▼ **Always think of your audience.** A skeptical public and a leery press need information that is fully referenced. Document everything. Every statement, fact or bit of material used against your opponent must be backed with a source that can be understood by your audience.

▼ **Always think like your opponent(s).** Your opponent will scrutinize your record in detail; be prepared. Your opponent is not above resorting to misrepresentations and half-truths. Conduct opposition research on yourself as if you were running against yourself.

As a gay candidate, you cannot afford to lose control over the debate. The more you understand your opponent's record and your own, the more prepared you will be to respond to negative charges quickly, and the more you will command the campaign dialogue.

What you should know about your opponent

Conducting opposition research (also called "comparative" research) involves investigating your opponent's background, financial record, campaign finances and stance on the issues. Effective comparative research isn't an exact science; in fact, the mechanics rely more on political intuition and following these basic guidelines.

Research your opponent thoroughly

You want to know everything about your opponent. Information is available from the following sources:

▼ **Newspapers, magazines and journals**

Get a copy of every reference mentioning your opponent. You should consider conducting an exhaustive clip search utilizing an on-line service, such as Lexis®-Nexis®, DIALOG, or DataTimes.

▼ **Birth, marriage and divorce records**

Official records of births, marriages and divorces are kept in the locality in which the event occurred – most likely in the city or county clerk's office.

▼ **Courts**

Courts – including municipal, state and federal – have public records of any civil or criminal cases in which your opponent was named as either a plaintiff or a defendant. Do not forget divorce files because they frequently contain hard-to-obtain tax filings.

▼ **Real estate records**

Personal and business property holdings are available through the county land records or deeds offices. In some localities, the state handles these matters. Property assessments and tax records are generally open to the public. Check with the county assessment or finance/revenue offices.

▼ **Motor vehicle records**

Department of Motor Vehicles records are publicly available in some states, so check with the state DMV. Records may reveal vehicles owned, social security numbers and outstanding traffic violations.

▼ **Voter registration records**

Voter registration records may reveal social security number, party affiliation and date of registration. Many offices keep back files, which will enable you to check if your opponent has ever belonged to another party and has exercised his/her right to vote. Check with the County Registrar of Voters.

▼ **State, federal and professional licensing agencies**

Check with state medical boards, bar associations, real estate commissions, etc. to confirm membership and standing.

▼ **Academic records**

Check school yearbooks, college registrar's office and student newspapers to verify completion of studies and check student activities.

Double-check everything your opponent says

Once you've compiled as much information about your opponent's background as possible, you want to confirm every biographical detail. Don't forget to obtain your opponent's official campaign biography. Your campaign should check into the following:

▼ Family
▼ Education/degrees
▼ Career/jobs
▼ All places of residence
▼ Club/organizational/professional memberships, legislative and civic awards, church affiliation
▼ Brief overview of previous offices held

Campaigns are not above embellishing their candidate's life story. For example, in the 1992 election for Texas Railroad Commissioner, Democrat Lena Guerrero's campaign became embroiled in controversy and eventually faltered after it was disclosed that she never earned the college degree or academic honors that she claimed.

Examine personal finances

In the public's mind, there is possibly no greater ethical lapse than financial impropriety, or even the appearance of it. The financial disclosure forms required of office seekers are mandatory reading for any researcher. For federal races, these statements are available from the Clerk of the House or Secretary of the Senate; and for state races check with the Secretary of the State. Lexis®-Nexis® also carries this information. Your campaign should check for the following, as applicable:

▼ **Honoraria/speaking engagements**

Determine yearly totals; categorize by interest group/issue; rank with state delegation. (Prior to 1990, members of the U.S. House of Representatives were allowed to keep honoraria from speaking engagements.) Cross-examine date honoraria earned/received with dates of missed votes (if incumbent).

▼ **Assets and income**

Track over time, check for conflicts of interest, and determine questionable holdings, such as ownership in a failed S&L.

Check with courts and regulatory agencies to ensure that holdings have complied with applicable laws, such as Social Security rules.

▼ **Gifts**

List all gifts and check for conflicts of interest, such as gifts from businesses bidding for a government contract.

▼ **Reimbursements**

List and cross-examine reimbursement dates with dates of missed votes (if incumbent) and check for conflicts of interest.

▼ **Transactions and liabilities**

List and investigate nature of dealing and other parties involved (such as the lender) and check for conflicts of interest.

Remember to cross-check what your opponent disclosed on the financial forms with what you have uncovered from your investigations into divorce records, court proceedings, motor vehicle registrations and real estate holdings.

Your opponent's financial dealings – whether it involves non-payment of an employee's social security taxes or ownership in a company with multiple complaints filed with the Better Business Bureau — deserve scrutiny. For example, in the 1990 race for a Mississippi House seat, Republican Tom Anderson lost the race because of his failure to report as gifts travel he had taken on private planes owned by a Mississippi businessman.

Investigate campaign contributions

In the race to raise money, many campaigns forget to play by the rules. Fortunately, the Federal Election Commission maintains a comprehensive database on all receipts and expenditures of federal candidates and party organizations as well as contribution records on PACs. Most states also require campaign finance disclosure for all state office seekers, usually through the Secretary of State.

Contact the FEC for a list of services, including computer searches, they can provide at no charge. The national party committees have databases on individual and PAC contributions.

Once you have obtained the most recent FEC reports and all past reports, you should organize the information in the following manner:

▼ **Summarize contributions by PACs**

Group these according to areas of legislative interest, and

rank total amount with state delegation. Cross-check the dates money
was earned/received with dates of missed votes (if incumbent).

▼ **Summarize contributions by individuals**

Group by individuals' employer for evidence of bundling, check
for any contributions by corporations (which are illegal in federal
races) or controversial individuals.

▼ **Summarize in-state/out-of-state contributions**

Rank total with state delegation.

▼ **Analyze campaign committee disbursements**

Note any unusual expenditures (such as luxury items, dry cleaning, etc.). Look for any evidence of dates of fundraisers (catering,
band, expenditures, etc.) and cross check with dates of missed votes.

As you investigate your opponent's FEC reports, look for
conflicts with your opponent's record or statements on campaign
finances. Also, get your hands on fundraising announcements and
look for violations of campaign rules. For example, in a 1988
House race in Oregon, Republican Congressman Denny Smith broke
house rules when he listed his congressional office number in a
fundraising appeal.

Compile your opponent's record on the issues

Gather every public statement your opponent has made regarding the issues. This can be obtained from:

▼ **Position papers**

Voters have every right to ask your opponent for his/her statements on the issues.

▼ **Press releases**

Every time a reporter asks for your comments on the
opposition's statement, ask for a hard copy of that statement or a
press release. Better yet, have a source in the media.

▼ **Interest group questionnaires**

Every time you submit your response to an interest group
questionnaire, ask for a copy of your opponent's response.

▼ **Exhaustive and on-going clip search** (Discussed above)

▼ **Legislative analysis** (Discussed below)

This information can provide evidence of broken promises,
inconsistencies and general character. For example, in the 1990
Hawaii Senate race, Democrat Dan Akaka blasted Republican Pat

Saiki for taking credit for voting for final passage of important legislation when in fact he had voted to gut it in committee or through amendments.

Running against an incumbent

Holders of public office leave a paper trail that is an opposition researcher's fantasy. Although the following tips are designed for researching congressional incumbents, they can also be used against state and local officeholders because many of the public disclosure requirements are similar.

All politics are local, and your opponent will try to portray him/herself as someone who's looking out for the best interests of the home turf. In terms of defining your opponent's effectiveness, your campaign should watch for the following:

▼ **Legislation/amendments introduced**

Make sure that the legislation is original and benefits the state/district. Check on its status and the number of cosponsors.

▼ **Committee activity**

List committee and subcommittee assignments, rank and relevance to state. Check committee calendar and transcripts for accomplishments or vulnerabilities.

▼ **Federal funds**

Determine the amount of federal dollars returned to the district compared with Federal taxes paid and returns to other state districts.

▼ **Constituent service failure/successes**

Check the clips for this. And, take a look at the "Clerk Reports" for the number of case workers compared to other members.

▼ **Travel back to state**

The "Clerk Reports" will show how often and for how long your opponent goes back home (and at what cost).

▼ **Out-of-state travel**

Compile a summary of out-of-state travel, including committee travel. This is time not spent with constituents. The "Congressional Record" and the financial disclosure statements can provide this information. Cross check travel dates with dates of missed votes and determine yearly cost of travel.

▼ **Attendance**

The *Congressional Quarterly Almanac*s list members' vote participation by rank and percentage for each year. Try to determine the reason for each of your opponent's missed votes. List any missed votes that were close or important to the state or to a certain constituency. Also, check your opponent's committee attendance at hearings and votes.

▼ **Legislative Analysis**

Your opponent's legislative record can be obtained from an on-line legislative service, such as Legi-Slate, Legis, or Washington Alert. Your campaign should check the following:

▼ **Legislation/amendments co-sponsored**

A co-sponsorship – or failure to co-sponsor – is as good as a public statement or vote on a particular issue.

▼ **Votes on the floor and in committee**

The above mentioned on-line services, as well as the national party committees, have databases that allow you to group floor votes by issue or theme. Check with relevant committees to determine availability of transcripts.

▼ **Statements in the "Congressional Record"**

These statements – taken from both supporters and opponents of a vote – provide good ammunition for criticizing your opponent for voting a certain way.

▼ **Interest group ratings**

Compile relevant interest group ratings (such as League of Conservation Voters or Chamber of Commerce) noting the votes or co-sponsorships utilized. Compare with state delegation.

Utilization of incumbent "benefits"

The political environment of the 1990s is decidedly anti-incumbent. Use this to your advantage. Your campaign should check for the following:

▼ **Mass mailings**

Contact Congressional Mailing Standards to review all past and current "Postal Patron" newsletter mailings. Check the "Clerk Reports" to determine cost of mailing, including postage, printing and mailing list.

▼ **Office/staff expenses**

The House and Senate "Clerk Reports" detail office and staff budgets by quarter. List total of expenditures and compare with state delegation. Examine expenditures for irregularities, such as staff turnover, expensive hotels and meals, frequent staff travel, etc. Be sure to check votes pertaining to legislative appropriations.

▼ **Foreign Travel**

List all official trips taken abroad, noting cost and dates. This information is available from "Congressional Record."

▼ **House Bank/Post Office**

Document any involvement (*e.g.,* bounced checks) or statements relating to these operations. Be sure to check any votes or legislation cosponsored involving Congressional reform.

▼ **Pay raises**

Check all votes and statements relating to Congressional pay, pension and other benefits.

One additional research tip: let others do the work for you. Congressional watch dog groups often can provide useful information. For example:

▼ **Common Cause** (state chapters)

Analyzes campaign contributions, especially PAC contributions, by state delegation.

▼ **Public Citizen/Congress Watch**, Washington, D.C.

Compiles data on Congressional trips paid for by companies or trade associations.

▼ **National Taxpayer's Union**, Washington, D.C.

Provides numerous studies, including members' franking expenses.

Although the task of researching your opponent may seem daunting, remember, there is a point to all of this. Research does have its benefits. If you do it thoroughly, it will point out both your own and your opponent's strengths and weaknesses. Based on your research — along with polling data and the political environment you can develop campaign themes.

Campaign themes: Yours

Your ability to link campaign themes with concrete examples and basic information about your opponent is crucial to bringing your message home to voters. For example:

▼ **Trust/broken promises**

Can voters trust your opponent to honor his/her promises? A 1992 campaign brochure titled "Abandoning the Middle Class" used this tactic effectively by comparing an incumbent's vote *against* a higher minimum wage and extended unemployment benefits (both of which would have benefitted his constituents) with his vote for his own pay raise.

▼ **Status quo/change**

Is your opponent for real change and reform? In a 1992 Florida House race, Republican Tillie Fowler opened her debates with this soundbite: "My opponent says he is for change but, if elected, the first vote he would cast would be to re-elect Tom Foley as Speaker." (Recall that Foley was taking a lot of heat that year.)

▼ **Out-of-touch**

Is your opponent pretending to be just like the folks back home? Your ability to tie your opponent to a group that identifies strongly with the Radical Right, such as the Christian Coalition, may help build a strong case that your opponent is out of the mainstream.

▼ **Ineffective**

What has your opponent done for the constituents lately? And don't forget that incumbents can be blamed for everything that goes wrong while they're in office. In the 1993 Los Angeles mayoral race, Dick Riordan made gains among suburban voters by criticizing Councilman Michael Woo for not doing enough to stem the crime rate in his district.

Well-identified themes — backed with localized or personalized research "nuggets" — will enable you to move your message quickly and consistently in free media, paid advertising and campaign literature.

Campaign themes: Your opponent's

As a gay candidate, it is imperative that you understand your record so you can anticipate attacks. Remember, the Radical Right will be scrutinizing your record – so should you.

Even if you don't have time to completely research your own record, it is strongly recommended that you take steps to prepare for standard right-wing thematic attacks. Some examples include:

▼ **Too liberal for our district/state**
▼ **Out-of-touch with constituents**
▼ **Beholden to special interest groups**
▼ **Anti-family, anti-Christian, un-American**
▼ **Single-issue candidate**

The Senate floor debate surrounding Roberta Achtenberg's nomination to a post in the Clinton administration provides a disturbing glimpse of how anti-gay forces can disguise their homophobia by dressing it up in patriotic or moral symbolism. This is what you are up against. Good research will help you fight this tactic.

Campaign research is the means by which you obtain information to support your candidate's message and make it stick in voters' minds. No one understood this concept better than the late Lee Atwater, explaining message development for the 1988 presidential campaign:

> **The strategic concept was developed way before we knew who the Democratic nominee was... Whoever it was, we had to paint him as a frostbelt liberal who was out of the mainstream... What we did was find actual issues that allowed us to paint the picture.**

Because you are a gay candidate, your opponent will have an easier time of painting a picture of you than you will of him/her. That is why you must begin your research efforts early and conduct it thoroughly. If you can make sure not only that you are a clean candidate but that your opponent's past history is completely out in the open, you will avoid mid-campaign crises pertaining to any attacks that might be made against you, and will be prepared to make any offensive maneuvers necessary to win your race.

The author wishes to acknowledge the generous assistance of the Democratic Congressional Campaign Committee, Washington, D.C., and Dan Carol and Company of Takoma Park, Maryland, in writing this article.

A research associate with the political consulting firm of Dan Carol and Company and a Hill veteran of four years, Agustin Paculdar has served as health care aide to California Senator Dianne Feinstein, as an opposition/ issues researcher for the Democratic Congressional Campaign Committee during the 1992 election cycle, and as a research assistant for Hawaii Senator Dan Akaka. Dan Carol and Company, of Takoma Park, Maryland, provides research and advice to Democratic campaigns and maintains a public affairs practice, representing clients on telecommunications, environmental and health care issues.

It's All in the Mail

John H. Leitner

GOOD mail is mail that gets read. Good mail is effective, dramatic and informative. And, most importantly, it motivates the reader to vote for you.

Why mail? Direct mail is an important tool in any campaign. Where radio and television messages are usually limited to 30 or 60 seconds, direct mail allows you to deliver a more sophisticated, perhaps more persuasive message. It's also your opportunity to target voters on an individual level. You can tailor your message to each voter based on a laundry list of demographic factors, like race, gender, sexual orientation, ethnicity, income or even previous voting patterns. For smaller campaigns or campaigns in large media markets, direct mail is often the only advertising available. Radio and television are beyond the reach of many campaigns, or are simply impractical in media markets that are much larger than the pool of eligible voters.

Yes, but who can afford it? Because of the flexibility of a mailing program, and because you know exactly which voters a mail piece is going to reach, a mailing program can be designed for almost any budget.

How to mail? Your mail needs to compete for attention, not only with your opponents, but with every other local advertiser, from charities to department stores. Like any other advertising, mailed literature is useless unless it catches people's attention. Good literature makes good reading, rewarding the reader with interesting information, ideas or engaging stories about local concerns and activities. Good literature begins by stimulating curiosity and then informs the reader by providing answers. People don't read without a reason. Make reading your mail worthwhile and people will find the time.

"Vote for me" isn't the message, because anyone can say that. The message you want to communicate is "Here's *why* to vote for me." When a group of religious zealots tried to take over the school board in New York recently, I designed a piece with the words "They're coming from far away..." on the cover. When the piece was opened, it continued "... to take over our local schools." Compare that with a piece that starts with the words "Vote for." Which are you more likely to read?

Designing good literature is like a balancing act. The more you write, the less people will read. (But write too little and you may not get your message across.) Voters aren't concerned with the intimate complexities of every issue. That's your job. You need to present a simple statement of your ideas and accomplishments.

Stay away from platitudes like "I really care." Unless your opponent is saying "I really don't," it's meaningless. Anyone can say it, and can't be proven wrong. And don't just tell us, for example, that you want to improve the schools. Who doesn't? Prove to the voters that you're qualified by giving them concrete examples.

Graphic design is also an important part of the package. Not only does good design get attention and determine the relative importance of the various parts of the text, it's also an opportunity to deliver a message, albeit a subtle one. A well-designed piece says something about you. Even to somebody who doesn't read it.

Gay and lesbian mail? A gay or lesbian candidate is a candidate. And his or her campaign should not be very different from any other. But unfortunately, sexual orientation is still a complex issue and it needs to be dealt with in campaign media. Because few districts are monolithic, direct mail gives a gay or lesbian candidate the opportunity to approach that issue in different ways around the district, as needs dictate. It lets you, not your opponents, control the issue.

Why hire a pro? A media consultant's job is to help reduce the risk associated with running for office. Running costs thousands of dollars, takes months of work, and, on election day, you could end up with nothing. But election day shouldn't be like a roll of the dice. A media consultant can help you take control of the dice.

You are not supposed to be a professional campaigner. Your job is to govern, to represent the people. Your consultant's job is to help you avoid the costly mistakes that campaigns make again and again. Some mistakes cost only money. Others cost votes and lose elections. Political direct mail consultants are specialized advertising agencies. Their job is to help communicate your ideas to the public, to make certain that the message you intend to deliver is actually delivered and to provide the talent and creativity to deliver it in a powerful and memorable way. One mailing that's read is better than a dozen that go in the trash.

Which pro? Hiring the right consultant is like finding a mate. You need to find the right match, someone whose style appeals to you, because it's your wisdom he/she's being hired to spread.

Because cost varies greatly, it has to be one of the factors you consider. But don't let it be your only one. Each consultant has his or her own personal style. And each operates in a different manner. Look for a consultant with an entertaining portfolio. If looking at someone's past work is a chore, it stands to reason that his/her work for you will also be less than effective.

Media consultants are communications experts, not experts about your race or district. Whether they're located around the block or across the country, they'll need to spend time learning the details of your election. Even from last year to this year, everything's different. Look for assurances that you will get adequate attention. Good consultants give every client individualized service. They can't operate like a factory, because every campaign is different. There are no formulas for decisions when running for office, and you need to be able to rely on a media consultant as one of your key strategic advisors.

Winning elections depends on effective communication, and effective communication depends on getting people's attention and making sure they receive your message. That's the only way to motivate voters to vote for you. A campaign needs creative advertising, just like any business. You can get your message across to even the most uninterested people if you apply the basic principles of communication.

Stimulate curiosity. Then people will pay attention to the answer. People won't vote for you just because they saw your name more than they saw your opponent's. They'll vote for you if you give them compelling, memorable reasons to do so. Ideas, goals, and accomplishments aren't enough — the voters have to know about them. That's what your career depends on. Any good candidate can organize a good campaign. All it takes is the determination to do so. And when the voters are well informed, the best candidate usually wins.

John H. Leitner is president of JH Leitner Inc., a political media/direct mail consulting firm.

1-800-Dial-Victory

Telemarketing in the Political Campaign
Kathy Swayze

L ET me guess – your first thought when someone mentions telemarketing is "those pesky phone calls during dinner." After all, you just hate it when some telemarketer calls you in the evening, and so does everyone you know. Although you realize that the phone may be an essential tool in your campaign, you're still reluctant. So, how can the phone help you win people over – as voters, as volunteers, as contributors?

Quite simply, the phone is *the next best thing to being there.* As a political candidate, there is no end to the ways that "being there" can help you. From very early polling and voter identification to fundraising and Get-Out-the-Vote campaigns, the phone is an essential tool you can use again and again to help you win an election.

Here are some of the advantages of telemarketing?

IT'S PERSONAL...

If you could shake hands with every one of your constituents, the odds of winning the race would improve dramatically. The phone helps reach the voters who you can't go out and meet directly, and in a more personal way than your media or campaign brochures can. Furthermore, because a phone call is a two-way communication, you can ask for what you need and get information back from prospects.

IT'S COST EFFECTIVE...

The phone is the fastest and least expensive way to communicate personally with your supporters. As printing and postal rates increase, the phone has become increasingly competitive as a cost-effective way to reach large numbers of people quickly.

IT GETS RESULTS...

The number-one response people give about why they didn't give money is that nobody asked them. The same might be said for voting for a particular candidate. When you make calls to contributors or voters and ask for their support, you will find many people ready and willing, and glad to be asked. Most importantly, results can be monitored and measured on a nightly basis.

IT UPGRADES SUPPORT...

Many of your supporters, whether they be financial contributors or volunteers, are committed to your cause. If approached directly and asked for additional help, many would be happy to comply. The phone is an effective tool to upgrade contributions and to turn volunteers into contributors and contributors into volunteers.

IT'S QUICK...

Campaigns move rapidly. A phone program can be set up fairly quickly and begin to produce results within the first few hours. Often it takes more time than you have available to develop a mailing piece or a new television commercial. The phone can help get your message out and contributions in — in a very short period of time.

AND IT'S FLEXIBLE!

One of the greatest advantages of the phone is that you can adjust your approach on a nightly basis to improve results or respond to recent media fires. How many times have we wished we could pull back that mailing which highlighted an issue that turned sour overnight? On the phone, we can simply rewrite the script.

There are a number of uses for telemarketing in political campaigns. They range from the inbound 800 numbers used so effectively by Jerry Brown in the 1992 Presidential race, to polls of registered voters, voter identification efforts, Get-Out-the-Vote campaigns and fundraising. Each of these applications has its own unique challenges; the following paragraphs summarize what you need to know to succeed with each one.

FUNDRAISING

Because winning elective office has become increasingly expensive, you'll want to use telemarketing to maximize the effectiveness of your fundraising efforts. Fundraising by phone is one of the most efficient means of securing gifts from individuals. A well-developed program of direct mail and telephone solicitation can yield a lot of cash for your campaign. Especially when you get down to the final weeks of your race, a phone campaign to previous donors is a great way to generate badly needed cash. These guidelines will help you make your phone campaign even more profitable.

▼ **Who to Call**

The first thing you need is a list of people to call. Your best chances for success on the phone will be when you are talking to donors who have contributed to your campaign previously. But if you are a new candidate without a strong list of supporters behind you, then the phone can be an effective tool for acquiring donations from new people.

The best way to generate your first list is to get all your friends and family together for an evening and ask them to bring their rolodexes. EMILY's List, a Washington, D.C. organization that gave more than six million dollars to Democratic women candidates in 1992, was started from the rolodexes of a handful of women. Whenever you do public speaking or attend public meetings, commit yourself to collecting names. Pass out blank index cards and ask people to write their names on them. In Jesse Jackson's 1988 bid for the Presidency, one of the most successful lists for our fundraising efforts was shoe boxes full of index cards with scribbled names and dollar-amount pledges. We spent hours sorting them into stacks by pledge amount — from $1,000 to $10. When we began calling, almost every person said, "I was wondering when Jesse was going to get back to me about that!"

Another way to expand your list is to ask your supporters to give you names of people they know who would care about your candidacy. Especially within the gay and lesbian community, your supporters will be glad to help you reach out to others. Organizations, including gay and lesbian groups in your area, may also lend you their list for fundraising — especially if they've endorsed your candidacy.

▼ **What to say**

Once you've decided who to call, the next critical task is figuring out what to say. Prepare a script for your staff or volunteers who will be making phone calls. Although you don't want anyone to sound like they are reading, you do want them to sound competent. If a script is well written and the caller well practiced, the call won't sound recited. It is not intended to be read verbatim, but to be used as a guideline to facilitate a more effective presentation.

A fundraising script should have these components:

a. Introduction
b. Thank donor for past support or interest
c. State the need and explain why people should give
d. Explain the opposition
e. State why it is urgent that they give now
f. Ask for a specific gift — two to three times higher than previous gift

Always include two to three tradedowns to ask for lower amounts. Most inexperienced fundraisers will have a tendency to give up after the first try — make sure you train people to listen, respond, restate the need and ask again.

A set of "Responses to Objections" for some of the more common questions you have faced. If you can predict which issues might come up and train the callers on how to respond to them, you will be more successful.

Close the call by thanking them for their gift, checking their address and confirming the amount of their pledge.

▼ **What results to expect**

Results will vary tremendously depending on the list, the callers, the timing, the strength of your candidacy and many other variables. However, these are some general guidelines of what you can expect from a phone fundraising campaign:

Percent of your file you will contact	50-70%
Dials per hour	40-65
Presentations or contacts per hour	7-12
Percent (of presentations) who agree to pledge	25-50%
Percent who agree to consider; "maybes"	5-10%
Amount of pledged dollars actually retrieved	65-90%

▼ **Getting the money in**

Although you've secured pledges over the phone, you still don't really have the money. Depending on the type of campaign, you may only receive 65 to 90 percent of the money that is pledged. You need to plan a follow-up mailing to each donor including a postage-paid return envelope in which they may send their gift. Send out initial confirmation notices within 24 hours of the call so that the donors receive them when the call is still fresh in their minds. If you delay in getting the letters out, your "pay-up rate" will decline.

Typically, the follow-up letter should be very short. Rather than a fancy direct mail package with a lot of inserts. It should be simple and concise and remind the donor of his/her commitment. The letter should thank the donor for the pledge, briefly restate how the gift will help, state the specific amount they agreed to and tell them exactly what you want them to do. Stress the urgency of this appeal and ask them to send their check right away.

If you still have not received their gift after three weeks, send a reminder. This notice should not be harsh like an overdue payment notice, but should tell them that you are still counting on their support. If a gift is not received after six weeks, a second reminder should be mailed. With all reminders, be sure to include a disclaimer — "If your gift and this letter have crossed in the mail, please accept our appreciation and disregard this notice."

▼ **Inbound 800 numbers**

A great way to show the voters how accessible you are is to establish a toll-free number to allow constituents and supporters to reach you. You should publicize this number at every opportunity: print it on promotional materials, give it out during "meet-the-candidate" nights and radio and television talk shows. It provides people with an easy way to contact you about voting issues, volunteering, contributing and more.

If you're running in a local race where all calls within your electoral district are free, then you can simply set up a local exchange. If you're running in a large district, an 800 number is preferable. The cost of 800 numbers has decreased dramatically over the past several years thanks to competition among phone vendors. You should evaluate pricing schedules from AT&T, MCI and other 800 suppliers to find the one that best suits your needs.

The biggest concern with an 800 number is "Who's going to answer it?" How you deal with staffing depends largely on the volume of calls anticipated. If you are simply printing the number on brochures and posters, the calls can probably be handled in the campaign office by the staff or volunteers. However, if you get into print, radio or television advertising, then plan on a large number of calls. Options for handling heavy-call volume include:

1. Having the number ring into your office (and roll over to a voice-mail system when all lines are busy).

2. Hiring an agency to act on your behalf and have all calls forwarded to them. They will offer increased capacity, round the clock access and experienced telemarketers to answer the phone.

Given the low cost of 800 numbers today, you can't go wrong by setting one up for your campaign. The rewards of making your campaign accessible to your constituency will be realized in the voting booth, your volunteer efforts and in fundraising.

GET OUT THE VOTE

Winning your election all comes down to one thing – getting people to go out and vote for you on election day. The biggest mistake campaigns make is spending all their energy to develop fancy messages or undermine their opponents, while forgetting the basic premise of a campaign: getting people to vote for you. Particularly for gay and lesbian candidates, who often have a strong chance of securing virtually *all* gay and lesbian votes, the efforts to ensure that the community turns out are critical.

Many people mistakenly think of voter turnout as something you do in the final days of a campaign, but to do it correctly, you should start weeks, even months in advance. Begin with a turnout strategy – how many votes do you need to win? And what coalition of voters are you going to put together to win that number of votes?

▼ **Voter Identification**

Using your targeted voter groups, identify voters by calling lists of possible supporters. These can simply be party registration lists, voter lists or lists from local groups who are supporting you, such as unions, gay and lesbian organizations, business leaders, etc. A voter identification call is very short, but its goal is twofold: to identify supporters and to identify what the "hot button" issues are for your candidacy.

A call that includes a third-party introduction is the best way to go: "I'm calling on behalf of Peg McGraw with the Fairfax Lesbian and Gay Citizens Allinace." This lends legitimacy to your candidacy and makes the prospective voters less suspect. It also helps you avoid questions like "why are you calling me?" and "where did you get my name?"

Then ask five to seven short questions to find "hot buttons" and to measure the degree of support. The last question should always be whether or not they've decided to support you/your candidate on election day. If yes, remind them of the election date and urge them to go out and vote. Transfer their name to the list of "identified supporters" who will be called from your Get-Out-the-Vote phone banks near election day.

If the response to your "Can I count on you to vote for me?" question is a clear "no," thank the person and move on.

▼ **Voter Persuasion**

Voters who are still identified as "undecided" are worth investing in. Following the identification call you should send the voter some campaign literature. Because the call has already aroused his/her awareness and interest in the campaign, he/she will be more likely to read materials received shortly after the call.

After a few weeks, arrange another persuasion call, making it as personalized as possible. Talk to the voters about information that will appeal to them, referring, for example, to their address, demographic information, voter history and organizational affiliations: "As a resident of the Park Heights neighborhood, I'm sure you're concerned about the threatened school closing."

This call will be slightly longer than the initial "voter identification" call because you will introduce yourself, spend a short amount of time describing yourself (if you are the candidate in a small race) or your candidate, highlighting the "hot button" issues that emerged in the identification calls. Once you have given the voter more information, ask again if they will be supporting you on election day. Continue making persuasion calls as your resources allow up until a week before election day in an attempt to move as many voters as possible into the "identified supporters" category.

▼ **Voter Turnout**

The Get-Out-the-Vote campaign requires tremendous resources be used in a very short period of time. This is where you need to utilize all your volunteer resources *and* a paid vendor to ensure that you reach as many of your voters as possible. There are many fine telemarketing firms that specialize in voter persuasion and turnout. Many are now automated which means that while they still use live operators, they have computers to handle the dialing so that callers spend more time talking to voters and less time listening to busy signals and answering machines. This type of equipment could be critical on election eve and election day when it is essential that you reach a large number of voters in a short period of time.

Depending on the resources and the number of identified supporters, it is ideal to give every identified supporter two calls. Place the first call four to five days before election day to remind supporters when the polls are open, ask if they need assistance getting to the polls and request a promise to vote before a certain time on election day. Make the second telephone call the day before or on election day itself. In addition to phone calls, all supportive voters should be sent a direct mail piece that urges them to go to the polls (or provides information on voting by absentee ballot) and gives them specific times and locations of polling places. Include a phone number for people to call for further assistance.

IN-HOUSE VERSUS OUTSIDE VENDOR-MANAGED CAMPAIGNS

Once you've identified a list of people to call and written a solid script, who's going to make the calls? Many candidates use volunteer phone banks for city- and countywide races. But most in Congressional, statewide or national races must rely on both volunteer and paid professional phone banks to accomplish their goals. Here are things to consider with both:

▼ **People Power**

Volunteers are especially hard to come by these days. Be realistic in projecting the people you can get and plan for a high turnover. If you are doing an evening phone bank where volunteers will come after work, plan to give them dinner and refreshments.

▼ **Physical space/equipment**

Decide where the calls will be made (e.g., from your office, from phones in a donated company office after hours, from a campaign headquarters)? Consider the parking and public transportation needs of your volunteers. Remember, if you still need to install phones it takes time. Plan ahead.

▼ **Script and training**

Prepare a script for each component of your telemarketing plan (fundraising, Get-Out-the-Vote, voter identification, etc.) as a guideline for others. (You may want to hire a professional to write your script.) If you write it yourself, make sure you read it aloud, and have others do the same. It doesn't matter how it looks on paper, the bottom line is "can they say it?" and "does it sound conversational?" (One of my favorite words to use in letters is "unprecedented," but I've learned the hard way that it is *not* a telemarketing-friendly word.)

In addition to the script,prepare a training packet including "talking points"and "responses to objections" in areas you feel your callers will be asked about. Make sure you use role playing in the training — if callers are too shy to practice with a partner during training, then they are probably not ready to be on the phone.

▼ **Management**

The biggest mistake people make when they decide to do volunteer phone banks is not evaluating the real resources required to accomplish it. While using volunteers can save you money, it is not free. You need to allocate at least one staff person to oversee the entire project, and if you have dozens of phones going each night of the week, you will also need two assistants to handle logistics, supervise shifts, etc. Remember, it will always take more time than you expected.

▼ **Prepare in advance for follow-up mailings**

Getting something in the mail shortly after the call is critical in telemarketing, especially when you're fundraising. Make sure you have systems established to make it easy to get follow-up mail out.

TELEMARKETING FIRMS

The main advantage of hiring a telemarketing firm is that you are not responsible for recruiting and managing personnel. This is critical because, as we all know, managing a large group of people is very time consuming. Furthermore, if for some reason you have a slowdown in available work, the firm can simply move callers onto another project rather than laying them off, or paying them for less critical work. Don't be shy about asking the firm how they recruit, train and manage their staff. The biggest drawback to a volunteer phone bank operation, or even paid staff in your own headquarters, is that people don't always come through and the effort often falls behind schedule. When you hire a professional agency, you agree up front on a pace of calling and completion date for the project. Telemarketing firms are more likely to complete the calls on time because their staffing resources enable them to shift more people onto the project if it is not on schedule. They can also handle or offer assistance in list selection, script writing and analysis of results.

Many people are afraid that if they hire someone from "outside" to do their telemarketing, the quality of their effort will suffer. They fear that giving up some control means that strange, rude people who don't care about their donors will get hold of their list. In reality, reputable telemarketing agencies have strict quality-control standards. Their callers are well trained and possess good communication and fundraising skills. Furthermore, the firms often have the technology to monitor calls (and allow you to monitor them) to ensure that your quality standards are being met. One important quality-control feature to look for in an agency is callback verification procedures. Ask what type of callback verification procedures they utilize and what percentage of the prospects receive these callbacks. Remember, when you hire a firm that has conducted a lot of political campaign work, you gain access to the experience gained from their previous programs.

Most telemarketing firms charge between $26 and $48 per hour depending on the complexity of the call. Some vendors also offer pricing on a cost-per-completed-contact, or cost-per-contract basis. When evaluating costs, make sure that you are comparing apples to apples. Firms use different terms and definitions to determine their prices. There are often additional charges for mailing of follow-up packages, data-processing work and creative services. (For example, a Washington D.C.-based firm that charges $31 per caller hour had developed a reputation for being "cheap" compared to competing firms offering rates of $38 to $45 per hour. In fact, although the firm had a lower hourly rate, they achieved far fewer completed contacts in each hour, so their overall cost per contact was much higher.) Make sure you really understand a firm's costs before you begin the program. Ask for definitions of terms used, such as "contacts" and "completed calls." Many companies use these differently so their prices will appear to be lower than they are really are.

Although it may be cheaper to set up your own phone bank and use volunteers, remember that going to an established firm will mean lower start-up costs and quicker start-up time.

FINDING ASSISTANCE

If all this seems a little too complex, relax! There are people out there who can help. First, you can probably find campaign personnel who have had experience working and managing volunteer phone banks because many young political professionals "do their time" in the phone center.

In addition, you can find consultants who specialize in telemarketing or firms that have professional phone banks you can hire. To find good consultants or telemarketing vendors, contact your local, state or national party offices, look in the "Campaign Professionals" section of this book and ask elected officials which firms they used. *Campaigns and Elections* magazine also publishes an annual guide to political professionals that lists everyone you'll need, from pollsters to speech writers to fundraisers.

Don't assume that you can find a telemarketing "expert" who will help you with all the types of telemarketing I've mentioned. If you do, you'll be very lucky. You will be more successful if you work with a variety of consultants and firms who specialize in telephone polling, voter identification, voter turnout and fundraising. The techniques, skills and procedures of telemarketing are so unique that it's best to find those who specialize in each area.

Not every campaign will use or even need all of the telemarketing methods I've discussed, but a campaign that dismisses the vital tool of the telephone will miss getting its message out effectively, and will waste precious resources by using more expensive, less effective methods of communication.

Now vice president of her own Washington, D.C. firm, Herzog Swayze, Kathy Swayze consults with nonprofit organizations to help them develop and manage telephone fundraising projects. Herzog Swayze offers vendor selection and management services and also provides assistance with in-house phone campaigns. Over the past decade, Swayze has implemented hundreds of telemarketing campaigns for clients such as the National Abortion Rights Action League, the Human Rights Campaign Fund, the Democratic National Committee, the Kennedy Center for the Performing Arts, Physicians for Social Responsibility, American Rivers, Common Cause, the Women's Campaign Fund and many others. In addition to her position at Herzog Swayze, Swayze serves as volunteer president of the board of Hannah House, a transitional shelter for homeless women in Washington, D.C.

Earned Media Operations
Kris Bess

*"Self-expression must pass into communication for fulfill-
ment."* — *Pearl S. Buck*

C AMPAIGNS live and die by their ability to communicate, both internally and externally. From press conferences to direct mail fundraising to volunteer phone banks,
communication moves the campaign from one place to the next,
from one set of polling numbers to another, from one constituency
group to the next. What to communicate, when to communicate,
where to communicate, how to communicate and with whom to
communicate become key strategic and tactical questions. The answers to these questions – right or wrong – can significantly impact
election-day results.

Central to a campaign's overall strategy and ultimate success
or failure on election day is its earned media or free press operation. (Most campaigners prefer to use the term "earned media"
because nothing in a campaign is truly free and any mention in the
press is usually the result of hours of hard work, whether yours or
your opponent's.) Campaigns never have enough money or enough
time. Consequently, the earned media operation is expected to
complement and even supplement the paid media, as well as act and
react quickly on any number of issues. How to most effectively and
efficiently do this is a question that campaigns struggle with on a
daily basis. It is also a question that I hope will, at least in part, be
answered in the next few pages.

Making a name

Credibility and persistence are the keys to the success of any
campaign's earned media operation and to "making a name" for
your candidate. Without them, you become only what the press and
your opponents want you to become. With them, you have the tools

to control the press (at least to some degree), get *your* message out to the public and make the kind of name *you* want.

Credibility and persistence, though seemingly different, are inextricably linked. You cannot effectively have one without the other, nor can you "make a name" (at least the kind of name you want) for your campaign without them. If the press does not view a campaign as credible, then coverage of that campaign will most likely be both limited and disappointing. If a campaign is not persistent in dealing with the press, it will all too often be ignored, or contacted only when the opposition initiates a story. That is why it is crucial for a campaign's earned media operation to take careful steps to establish credibility with the press and to be persistent (but not overly pesky) in working with the media.

Establishing credibility with the press begins the day the campaign begins and ends the day the campaign ends. Though certain members of the press may find your campaign credible in its first three months, you can be sure that your opponent's opposition research department is digging hard to find some way to derail that credibility. Never let down your guard and never assume that a reporter who writes a positive story one day will write one the next. Members of the press are generally more concerned with the status of their careers than with the outcome of your particular race.

There is no single blueprint for building credibility, but there are some general guidelines for working on that process. Many of these guidelines are listed in the following section, but first let's briefly address the necessity of cultivating relationships with the press corps and the crucial role of knowledge in building those relationships and establishing credibility.

To begin, the press liaison should cultivate relationships with the press, from assignment desk editors to political reporters to editorial board members. How to go about cultivating these relationships depends on the liaison's personal style and that of each member of the press corps. The process might involve lunch meetings, a quick cup of coffee, phone calls, sending regular, timely update memos or detailed and accurate information on a story they want to write. Whether the relationship begins by meeting for a cup of coffee or by simply picking up the phone and talking about a story, maintain an air of professionalism and loyalty to the campaign to ensure that when a press conference is held or the opposition launches its attack, the press believes what you are saying and writes the story you want written.

As those relationships begin to develop, knowledge and information will play key roles. Knowing the issue you are presenting backward, forward and upside-down is absolutely essential. If you give a reporter faulty information, whether an out-of-date statistic or a fabricated set of documents, it will come back to haunt you. Reporters' reputations are on the line every time their stories appear in print. If you endanger that reputation with misinformation, you will pay the price. Moreover, demonstrating to the press that your campaign is prepared, knows the issues and can talk about them with fluency will build and strengthen your credibility.

Knowledge *is* power, but only when you understand how, when and where to use it. The only way to get a story written the way you hope to have it written is by working closely with the reporter. Whether you choose to present the issue through a press conference, a press release, a phone call or over lunch, you will need to push the media to cover the story – and to cover it in the way you want it covered.

Campaigns always walk a fine line between being obnoxiously pesky and credibly persistent. However, a successful earned media operation must find that balance. The guidelines in the next section cover some of the basic rules that may assist in this process, but how to walk that fine line depends on the styles of the liaison and the press corps as well as the dynamics of the race. For example, you may find that many of the regional radio stations will not accept faxes (generally because they have to pick them up from another office and pay for them). If you continue to send fax advisories and releases to them, they may completely turn away from any stories pertaining to your race. However, if you call instead of sending a fax, you may find they are quite receptive. Of course, there are no guarantees, but it is certainly better than alienating them.

As an openly gay or lesbian candidate, credibility may be more difficult to establish because the press may find your sexual orientation more interesting than your reasons for running for office. Unfortunately, you may find a significant amount of your time with the press is spent fielding questions about your sexual orientation and dispelling stereotypes.

Persistence, then, will take on a new twist. You will not only have to be persistent in getting reporters to cover your campaign, but also in persuading them that your sexual orientation and the stereotypes that follow it are not the key issues in the campaign. But, remember, just because the press asks you a question does not mean that you need to answer it — at least not directly. Keep in mind that neither you nor your candidate are running for office because you or he/she are gay or lesbian. You are running for office or helping someone else run for office because you or he/she wants to work to create sound policy, make a difference and build a better future for the people in your community, district, state or country. And you need to let the press know this.

Rather than allowing the press to control the agenda with questions about your sexual orientation, respond to some of those inquiries by spinning your message into your answer. For example, if a member of the press asks you a question about being gay, you might respond with a statement such as the following: "The issue in this election is not my sexual orientation or that of my opponent, but how we are each going to deal with the issues facing our community, issues such as jobs, health care and protecting our environment (or whatever the key issues are). Voters are interested in a candidate who will stand up and fight for them and they have a right to know where we stand on these issues." By making this kind of move and spinning your message back into your answer, you are not only taking control of the dialogue, but setting the agenda for the press, your opponent and the public.

Playing the game

Working with the press can be both enervating and frustrating. A great story makes for a great day at headquarters. But a terrible story or an off-message quote can not only put the candidate in a bad mood, but all his/her supporters as well. All too often campaigns and reporters don't see eye to eye. You have a story you want written and the press has a story they want to write. Generally, they are not the same. To minimize those "bad press" days and create a solid, credible working relationship with the press, your earned media operation should follow some simple, basic rules.

While the basic rules offered here have been applied both in successful and unsuccessful campaigns, from state house races to U.S. Senate races to elections abroad, they are not set in stone, nor are they all-inclusive. Every campaign has its own style and its own unique dynamic, just as every news outlet has its own. Part of "playing the game" means knowing when to bend, break or recreate the rules to fit those styles. What follows, then, are some basic suggestions to help you work more effectively and efficiently with the press and establish credibility for your campaign, your candidate, and your press liaison.

A. Setting up the Press Conference
    1. Know the reason for your press conference and why it is "NEWS."
    2. Know the campaign message and make sure your press conference reinforces that message.
    3. Target the message and the press conference to your audience. For example, if you need to appeal to males age 65-plus, don't do a press conference on day care.
    4. Pick up the national angle, especially if you are in a federal or high-profile statewide race. Frame your story within the larger story.
    5. The site of your press conference should reflect the message to some degree. A hotel room or campaign headquarters says very little about health care or crowded prisons. It also makes the event look political.
    6. Send the press advisory out one to two days before the event, depending on the nature of the press you are dealing with and the sensitivity of the issue.
    7. Be careful not to give away too much in the press advisory. The advisory should include the date, time and location of the event as well as one or two sentences on the basic topic to be addressed.
    8. Call the press outlets after you send the advisory to make sure the proper person received it and made a note of it. During busy election cycles, it is easy for political press advisories to get lost in a heap. Don't forget to ask the reporters and/or assignment editors if they will be attending or sending a reporter. They probably won't give you a definitive answer, but this allows you to make an initial plug for the event.

9. Call the press outlets the morning of the event. This will allow you to push for coverage and give them more of a "hint" — if needed — about the topic for the conference.

B. The Press Conference

1. Make sure that both the press liaison and the candidate are fully briefed on the topic *and* on any "hot" news of the day. Reporters often use press conferences as a way to get at the candidate on other issues.

2. Make the press conference "real." Gimmicks rarely work and they often make the candidate look foolish. Those pictures may also come back to haunt you.

3. Visual aids, such as graphs and charts, can add emphasis and credibility. Make sure that you choose visuals that are easy to read and easy to comprehend in a 30-second TV report or a small picture in the newspaper. Providing reporters with photocopies of the visual aid can help ensure that your point is made.

4. Use rhetoric that broadens your coalition. Although you may be targeting a specific group, make sure that you are not alienating other key constituencies.

5. Know the key words and phrases of your campaign message. Create a statement that repeats and reinforces the campaign message. Be sure to include a few crucial sound bites. What do you want to see most in the headline or news lead? What do you want to see most in the article/ news report? What don't you want in the story?

6. Make it easy for the press to write the kind of story you want written. Be prepared and assume the reporters will be unprepared. Have sufficient copies of press releases, background information and photographs.

7. Allow time for questions, but know that you can limit that time.

8. If you do not have an answer to a question, don't fabricate one. Depending on the question, either indicate that you don't know the answer or spin your answer in a way that taps back into your message.

9. Do not allow the candidate to "hang out" with the press. After questions have been fielded, the candidate should be accompanied out and any further dialogue should be directed to the press liaison.

C. After the Press Conference

1. Send press releases to all news outlets that did not attend.
2. Follow up with reporters who seemed interested when you sent the advisory, but then chose not to attend.
3. Follow up immediately with reporters who attended the conference, but requested additional information.
4. Send actualities out in the next drive time closest to the press event or the drive time that will give you the most air time without throwing it into the category of "old news."

D. Day-to-Day Press Relations

1. Try to find ways to get press without the candidate present. Surrogate speakers or events held in different areas of the district or state can often draw a good deal of press. (Of course, you'll want to know what the surrogate speaker is going to say ahead of time.)
2. When talking to reporters, know your agenda. Be clear on your purpose and your plan before talking with reporters.
3. Again, never discuss any issue with a reporter without being fully briefed.
4. Know the deadlines of every major news outlet. Respect reporters' time limitations.
5. Don't be afraid to let a reporter know she or he was wrong. But before you do, make sure you are right. Have the documented proof at your fingertips and compiled in a way that allows you to quickly fax or mail it to the reporter.
6. Don't allow any member of the campaign team to field questions and/or calls from the press except the press liaison. This will give the campaign better control of the message and media. Reporters will try repeatedly to go around the liaison. Don't let this happen.
7. Remember, campaigns are not won with a single statement, but you can definitely lose ground with one.
8. Above all, work to ensure that any interactions with the press help your campaign, your candidate, and your press

press help your campaign, your candidate, and your press liaison establish credibility with the press and increase their ability to control the message when translated and transported by the press.

Final note: *Sometimes, when all else fails, you just gotta go with your gut.*

As senior associate of Ridder/Braden, Inc., Kris Bess specializes in message development and implementation, earned media, issue development, research, speech writing and corporate and nonprofit public relations while running the firm's Washington, D.C. office. Prior to joining Ridder/Braden, Bess served as press secretary and communications director for two U.S. Senate campaigns. Her experience also includes two years of teaching writing and communications at the university level, writing, researching, and lecturing at the U.S. Supreme Court and working as a film writer and editor.

Respecting the Media

William Waybourn

BECAUSE the media can make you or break you as a viable contender for public office, it is of vital importance, if not survivability, that you be "media savvy."

First of all, never, never, never lie to a reporter. You will only regret it. Remember that good reporters will always check out what you tell them. They are human, of course, and form opinions based on what they hear and see, just like we all do. But they are also trained to check out the facts. You don't have to tell the *whole* story, but lying will definitely get you in trouble. You will never regain your credibility with that reporter, and chances are you will also lose credibility with the public because the media is your conduit to a positive image and/or public reputation. You can avoid putting yourself in a situation which might encourage you to lie by giving reporters only as much information as you feel comfortable giving them. (Frankly, most space constraints don't allow for two-thirds of the stuff you will give them anyway.)

Talk directly to the reporter whenever possible. It's better that the information comes from you rather than from a spokesperson or someone who may not have as much first-hand knowledge. Do what you can to make the reporter's job easier. Keep what you say as simple as possible: think – and speak – in 12-second soundbites. Don't expect reporters to wade through reams of material just to fish out a quote from you.

Don't blame the media for presenting both sides of an issue (*e.g.*, homosexuality). In fact, seeing the other side can help readers (also known as voters) realize that they don't want to be considered bigoted or narrow-minded. Remember the lesson of the 1992 Republican Convention of hate and prejudice – it probably got Bill Clinton more votes than anything George Bush did while he was in office.

Your biggest media obstacle as a gay candidate is to avoid being characterized as a single-issue (i.e. homosexual) candidate. Here are some ways to avoid the media's attempt to make you into a single-issue candidate:

▼ Offer them your positions on a wide range of issues and point out that only their own bias can make you a one-issue candidate.

▼ Demonstrate examples of your coalition-building skills with other groups, organizations and professional societies.

▼ Show them the endorsements you have received, especially those that are *not* from groups and individuals who can be written off as "typical gay supporters" (for example, citizens groups, church groups, rabbis, priests and ministers).

▼ Never run from the lesbian/gay issue. Any level of discomfort you show will be directly proportional to the amount of space you get for it. No candidate has ever lost because of his or her homosexuality alone. Some may not have won because of it, but generally there were other factors to consider, such as low name identification, lack of money, and an inability to articulate responsible positions on a wide range of issues.

▼ If a reporter asks how being lesbian or gay affects your race, don't be defensive. Face the question head on ("Well, to tell you the truth, it's hard to get the press to concentrate on my race rather than on my sexual orientation.") then, gently but firmly guide them into other areas: "I'm not sure how whom I sleep with is relevant to this race. By the way, are you familiar with my position on zoning (schools, street repair, crime control – pick any subject that *is* relevant to your race)?" Or, "I'm more than happy to talk about my candidacy and my sexual orientation – and how do you plan to cover similar sexual identity issues with my opponent(s)?"

▼ Never accept coverage that holds your campaign to a different or higher standard than that of other candidates in the race. We are, after all, working for equal treatment, if not equal standards. A reporter once asked me if a Victory Fund recommended candidate's failure to note his sexual orientation in the straight media meant that he was acting "gay in gay circles while appearing straight in straight circles." I answered with a question: "Will you (the reporter) be conducting a similar study of the opposition's ads to see if they all note his heterosexuality?" The reporter thought better of the question and said that if his editor required a higher standard for the gay candidate he would call back. I never heard from him again.

▼ Don't let fear of the press make you avoid your gay or lesbian supporters. There is nothing wrong with candidates appealing to their own communities and constituencies. Black candidates, Hispanic candidates and female candidates do this routinely and no one ever questions it. So, if you appear at a gay function and they try to pigeonhole you as a single-issue candidate, call them on it.

Believe it or not, most reporters are our friends. Editors, however, are a different matter entirely. Reporters are on the scene, view particulars, and report facts. Editors are behind desks wishing the reporter saw something they didn't, trying to include something that wasn't in the story because the reporter *obviously* misunderstood the intent of the assignment. Reporters frequently have personal relationships with the subjects they cover. It is impossible for a trained journalist to interview someone and not gain an awareness of the person's vulnerabilities and strengths. Editors, however, are rarely privy to such relationships and are nervous about such closeness with subjects.

If you are wronged by a story, don't hesitate to complain. Call the reporter first as a matter of courtesy. Let the reporter know of your concerns. Frequently, mistakes can be corrected at this level. But if they aren't, skip everyone else and head straight to the top. Don't spend time with mid-level managers/editors. As a former editor, I know that the front-line defense of reporters in *all* situations is crucial and editors are not likely to take your side or find fault with their reporters' work. The corporate brass is different, however, and the last thing executives want is someone screaming in their offices that their newspaper's report is severely flawed. Reach the highest ranking executive/official of the paper or station to whom you can get through, even if it means camping outside their office. Present the facts that show bias and prejudice and stand your ground. No credible news organization can exist without correcting errors of its own making. Going straight to the top might not gain you any friends, but it will gain you respect.

The quickest way to get a reporter's attention is to accuse him/her of bias in their coverage (or lack of coverage) of your campaign. This is risky, so be prepared to back it up with facts showing coverage of similar or previous races. I once told a TV reporter that his gay-related questions of my candidate at public forums were making him a single-issue candidate. Of course, he denied this, so I gave him a videotape that showed him directing questions related to the issues (crime, zoning, privatization of city services, etc.) to the other candidates, then asking my candidate, "Do you think lesbians or gay men should be allowed to serve as police officers?" Previous forums were the same. The reporter couldn't believe he would do something like that until he saw himself on the videotape. He changed his line of questioning thereafter.

If your race is assigned to a closeted gay or lesbian reporter, ask him/her to voluntarily remove him/herself from covering your campaign. Inform the reporter that you will ask for a straight reporter or an openly lesbian or gay reporter if they don't. Follow through if necessary. A straight or openly gay/lesbian reporter has nothing to hide. A closeted reporter may bend over backwards to be tougher on you to prevent anyone from thinking that he/she might be gay.

I once arranged for a candidate to campaign door-to-door with a bevy of reporters in tow. At every house, my candidate asked the occupants for their input and their concerns relevant to the district. After the discussion ended at one house, the voter-occupant asked my candidate about a hanging plant on her porch that was obviously not doing well in the bright sun. The candidate, wanting to be helpful, spent a few seconds advising her to move it into the shade. The next day the closeted gay reporter's story announced, "... the first gay candidate to run for city council handed out landscaping tips as he campaigned door-to-door." I protested that such coverage was not typical of any of the discussions and asked the reporter to seek voluntary reassignment. He refused. I then went to the paper's managing editor and sought the reporter's removal on the grounds of personal bias. The reporter was reassigned after much deliberation among the paper's editorial management. Of course, I took a big chance. But I strongly believe that coverage of open and honest debate requires reporters who can be open and honest with themselves first.

Be open and honest with reporters. If you withhold information, it will only invite more questions. Most reporters will welcome the opportunity to understand complex issues and factors affecting your candidacy. Being open invites their attention. Voters respond to this same openness. Witness how the public viewed Janet Reno after the David Koresh debacle. Meeting issues head on will gain you respect.

And just how will reporters know that you meet issues head on? You have to tell them. Call them — every day if you have something to report. Remind them of forums, events or situations that show you in environments other than strictly gay or lesbian. They will welcome insider "tips" about the campaign, plus it will educate them to aspects of your candidacy that they may not see otherwise.

Finally, always be cautious in what you say, no matter what the situation, because reporters are always working. Anything you say to a reporter can (and probably will) be used. The concept of "off the record" is frequently misunderstood and is used less and less. Reporters can also confirm what you reveal through other sources, and if they do, the information you gave them becomes fair game. Don't complain if reporters print what you tell them. That's their business.

William Waybourn is a cofounder and the executive director of the Gay and Lesbian Victory Fund, a political action committee founded in May 1991, that has raised hundreds of thousands of dollars to support qualified openly lesbian and gay candidates for public office. Waybourn is the former president and member of the board of directors of the Dallas Gay and Lesbian Alliance and the Foundation for Human Understanding. He also cofounded the AIDS Resource Center, the Nelson-Tebedo County Community Clinic for AIDS Research, the AIDS ARMS Network and the Dallas Gay and Lesbian Alliance Credit Union. In addition to service on various boards of directors of other organizations, Waybourn worked on the staffs of daily newspapers as a reporter and as an editor for over a decade before entering the field of public relations, and has also managed and worked on many political campaigns.

What a Queer Thing to Say
Dawn Laguens

IN today's world, most people's *primary* relationship is with their television set; their eyes, ears and brains are accustomed to receiving and evaluating information delivered through electronic medium. **The core of today's political campaign is communication.**

You, too, can grow up to be a demagogue.

People, especially candidates, want to believe that a campaign is an intellectual endeavor won by the smartest and best-prepared person. In fact, few things approach the level of sheer demagoguery involved in a political campaign. It is not an intellectual enterprise (in which case we could just issue some position papers), but an emotional one. Campaigns are, at their root, cults of personality. They are about creating an emotional bond between candidates and voters, and the victor is most frequently the person who can best manipulate these emotions. Voters want candidates to articulate a faith – a way and reason to belong – where they can feel meaning and significance.

It is critical that candidates channel issues into emotion to provide resonance and a connecting point. This perhaps was Clinton's greatest achievement – wrenching every ounce of emotional significance out of any issue. This point could not be more important to lesbian and gay candidates. It is the emotional nature of politics, this search for shared meaning, that puts gay and lesbian candidates at a disadvantage. For this reason, lesbian and gay candidates must move proactively to eliminate barriers that would separate them from the average voter.

Here's lookin' at you kid...

Fairly or unfairly, the way a gay or lesbian candidate and his or her supporters present themselves to the outer world is an important part of the message. The first emotional hurdle for the gay or lesbian candidate is to send the message "I am like you. You can feel safe with me. Our interests are the same." There is a time for throwing stereotypes in people's faces and saying "deal with us," but that time is not during a campaign for elected office. Attention to outward signs and symbols also helps deflate your opponent's ability to make you an unrecognizable other. A twisted example of this is how Neo-Nazi/Klan Wizard David Duke's clean-cut, moderate exterior made it hard to get people to believe he was this horrible creature. He didn't look like his opponents said he did, so it took more money and time to make the negatives stick.

Additionally, gay and lesbian candidates are sometimes distracted from presenting a winning message by the neediness and demands of their own community. Campaigns are less about communicating with your friends and supporters than about your ability to reach undecided voters and to damage your opponent. This is why a poll is so critical to the process of determining a message. Many candidates fear being "re-made" in the image of a poll, but the poll helps you know what voters want to hear, as opposed to what you want to say.

There are two themes in the world. Really.

If you embark on the great genealogical search for the parents of the modern political message, you'll always end up with the same two names: Status Quo and Changing the Status Quo. These themes, combined with the voter's psychological (definitely psycho and rarely logical) dynamics at the moment of the race, define the issues. The battle in most political campaigns is really for the mantle of change. The challenge for the lesbian or gay candidate is to utilize his/her inherent "outsider" status without appearing "frighteningly" different.

The zen nature of message.

Message can be loosely defined as the key concept or thought, expressible in less than a paragraph (and sometimes in a sentence), that is the main thrust of all positive campaign communications. It is the basic or fundamental truth of the campaign and should be chanted like a mantra. The positive message is the question to which you are the answer. Message is proactive, not reactive. Don't forget that message is a twin: the negative message — the case against the opponent — must be defined and managed as well. An example:

Theme: *Change*
Campaign Issue: *The Economy*
Positive Message: *I feel your pain.*
Negative Message: *My opponent is out of touch.*

A major task of your campaign will be to develop an integrated message delivery system. Message discipline and integration in canvassing, phone banking, earned media, direct mail, candidate speeches and any broadcast media is a challenge to even the best run campaigns.

I smell a dirty rat... or, who's the single-issue candidate?

Prepare to be attacked. Marginalized. Radicalized. Attack of the 50-foot lesbian! As stated previously, if you are asking friends and acquaintances for lots of time and even more money, you have the responsibility to do whatever possible to minimize the effects of very predictable attacks. Your ease with your "gayness" is going to set the tone for how many others deal with it as well. You can take some of the power out of your opponent's attacks by addressing the gay issue first. But hey, they're still going to come after you. And they won't always do it directly. Your personality will, to a great extent, determine which response is most effective. Humor is one of the great political weapons, and gay and lesbian candidates across the country have used it to deflect image attacks. A bit of confident humor can strike at the heart of the ridiculousness of your opponent's claims about you.

Anger and outrage are another avenue of response, but are risky for a number of reasons. People are frightened of righteous anger and will avoid it if possible. The only time people embrace anger is when it gives them the opportunity to be against something they feel is weighing them down personally. Because so many "moderate" people still feel uneasy about the gay issue, it is hard to bring them into solidarity with you. Some attacks, however, are so awful that anything less than *controlled* anger will make you look like a wimp.

Next to perfectly timed humor, the best responses to anti-gay attacks are usually rooted in the personal experiences of the candidate, which allow for an emotional connection with voters in the response. An example is the openly gay candidate whose response to an attack was to say "How sad that when we are here to talk about the drunk drivers who killed my brother and who threaten the brothers and sisters, daughters and sons of all of us, my opponent remains a single-issue, or more truthfully, a no-issue candidate." Define your opponent as the single-issue candidate before he or she can define you.

So, should I be on TV?

Cathy Allen, in *Political Campaigning: A New Decade*, makes this point about paid advertising and the small campaign:

> The best field operation in the world cannot make up for the name recognition you can receive from broadcast advertising. TV and radio ads now account for more than half of the dollars spent on political campaigns. Broadcast media is more expensive than other items in your budget, but few other investments result in as many votes. Both television and radio allow a personal connection to be established between the candidate and the voters. The ads must be well-thought-out, well-produced, and smartly distributed. If any of these three characteristics fall short, more damage than good may come from your broadcast investment. [In the modern political world] the power of broadcast media is so dominant in determining winners and losers that a campaign may need to limit other campaign costs in order to finance the best possible broadcast strategy.

One of the major mistakes of small campaigns is to spend *some* money on radio and television, but not enough to make a difference. From a strategic viewpoint, if a campaign cannot spend enough money on electronic media to sufficiently reach its targets, it is better off shifting the resources to another use. However, there are sometimes tactical reasons – to reach a particular constituency or demographic group or to establish the viability/credibility of the campaign – to buy small amounts of radio or TV time.

Close to the end.

Just as there is no one formula for gay and lesbian candidates to follow to electoral victory, there is no one message that works. But the one message that is almost sure to fail is a narrow gay-rights agenda. You will have any number of constituencies who will want you to be their champion — your gay and lesbian supporters, the national organizations that are giving you technical support and funding, etc. — yet there is hardly a district in the country where crime, jobs, taxes and ethics aren't the main issues. A good poll, thoughtful targeting and message discipline are three keys to a solid campaign for any candidate.

You must overcome the average voter's fear that your agenda as a lesbian/gay candidate is different than their own. You must take advantage of your uniqueness, though you know that your uniqueness can, and probably will, be used against you. This is courage. Good luck.

The end.

Dawn Laguens is an owner and partner in the media and general consulting firm of Seder/Laguens, Inc. Her specialties include campaign strategy and message development, television and radio production and independent expenditure campaigns. The firm has received numerous awards, including recognition with ADDYs, Pollies and the 1991 Clio for the best political ad in the United States. Laguens has worked as a campaign professional in local, statewide and Congressional races and served as the campaign director for the Louisiana Coalition Against Racism and Nazism. In 1992, she served as the Press Coordinator for the Women's Caucus at the Democratic National Convention. In addition to her work on campaigns and at Seder/Laguens, Laguens teaches seminars on media, campaign strategy, free press, field operations and independent expenditure for numerous organizations and publications.

Reaching a Broader Audience
Barney Frank

THE single most important piece of advice I can give to openly gay or lesbian candidates is to resist the effort that will almost certainly be made to portray you as someone who will focus almost all of your energies on gay and lesbian issues to the exclusion of all other issues. However, it is neither politically sensible nor morally acceptable for a gay or lesbian candidate to weaken his or her positions on substantive issues involving gay men and lesbians. All this will accomplish is to make you feel badly about yourself because none of those who are strongly motivated to be anti-lesbian or gay will vote for you in any case. The political problem will come from those homophobes who are more subtle in their approach, and who may succeed in winning over people who are not especially homophobic to a negative position on your candidacy if you are not especially vigilant.

The tactic they will probably use is to argue that while they are not opposed to the fact that you are gay or lesbian, they are concerned that because of your sexual orientation you will spend almost all of your time, political capital, etc., on gay and lesbian issues and thus neglect the concerns of others. Unfortunately, to many people this will be plausible, especially to those who are not familiar with the fact that lesbians and gay men function pretty much as does everyone else in most situations. There are two important ways to counter this.

First, make sure that you address the full range of issues. This should not be difficult because you will be interested in that full range of issues and will in fact be running not simply because of your concern about homophobia, but because you are interested in improving conditions for people in general. Do not take it for granted that people will understand this. If it seems to you and your campaign workers that the argument that you will focus exclusively or excessively on gay and lesbian issues is gaining currency, I strongly recommend that you address it openly. It used to be conventional political wisdom that you should ignore negative charges. Most of those who have followed that wisdom are now former office holders. In the current political climate, negative evaluations are often readily accepted by a public skeptical of all elected officials and candidates for elective office, so it is important to take these falsehoods on and refute them. You can do this easily by addressing the full range of issues in a knowledgeable and thoughtful way.

Second, you will have to resist the well-intentioned tendency of your gay and lesbian friends and supporters to overdo their support. Remember that the scarcest resource you have is your claim on the attention of the voters. Citizens have a great deal to do — they have jobs, families, recreation, etc. The amount of time any individual voter will spend on your particular race — unless you happen to be running for President or maybe governor — is not very great. If you appear on a daily basis at gay and lesbian events where you will be given a great deal of emotional support and will have the chance to make yet another good impression on people who are already firmly committed to voting for you as many times as the law allows, you will forfeit your chance to make an impact on people whose primary concerns are other issues.

Indeed, given the tendency of the press to focus on the unusual, and given the fact that openly gay and lesbian candidates are unusual in most places, you will run the risk, if you appear too regularly at gay and lesbian events, of giving credence to the frequent falsehood that that is all you care about. Your gay and lesbian supporters should understand that the important thing for them to do is not to gather together to repeat their fervent support for you on frequent occasions, but to help you build on that support to reach out to others in the community.

There is nothing remotely dishonest in this because in any job I can think of — city councilmember, county commissioner, state legislator, etc. — you will in fact be spending most of your time on issues that are not of special relevance to gay men and lesbians. Fighting homophobia is important, but it could not conceivably take up more than a small percentage of your time in any office that I am aware of because the full range of issues — which of course affects all people, gay and straight – is so all encompassing.

Thus, my advice is to be explicit about your support for gay and lesbian issues, but to resist the tendency of both your worst enemies and your best friends to give people the impression that these issues will be the focus of your work while in office.

Now serving in his seventh term in the U.S. House of Representatives, Barney Frank chairs the Subcommittee on International Development, Finance, Trade and Monetary Policy of the Committee on Banking, Finance and Urban Affairs. He also serves on the Judiciary and Budget committees. Although not "out" when first elected, Frank voluntarily acknowledged that he was gay in June 1987, and has since been reelected three times by between 65 and 70 percent of the vote. Frank was an active leader in the fight for gay and lesbian rights before coming out and was the first member of the Massachusetts legislature to sponsor a gay rights bills.

The Gay Label:
How It Helps and Hinders
John Laird

S INCE I finished as runner-up in the August 1993 Democratic special primary for the Monterey Bay area seat in the California State Assembly, the question I've been asked most frequently is whether I thought I was helped or hurt by being an openly gay candidate. There is no simple answer. Rather than discuss the question, I thought it would be more interesting and informative to give the background of the race and present anecdotes telling what it was like to run as an openly gay candidate.

California's 27th Assembly District has a population of more than 375,000, including over 220,000 registered voters. The assembly vacancy for which I ran was created when then Assemblymember Sam Farr was elected to Leon Panetta's congressional seat in a special election after Panetta stepped down to become budget director for the Clinton administration. Because these were the first legislative vacancies in 13 years, 26 candidates filed for the congressional seat and nine candidates for the assembly seat. My race for the assembly included another major liberal Democrat among the four Democrats, as well as three Republicans.

I brought to the race solid credentials, years of Democratic Party activism and nine years of experience as an elected official, having served as a city councilmember and mayor of Santa Cruz, the largest city in the Assembly district. Sixty percent of the district is in my home territory of Santa Cruz County, where I was well known and had an identity much greater than just being openly gay. But 40 percent of the district was in new territory in Monterey County, generally reputed to be more conservative than the Santa Cruz area.

▼ When the rumors of my possible candidacy first made the front page of the *Santa Cruz Sentinel* in early January 1993, the major news angle was that if elected, I would be the first openly gay or lesbian state legislator in California history.

▼ A few weeks later, a politically connected friend of mine was talking to a longtime member of the State Assembly about my candidacy. The assemblymember said he did not understand why I would run, commenting: "That's not a 'gay' seat."

▼ The Gay and Lesbian Victory Fund recommended my candidacy to its donor network at the end of February. By early September, I had received over $27,000 directly from Victory Fund members, 15 percent of the $180,000 I raised for the primary.

▼ When my major liberal opponent addressed the Building Trades Council in Monterey County in February, he was asked to describe his potential opponents. He included me, and the fact that I am the former mayor of Santa Cruz. The only other descriptive item he listed was the fact that I fight for lesbian and gay rights.

▼ In early May, I traveled to Salinas to meet with unsuccessful congressional candidate Bill Monning and five of his key supporters. Monning, an attorney with a longtime record on progressive causes, had run a surprisingly successful insurgent campaign attacking the other two major Democratic candidates from the left and finishing second in the primary. During the course of a generally friendly and wide-ranging meeting, one of his supporters made the comment that he did not think I could win because "people on the Monterey Peninsula would not support a gay candidate. Had I experienced this before?" I responded that I had experienced that attitude every day of my life. Everyone but the person making the statement laughed, but I later regretted not asking him to substitute "Latino" or "African-American" for "gay" in his electability premise to see if he could understand more clearly how his own feelings were embodied in his question. Monning endorsed another assembly candidate, and I felt that his silence during that exchange reflected his lack of understanding about discrimination against lesbians and gay men.

▼ In late May, my campaign made arrangements for a poll to

gauge, among many different things, the attitude of district voters toward an openly gay candidate. Our pollster advised us that the best way to test voter homophobia was not to ask directly if the person supported civil rights for gays or if he/she would vote for a qualified openly gay candidate, but rather to ask if he/she thought an openly gay candidate can win – the exact premise included in the question during the Monning meeting. This is because people who might not be direct about their own homophobia in a question about civil rights will let it show in a question about electability. When the poll results came in, respondents said (by a two-to-one margin) that they believed an openly gay candidate could win election to the assembly – less than the three-to-one margin by which respondents indicated they supported lesbian and gay civil rights.

▼ The first endorsement forum was held by the Democratic Women's Club in May, before the assembly seat was even vacant. Gary Patton, a County supervisor and my major Democratic opponent, and I were the only candidates seeking the endorsement. I did not mention during my presentation that I was gay or that my election would make history. I later heard that some of the club members thought I didn't mention it because the press was present.

▼ Two gay men from outside the area came onboard to run the field operations in Santa Cruz and Monterey Counties. They made personal sacrifices to be part of the campaign, but were willing to do so because of their belief in its historic importance.

▼ The Santa Cruz Action Network (SCAN), a progressive political organization in Santa Cruz County, held its endorsement forum in July. I was approached a few days before the forum by a SCAN member who supported another candidate. The member said he was bothered by the fact that my major issues handout did not mention my sexual orientation. He said that he believed the historical importance of my election was a strong reason to consider my candidacy. I told him that my sexuality had been covered on the front page of the local newspaper as recently as last week, and I did not see a need to talk about it in every single campaign flyer. He warned me that he would ask about this at the SCAN forum. I saw him there, but he did not ask the question.

▼ Because anyone can join SCAN on the night of the forum, many gay men took the opportunity to join so they could vote to endorse me. A supporter of another candidate expressed nervousness about the fact that there were so many men in the audience she didn't know. This was a clear statement of how the gay community did not necessarily overlap with the progressive political activists.

▼ After the forum, the candidates were excused from the debate on whom SCAN should endorse. Someone who identified herself as a lesbian expressed support for a straight candidate, stating that he "has an intuitive sense about oppression."

▼ Every day, our campaign volunteers manned tables outside local supermarkets, drug stores, the farmers market and the community credit union. Homophobic responses – usually at the rate of one or two a shift stunned the straight volunteers and became a valuable lesson for them. When I was working a local market one day, I asked a man to vote for me and he said "Isn't he homosexual? Why would I want to vote for him?" At another supermarket a volunteer was asked, "Isn't he a lesbian?"

▼ I met with building trades labor leaders about my candidacy. Although I was the logical candidate for them to support, I knew they were hesitant to endorse me because I am gay. I decided to address the issue directly, pointing out that although some city employees were initially concerned about my sexual orientation, I was a city council leader on many issues of importance to them. Later, a friend told me that the labor leaders were surprised that I brought "it" up, saying that they were "past that." The person who got that feedback told me he jokingly suggested that the next meeting should be held at the Blue Lagoon, a local gay bar. (It wasn't.)

▼ The fact that I ran extensive television ads was due primarily to the fact that I am openly gay. Other candidates had more leeway to make the strategic choice to allocate resources to television, mail or a field operation. I needed to buy television time and run advertisements showing that I was well-versed on all of the issues and did not fit the stereotype that voters in Monterey County – where I was not well known – might have had about an openly gay candidate.

▼ Our television advertisements contained a series of headlines about my service as mayor. My campaign staff and I thought it was important to include a gay-related headline and we chose one from an article written during my second term as mayor: "Santa Cruz's Gay Mayor, It's Not a Big Deal Anymore." A media analyst asked by the *Santa Cruz Sentinel* to comment on the campaign ads called the use of this headline "inoculation," and gave me credit for raising the issue myself. However, he then compared it to Bill Clinton posing next to the polluted Arkansas River during last year's Presidential campaign – not a comparison I would have made.

▼ My strongest liberal Democratic opponent's major television ad included his family. His first major mailer – requesting that supporters vote by absentee ballot – featured a photo of his family on the front. My gay supporters were outraged, and the media analyst commented on the "family values" nature of the advertisement.

▼ Unbeknownst to me, my parents, who live to the north in the San Francisco Bay Area, had subscribed to the Santa Cruz daily newspaper to keep tabs on my race. My mother was so irritated with the news article on the "family values" nature of my opponent's television advertisements that she drove down to the campaign office unannounced to deliver family pictures that she thought I might be able to use in my campaign materials. "Where do they think you came from?" she asked.

▼ In early August we held a campaign benefit at the Boulder Creek home of a National Gay and Lesbian Task Force board member. We sent invitations that said "Help Elect California's First Openly Gay Legislator" to Santa Cruz-area contributors. I got a note from a former Santa Cruz school board member, a supporter, telling me that she supported me not because I am openly gay, but because of the good qualities I had shown as an elected official.

▼ The California lesbian and gay community outside of my district was heroic in its support of my candidacy. They held fundraisers in Sonoma County, Marin, San Francisco, San Mateo, San Jose, Berkeley, Sacramento, Los Angeles and Orange County. There was a clear understanding of the importance of making history in the

California legislature. Keith Meinhold, Zoe Dun-ning, and many of California's openly gay and lesbian elected officials helped.

▼ Out-of-the-district straight politicians helped as well. San Jose Mayor Susan Hammer endorsed my candidacy, Congresswoman Anna Eshoo appeared at a fundraiser and various San Francisco politicians were also helpful, as was Assemblymember Terry Friedman.

▼ When we filed the second round of campaign finance reports in August, a reporter from Monterey County said he wanted to ask me "the obvious question." I thought the obvious question for him was what the balance of donations was between Santa Cruz and Monterey County contributors and why I didn't have more contributors from Monterey County. The "obvious question" turned about to be what my reaction was to having received so much "out-of-the-area *gay* money."

▼ A female campaign staff member accompanied me to a Monterey County fundraiser. While I was working the room, people asked her if she was my wife. It really frustrated me to realize that after ten years of lead stories focusing on my sexual orientation, I *still* had to come out to people every day in this campaign.

▼ My major campaign themes were boosting the Monterey Bay Area economy, supporting public education and opposing November's school voucher initiative, pushing for campaign reform and reexamining the state budget. This message resonated, and I was endorsed by the Monterey and Santa Cruz Labor Councils, the California Teachers Association, the California Nurses Association and State Assemblymember Terry Friedman. Despite this, many press references to me or my campaign only made mention of my sexuality. The local reporter covering the race said I wanted it both ways, to get gay support and to be viewed primarily for my record on non-gay issues. I insisted that one could be openly gay *and* recognized for issues and hard work on traditional governmental issues, just like any other candidate or elected official.

▼ I originally thought that in a strong anti-incumbent atmosphere I had an electoral advantage by not being an elected official. As the campaign wore on I realized that incumbency would have been an advantage for me. When I held public office I was regularly covered in the press on nongay issues, and did not have to struggle to avoid a single-issue tag.

▼ The media constantly identified me only as Santa Cruz's "first openly gay mayor" or as the candidate that had received lesbian and gay political action committee support. During my endorsement meeting with editorial board members *Monterey Herald*, I was asked if I thought that being gay would be a negative issue. The *San Jose Mercury News* endorsement editorial indicated that I would focus on education and gay issues if elected. The major *Santa Cruz Sentinel* profile on me the week before the election devoted a large portion of its content to the fact that I was gay, with the headline about my struggle to keep from being perceived as a single-issue gay candidate.

▼ A leading Santa Cruz gay activist sent me a card questioning the years I had spent supporting the mainstream Democratic Party. He felt that the party did not return the favor and that lesbian and gay activists should question their allegiance to the Democratic Party.

By primary day, I had raised about $180,000 from 1,700 individual donors and had over 400 volunteers. I lost the Democratic primary by eight percentage points. Three-quarters of that margin was in the Monterey County portion of the district. I did the best in the three Santa Cruz County cities, coming in as the second-place Democrat by one vote in Capitola, twenty votes in Scotts Valley, and ninety-nine votes in Santa Cruz.

There were two recurring themes among the many calls, cards, and visits in the weeks after the election: one, that many lesbians and gay men who had never been involved in politics had been drawn into the political process by my race and would be politically active from now on; and two, that many straight political activists had come into contact with lesbians and gay men in a way that they never had before — and it had changed their attitudes. Though I would have *preferred* to have received one vote more than my opponent and to have been recognized more for my campaign themes and well-rounded qualifications than for my sexuality, that made the entire campaign worth it. To be sure, there were many other factors in the race and its outcome – my opponent's strengths, various endorsements, the way each candidate was positioned in the race and the fact that it was a summer election with many people, including our large university campus, gone on election day. But being an openly gay candidate also had a large impact on how I had to run my campaign. I was probably the only candidate in 1993 who was at a disadvantage because I was not an incumbent. And I had to make certain choices, like going with television ads, that I might not have made if I were not gay. Then again, I do not know if I could have motivated such a dedicated corps of volunteers and contributors if they had not wanted to see history made in the race.

One thing is for sure, the campaign was a credible effort and helped bring us closer to the day when an openly gay man or lesbian will sit on the California legislature. It's about time.

Currently executive director of the Santa Cruz AIDS Project, which he helped to establish in 1985, John Laird was elected one of the country's first openly gay mayors in 1983. Laird has led the Regional Council of Governments, the Water Planning and Redevelopment Agencies and the Senior City Advisory Council, as well as serving as president of the Association of Monterey Bay Area Governments. Long active in the Santa Cruz gay and lesbian community, Laird founded groups such as BAYMEC (a political action committee) and a gay beach-volleyball team, and was instrumental in the codification of municipal employee domestic partnership programs in the city and transit districts.

Running Against the Right
Glen Maxey

FROM the beginning of my campaign for the Texas House of Representatives, I knew that running as "the gay candidate" was not going to be easy. District 51 has historically been a "minority" district. It is 45 percent Hispanic and 15 percent African-American. For almost two decades a Hispanic legislator had held the office. This is not a gay-identified district and most of the consultants told me that the timing was not right for a gay candidate to run. Many questions came up in those deliberations: Could I win this race if I did not have the "political handicap" of being homosexual? Is there an underlying anti-gay sentiment that can never be turned around? Would there be openly hostile opposition?

My experience has been that the first defense against the forces of darkness (however you define them in your locality: the Radical Right, conservatives, Republicans, the Democratic establishment) is a very good offense. When I ran my first race for the House of Representatives, my offensive battle plan was to be the candidate of those constituencies that make up the voters of my district. If I were the environmentalists' candidate, I reasoned, how could people in that group make me into a single-issue candidate? If I were the candidate supported by teachers, consumers, women, the elderly, students, organized labor and public employees, no one could charge me with being a single-issue politician.

This may seem very obvious, but I think all of us who have been successful openly gay/lesbian candidates will agree that you cannot run for office just because you are gay or lesbian. Making a case for having gay and lesbian voices at the table of power is a very important message for our community to understand. However, that message alone doesn't resonate well with the voters unless you have the luxury of running in an area where a substantial number or majority of voters are gay and lesbian.

Just as the Radical Right has been successful in packaging our civil rights as "special rights," they will immediately target you as a "single-issue candidate" unless you are well prepared before entering the race. If your candidacy for the local school board is based only on bringing gay/lesbian issues to the forefront, you're going to lose. If you have ideas about quality of education, saving taxes and improving the schools, you may have a good shot at winning. Then, after you win, your constituents will probably listen when you talk about the issues faced by gay and lesbian high school students or why we need AIDS education in the schools.

Although a minority of voters are hateful, homophobic, extreme right-wingers with whom you shouldn't waste your time, the majority of voters who are not progay (or at least gay tolerant) constitute a possible swing vote for your campaign – *if* you reach out to them. When dealing with these more "conservative" elements in our elections, it becomes really important for the voters to learn that gay and lesbian candidates are "people just like them," and that our issues are their issues. Of the many voter contact techniques available to a campaign, none surpasses direct voter contact. No phone call, brochure or television ad from an opponent will change a voter's mind if that voter knows you personally as a candidate or an elected official. This is especially true for openly gay and lesbian candidates. All studies have shown that when a straight person knows someone who is gay, they are less likely to hold anti-gay opinions and more likely to support our civil rights.

When I ran for reelection after my first year in office (I had been elected in a special election to fill a vacancy in the Texas legislature), I faced a well-financed, attractive opponent. My consultants and I agreed that the best way to reassure those voters least likely to support me – especially older, conservative voters – was to meet them personally. We therefore devised an intense door-to-door walking program in those election precincts where the voters were less than likely to vote for me based on my sexual orientation alone.

Except for the list of registered voters, which can be obtained from any local registrar, we had few tools to tell us who the voters were. In Texas, the voter list is printed in house and street order with the names of all the registered voters, their voting history and their ages. That's all we knew about the people upon whose doors we were about to knock. So I learned early on to reconnoiter each home as I walked up the sidewalk or driveway, looking for clues which might tell me which subjects would interest the voter. A tricycle and toys told me that early childhood education and children's issues might be an important topic. If I saw a rainbow-flag bumpersticker or a flock of pink flamingos in the flower bed I assumed that the voter might be more receptive to my message.

One cold afternoon, I was walking in the Battle Bend neighborhood adjacent to the Air Force base located within my district and populated with many retired military families. I approached a home where the voter's list showed the residents to be a couple, both over eighty years of age. Operation Desert Storm was underway and yellow ribbons were tied around every tree, shrub and bush. A barbecue pit on wheels the size of a Volkswagen Beetle sat in the driveway next to the pickup truck with a rifle rack and an NRA sticker on the window. Not exactly the kind of voters that would support an openly gay, decidedly liberal legislator, I surmised. So, with some trepidation but with an eye on my promise to reach out to all my constituents, I stepped up onto the porch and rang the doorbell.

Through the screened door I saw a small, wiry elderly gentleman. "Hi, I'm State Representative Glen Maxey and I'm running for reelection," I began. He cut me off almost immediately saying, "I know exactly who you are! I know all about you." He seemed to spit out the words like they were venom. I decided that this was not a conversation on which I should waste much time, so I thanked him and began my retreat. Just as I turned to walk away he said, "I heard you speak at the VFW hall. All the guys at the VFW hall are going to vote for you." At this point, my curiosity was piqued. I stepped back up to the door. "Why is that?" I asked. "Well, we invited the whole legislative delegation from Austin to come talk to us and you're the only one who showed. And besides, you're the only one we can count on to be against that damned bingo tax!"

Besides winning this man's vote, I had won a private victory. I knew I had turned the corner and was no longer seen as a single-issue gay candidate. This voter had just proven my thesis for being a successful gay or lesbian candidate: *The voters won't care about your private life, the voters will even give you room to be vocal and active on gay issues, if you can prove to them that you will articulate and represent their concerns just as vocally and actively.*

In the 1991 special election, I faced 13 opponents and received 28 percent of the vote after only a six-week campaign. About three weeks later, I won the runoff with 52 percent of the vote. In the spring of 1992, I defeated my well-financed, establishment-backed opponent with 55 percent of the vote in the Democratic primary. That fall in the general election, I faced a radical fundamentalist Republican opponent who had been recruited by the local far right organizers. He made all of the charges you'd expect: breakdown of the family, special rights, promotion of promiscuity, *ad nauseam*, but I felt confident taking him on because I knew that a great foundation had been laid. I beat him with 72 percent of the vote in November 1992.

When I ran for reelection for my second term, I attended dozens of community forums such as the Women's Political Caucus, the Sheriff and Police Officers Association, the Teachers' Association, the local AFL-CIO Council, the Sierra Club and many neighborhood and Democratic clubs. At the end of the process, I had won endorsement of all but two (and the only two I lost were ethnically based groups whose purpose was to endorse Hispanic candidates). In every case, I was presented to the membership as "their" legislator. I was the environmental legislator, the leader on ethics reform, the spokesperson on labor issues, the teacher advocate and the proponent of minority issues. And I only happened to be gay. With that kind of record and outreach, I am also one of the leading spokespersons on gay and lesbian issues in Texas. The media calls me first for a comment on every local, state and national issue of our community. I can proudly and loudly take up our cause and not worry about the Radical Right because my constituents know me as "their" legislator first.

As we enter another election cycle, I face the recruitment of yet another conservative, fundamentalist opponent. The battle is never over, and we must continue to educate the voters. I know that I must run a full campaign to make sure the voters know my record and my activities on those issues most important to them. From the beginning of my campaign, I knew that running as "the gay candidate" was not going to be easy. I know I will always face a minority of voters who will never accept nor tolerate my sexual orientation. However, with a provocative performance as an elected official and with a well-defined and disciplined campaign message and theme, that minority will continue to be isolated as the fringe constituency that they are.

———

Elected to the Texas House of Representatives in a special election in March 1991, Glen Maxey is the first openly gay legislator elected to represent a minority district. In 1992, he won reelection in the Democratic primary, and has been heralded for his 100 percent voting record on civil rights, and on environmental and consumer issues. Prior to being elected to the state legislature, Maxey was employed as a fifth grade teacher and served as legislative aide for Senators Kent Caperton and Oscar Mauzy, for whom he coordinated legislation on education, redistricting and the environment. He served as the executive director and lobbyist for the Lesbian/Gay Rights Lobby of Texas from 1987 until his election in 1991. Maxey's varied political experience includes work on many campaigns for state, local and federal office, including service as field coordinator for Jim Hightower's 1982 race for Agriculture Commissioner, Lloyd Doggett's 1984 U.S. Senate race and Ann Richard's campaign for Texas Governor.

Running as HIV-Positive
Tom Duane

IN 1991, I won a seat on the New York City Council as the first openly gay, openly HIV-positive candidate to run for and win elective office in the United States. Although I did not know how "coming out" as HIV-positive would affect my race, I wanted to disclose my HIV status because I was ready to do it, and I felt that it was really important and the right thing to do. I hoped that disclosure would be empowering to other HIV-positive people and help break the silence and shame that often surrounds HIV. I also wanted to send a message to everyone that the lives of people with HIV are full and active. I wanted to let HIV-negative people known that an HIV-positive person could run for and hold office, an arduous process and career consisting of busy 14- to 16-hour days. So, in August of 1991, I sent this letter to my constituents:

Dear Neighbor,

In the coming weeks, the campaign to choose our next City Councilmember will begin in earnest. It ought to be an election campaign about issues, about who has served our neighborhoods and who will serve us best on the New York City Council. So I've made a difficult decision, to speak frankly and personally at the outset of this campaign, as I will speak frankly on the issues that face New York City as the campaign progresses.

In one sense, it's nobody's business that I've tested positive for the presence of the HIV virus in my blood. But I am a candidate for public office, and I believe in being candid. I've never denied who I am — or what I believe — and I can't imagine starting now. You should know that I'm not sick. I likely will be someday — but nearly everyone can say that. And I've undertaken a difficult task: to run for the City Council, and to try to make a contribution if elected. You simply can't attempt such a task without a lot of stamina, and in that, I'm very lucky. I'm running with confidence — I'm experienced, qualified, and ready to serve. I've got a long history, too, of fighting for our neighborhoods and this city.

I've long considered support for research and treatment for AIDS to be fundamental, and worked for increased funding for AIDS programs. And more, I believe that health care – and health education – ought to be top priority, because so many people need help. The federal government has abandoned old and poor people, while the flaws of Medicare and Medicaid have become more apparent. City hospitals and community-based clinics must fill the void. We must provide treatment, especially for those without insurance. We must provide help for every addict who seeks to kick the habit. And a woman's right to choose — under assault by the United States Supreme Court and the Bush Administration – must be guaranteed here, in our own health system.

So support for City health care is critical to me, to help everyone who is ill, or will be someday. And support for health education, to prevent disease and dispel ignorance, is essential as well. That's what I believe, and have for a long time. Maybe I believe it a little more strongly because of my own circumstance. Because I know that, no matter how healthy I am now, some day I'll need help, too – the help that, together, we can bring to all New Yorkers.

I'll fight for human needs – including health care – on the City Council. Like so many people in New York City, my life depends on it.

Sincerely,
Tom Duane

I must admit I was nervous about the response I might receive from the people in my district, but the vast majority of the mail and comments I received after I disclosed my status was wonderful. I was overwhelmed by the support I received from so many different people. Other HIV-positive people thanked me for what I had done and HIV-negative people thanked me for my honesty and offered me a great deal of heartfelt support. Sometimes now when I start to feel discouraged or burnt out, I pull out the letters I received after the disclosure and read them. They always renew my energy and help me keep fighting.

I won my Democratic primary with 60 percent of the vote (my two opponents received 26 and 14 percent of the vote) and went on to win the general election with 75 percent of the vote. Running as the country's first openly gay, openly HIV-positive candidate was an intensely positive experience for me and one that has opened the door for others to do the same.

I am grateful to the late Minneapolis Councilmember Brian Coyle for his courage and for the beautiful and empowering way in which he disclosed his HIV status.

In 1991 Tom Duane was the first openly gay, HIV-positive candidate in the United States to run for elective office — and win. Prior to his election to the New York City Council, Duane served four terms as Democratic district leader in the 64th assembly district and was appointed to the community board where he served as chair of various committees. He was also a member of the New York County Democratic Executive and Judiciary Committees, helping to elect, among others, Joan Lobis and Dick Failla, the first openly lesbian and gay judges in New York State. As a longtime tenant activist, Duane fought to secure succession rights to rent-protected apartments for partners and family members of lessees.

High-Impact Public Speaking
Lillie R. Brock

BEN Franklin said, "Well done is better than well said." Too often, however, political candidates concentrate solely on *what* to say and leave to chance all the other skills that are necessary when delivering a public message.

Effective public speaking is one of the most important skills a candidate can master. Expertly managed and well-funded campaigns often lose because the public message from the candidate is weak in delivery and low on impact. Consequently, the greatest weapon a candidate has is the ability to communicate in public and create a decisive image and recognizable style. Every politician has a style. The secret to winning is finding the style that communicates the message you intend and gets the votes you want. So, instead of creating a style and image by accident... create one on purpose!

There are three keys to effective public communication:

1. Create short, high-impact messages. Studies have shown that, when delivered in public, a candidate's message is received in this way: 7 percent words, 38 percent tonality, 55 percent physiology. When preparing a presentation, keep in mind that the words are just a small part of the whole. The other elements hold great power and must be mastered as well. The use of language is critical. Placing high-impact phrases in strategic places will give your speech power and focus. Additionally, appropriate use of certain words can greatly increase impact. For example:

▼ **NOT**

It is easy to get in the habit of saying what you don't want instead of what you do want. Because the brain refuses to process the word "not," you may frequently send a message that is the opposite of what you intended. For example: "Do **NOT** think of a pink elephant" immediately brings to mind a pink elephant. Learn to say what you want people to hear.

▼ **BECAUSE**

Give everything you say a reason. Studies show that even if the "because" makes no sense, people accept the statement better than if there is no stated reason. For example: "We want change now **BECAUSE** it is time to move forward."

▼ **BUT**

Remember that everything that precedes the word "but" in a sentence is negated. This can work for or against you, so use it carefully and deliberately. For example: "I know that it is difficult to get to the polls **BUT** we need your vote" sends a positive message. "I will fight to improve our health care system **BUT** it's a long, hard struggle" does not.

Always plan your speeches with *change* in mind. Every political election is an issue of change. We often speak about change as though it is an event. The truth is, change is a process and your message must assist people in that process.

2. Develop rapport. Rapport is the ability to enter someone's world, to make them feel that you understand them and that you have a strong common bond. When spending one-on-one time with another person, rapport can happen naturally, but when addressing a crowd, you must establish rapport consciously and deliberately.

The critical skill for establishing rapport is matching or mirroring. This simply means that you must study who your audience will be and match/mirror them in as many ways as you possibly can. Notice how they dress, how they speak, what professions they are in, their socioeconomic class, their living conditions, their level of education, etc. President Clinton is an excellent model of public rapport building. During the Presidential campaign, he and Al Gore threw a football with each other alongside the highway on their bus tour. When he visited the "heartlands" after the flood, he dressed in khakis and a pullover shirt instead of looking "presidential." The unspoken message here is "I'm just like you, and I am part of your world." Here are some ways to use mirroring to build rapport:

a. Share stories or jokes that fit the audience.

b. Eat their food, wear/use their gifts, etc.

c. Speak their language.

d. Match their physiology (i.e., if they are stiff, distant, conservative, don't try to embrace them or be too personal — assume their mannerisms, *mirror them.*)

Establishing rapport is especially important for gay and lesbian candidates because it is a tangible way to overcome stereotypes. One of the elements of homophobia is the fear of someone who is different. Rapport by its very nature is a strategy for "becoming like" someone else to establish trust and common ground. So, despite whatever resistance you may have to doing what other people "expect," remember that building rapport is merely a strategy for giving you more power and more access.

3. Deliver with congruence. Congruence means that body movement, voice, tone, pace and words must all deliver the same message. When a candidate says "If you elect me, I will see to it that the rights of all people are protected," while moving his/her head from side to side (like saying no), then an incongruent message is being sent that the audience unconsciously registers. When you hear audience members say things like " I don't trust him/her," or "he/she is just saying what we want to hear," or "he/she talks a good game but can't possibly deliver on that promise," you can be sure that something about the delivery is incongruent.

It is important to understand that when the brain takes in information, it produces an internal representation of the information in a matter of seconds. This internal representation is in visual, auditory or kinesthetic form. That is, it will evoke a picture, words or a feeling. Behavioral response is the result of these internal representations. Each individual tends to create one kind of representation more than the other two, although all three models are present in everyone. The effective public speaker must, therefore, use physiology, tone, pace and words to create representations in all three models to reach everyone in the audience. For the delivery of your message to be congruent, all of these elements must match up.

The following chart demonstrates the change in physiology, tone, pace, hand movement – coupled with certain words and phrases that create the differences between visual, auditory and kinesthetic presentations. To give your message the greatest impact, use the following formula when planning your delivery:

▼ When calling for action, use visual words, voice and physiology.

▼ When giving information (facts, statistics, policies, specifics), use auditory words, voice and physiology.

▼ When attempting to make the audience feel the effects of an issue, use kinesthetic words, voice and physiology.

	Tone	Pace	Hands	Words
Visual	Higher pitched	Faster than normal	Held out from the body and above the chest	*"Picture this..."*, "We can *see..."*
Auditory	Resonant, somewhat monotone	Even tempo	Held out from the body at waist level	*"Hear* me when I *say..."*, "It *sounds* like..."
Kinesthetic	Softer, quieter	Slower than normal	Held close to the body, around the torso	"To *grasp* this point...", "It *boils* down ..."

The hardest thing for speakers to overcome is the tendency to stay in the mode in which they are most comfortable. Be sure to mix all of the components and always end your presentation in the visual mode. This will give strength to your presentation and enable you to reach everyone in the audience.

The candidate's challenge as a public speaker is to enter another's world and gain common ground, giving the listener a congruent message that powerfully leads them through the process of real change. Too many qualified candidates with good things to say have been defeated because their delivery of the message was weak. To be successful you must stay on the cutting edge of what we know about communicating effectively to the masses.

Before you run for office, get an honest, impartial evaluation of your public speaking skills and do whatever is necessary to improve them. You can never put too much time or effort into becoming a better public speaker. Mastering the skills to create your message and deliver it effectively is your key to success in the political arena. Whatever the commitment, make it now, and become the most powerful communicator possible.

Lillie Brock, president and co-founder of Interchange International, a company whose mission is to significantly impact the quality of the work experience by assisting others in preparing for change, has more than ten years' experience as a professional speaker and trainer, and as president and chief operating officer of Citizens Against Crime, Inc. Through Interchange International, Brock has made presentations to such groups as Walt Disney World, Martin Marietta, NationsBank, AT&T, Florida Power and Merrill Lynch. She also co-authored the book, Managing Life Means Managing Changes, *and published several articles on change in the political process, women in the nineties and managing change in the workplace.*

An Army of Volunteers

Dave Fleischer

S UCCESS in local politics depends on smart, thoughtful planning; a broad, diverse base of support; a strong campaign team; lots of money; reasonably favorable electoral circumstances; and numerous, dedicated campaign volunteers. It sounds tough, and it is. It's never easy to assemble this combination of resource and opportunity.

In particular, if you're like most first-time candidates, you may not believe it's possible to find more than a handful of volunteers. If you've worked in struggling community organizations, you've almost certainly lived through tough times when there weren't enough people to get things done. Or maybe you don't know what you need volunteers for. If you have volunteered for campaigns where your time was poorly used, you may wonder if volunteers really are important to your campaign.

Before you let ignorance or skepticism determine your strategy, take a moment to focus on the possibility of putting together a volunteer army. In my experience, mass mobilization of volunteers makes the difference between losing and winning, particularly in the campaigns of openly gay and lesbian candidates.

Suggested Volunteer Projects:

▼ Mailings: folding, stuffing, sealing, stamping, zip code sorting

▼ Computer data entry

▼ Getting records ready for data entry: looking up zip codes and phone numbers, coding contributions, tallying totals

▼ Running off thank-you notes, and matching letters to their addressed envelopes

▼ Pricing the cost of items in the budget

▼ Staffing the front desk and greeting people who come in

▼ Proofreading all campaign documents, including letter and data printouts
▼ Doing heavy lifting after a delivery arrives
▼ Updating the press list by scanning the media for names of key writers, and calling to get their direct line, address and fax
▼ Clipping relevant coverage from community newspapers
▼ Pasting up news articles
▼ Bundling RSVP cards in piles of 120 each for house-party hosts
▼ Faxing a campaign update to your "Good News" list
▼ Organizing refreshments for the office-volunteer crew
▼ Sweeping and cleaning the office

WHY DO YOU NEED VOLUNTEERS?

1. Volunteers make it possible to get your message to the voters.

Statewide campaigns buy lots of TV time for their ads, and receive extensive free media coverage on the news and in the daily papers. But because most gay and lesbian candidates need to start out by running for entry-level positions that receive scant attention, it is necessary to use more direct, personal tactics to get the voters' attention. Direct contact with voters is one of few affordable and powerful ways to do it, and utilizing your volunteer army to make these personalized visits and phone calls, and to write the follow-up letters promptly, enables you to reach more of the people who you need to go out and vote for you in the primary and on election day.

2. Volunteers break through voters' stereotypical homophobic assumptions.

Openly gay and lesbian candidates also need direct contact with voters to dispel ridiculous but common misconceptions and prejudices. Many voters believe that they have never met a gay or lesbian person; even better-educated straight people may assume that you're a single-issue candidate. Direct contact with these voters where you or a volunteer listens sympathetically to diverse concerns – proves to them that you can represent *everybody*.

But it is usually impossible for you to meet all the voters face to face. In all but the smallest local races, you simply may not have the time to touch the 10,000 voters you need to win. But if you augment your own visits with visits from your best volunteers — a close relative, like your mother or brother; local community leaders who will speak on your behalf with voters they know personally; or any other dedicated volunteers — gay or straight — you will not only reach the voters on a personal level, making them aware that their concerns matter to you, but you will also dispel the false perceptions they may have of gays and lesbians.

3. Volunteers save money.

Saving you the cost of hiring clerical staff to keep track of your lists and put out your mailings is only one of many ways having a strong army of volunteers can save your campaign money. Highly skilled volunteers will help raise money, introduce you to potential supporters, gather necessary data, handle campaign legal matters, circulate the petitions to get you on the ballot, translate your literature into all relevant languages, provide free typesetting and graphics, introduce you at events, and fill in an astonishing range of positions. In a down-ballot race, you can't afford to hire staff to do all the work required. Any realistic campaign budget assumes that volunteer labor will fill in critical gaps.

3. Volunteers get you good press.

A large volunteer operation shows

▼ Translating campaign literature or training materials into another language

▼ Typing or word processing letters

▼ Hand addressing key fundraising invitations and phone bank follow-up letters

▼ Collating or stapling documents to prep for a mailing

▼ Highlighting district maps, as directed, to color code key areas

▼ Making a list of all gay and lesbian businesses that advertise in the local gay paper

▼ Copying quotes, statistics and other materials the candidate wants handy for speeches onto index cards

▼ Taking inventory of office supplies, and reordering what's needed

▼ Making signs for around the office, *e.g.*, the schedule for the upcoming week, a key upcoming campaign event or a good news headline

▼ Going through assorted lists and eliminating dupes

▼ Taping the candidate when she/he is speaking

▼ Updating the office bulletin board

▼ Providing child care at large-scale campaign events

▼ Calling new volunteers and scheduling them to come in

▼ Answering the main phone line

▼ Doing reminder calls for volunteers scheduled to come in the next day

▼ Calling potential donors, either to follow up on a mailing or on an invitation to an event

that you have broad, populist appeal. Neither the press nor your opponent will be able to dismiss your base with the usual anti-gay stereotypes when you have a large, diverse group of volunteers helping you. Make sure they are visible, vocal parts of all your events; thanking a long list of volunteers, especially ones who are prominent members of the community, in public makes it clear that you are a candidate for all, not just for some.

4. Volunteers get your supporters out to vote.

Many gay and lesbian candidates find that their critical election is not the general, but rather the low-stimulus, low-turnout party primary. Identifying your known supporters and getting them to the polls can easily account for 5-15 percentage points, and the difference between winning and losing. It's prohibitively costly and often ineffective to try to buy this critical service. You can only accomplish it with your volunteers.

5. Your large volunteer base will produce our next generation of leaders.

Our community has enormous talent, but we rarely take the time to organize and develop it. Even if your campaign is well-run, 75 percent or more of your volunteers will be new to politics, and many will never have done gay and lesbian community work of any sort. Your campaign is, therefore, a terrific opportunity to teach political skills through constant action, and its legacy will be new leaders inspired by you.

NOW THAT YOU WANT THEM, WHERE DO YOU GET THEM?

Most candidates reach out to existing gay and lesbian community organizations, AIDS organizations and women's groups to find their volunteers, but the single best way is to inventory your own public relationships. Make a list of everyone who you will ask to do more than vote for you. (If this list has fewer than 200 names on it, don't run for office.)

Think of everyone you know, in the past or present, who might give any amount of time, or who might help in any way, no matter how limited. Call them, ask for their help, and invite them to a work session. Meet one-on-one with anyone who has unusually high-level skills, or who might volunteer 10 hours or more each week. Have your campaign manager or volunteer coordinator meet with the rest.

ONCE YOU'VE GOT THEM, HOW DO YOU KEEP THEM?

Here are the five secrets to keep your volunteers coming back for more:

SECRET #1: Value their time.

Don't you hate it when people waste your time? Don't waste your volunteers'; they won't come back.

Your campaign manager and volunteer-night coordinator should always have

▼ Calling donors from whom the campaign needs information for filing campaign finance disclosure forms
▼ Delivering packages
▼ Picking up materials from the Board of Elections
▼ Dropping off RSVP cards to house-party hosts
▼ Erecting yard signs
▼ Going back and forth to the printer
▼ Hanging posters
▼ Handing out flyers to the general public, *e.g.*, at busy intersections, subway and bus stops, senior centers, churches after services, forums where the candidate is speaking
▼ Handing out flyers to the gay and lesbian community, *e.g.*, at bars, clubs, community centers

▼ Scouting a building or neighborhood where the candidate is going to appear

▼ Driving the candidate to events

▼ Advancing the candidate at events

▼ Schlepping, building or buying office furniture

▼ Phoning voters

▼ Going door-to-door and handing out campaign literature

▼ Going door-to-door and talking to voters

▼ Carrying signs that promote the candidate at events where the candidate can't be present; being part of a human billboard

▼ Staffing tables at strategic locations to distribute literature and recruit more volunteers

▼ Registering targeted people to vote

a list of volunteer projects that need attention. Structure a wide variety of projects so people with different levels of skill and commitment can all make a contribution.

Hold a regular weekly volunteer night – always at the same time and place where your regulars get to know each other and develop camaraderie. Always take a break in the middle to give an update on the campaign.

Whenever you need to deploy large numbers of volunteers, plan to have a mass meeting of your volunteers the week before, when you brief everyone thoroughly, train them to do the necessary work and sign them up for specific shifts. It's fine to do actual campaign work at the mass meeting; if 80 volunteers are there to learn how to gather petition signatures, they can knock out an extra mailing at the end of the meeting.

SECRET #2: Always train your volunteers.

Prepare training materials and hold training sessions. The trainings can be informal, particularly when teaching easy tasks. But always take time to greet, seat, assemble all needed materials for and train each person, and be clear about your expectations and standards. Set them up to succeed, and they'll do a good job, know it, and be eager to return. Training will not only help every volunteer perform better, it will also help you spot your best new talent.

SECRET #3: Promote your best volunteers.

Always be on the lookout for volunteers who excel at their work; they need to be promoted right away before they get bored, and you need their talent and energy. One way to give an outstanding volunteer more responsibility is to have him or her train and supervise the other volunteers on the project with which they're already engaged. Or you may ask him or her to take on an entirely new project. Either way, be sure to train them for their new responsibilities.

Check in frequently with all newly promoted volunteers to see how they do with their new tasks. Get ready to promote them again — or to move them to some more simple task if they aren't quite as good as you had thought.

SECRET #4: Provide public appreciation.

Take time to thank everyone personally each time they come in to work. Use volunteer night and mass volunteer meetings to publicly thank the people who have worked the hardest. Single out your house-party hosts, your top leaders, your most promising new stars, and your most reliable regulars. You could not run this campaign without them. Make sure they know it. Just as importantly, make sure they know *you* know it. The operating principle: Give your volunteers maximum ownership of the campaign — and the accompanying responsibility and appreciation. Remember, no one likes to be taken for granted.

SECRET #5: Always make reminder calls.

The day before you expect volunteers to come in, call and remind them of the date, time and location. **Always make your reminder calls!** Or have a reliable volunteer make them (and be sure to make your reminder call to the volunteer who is supposed to make the reminder calls!). If you make the calls, the volunteers (mostly) will show up, and show up on time. If you don't, they won't. It's simple.

THE BIGGEST MISTAKE

The biggest mistake a candidate can make is to ask too little of his or her volunteers. Most make this mistake over and over again.

Never say "No" to a capable volunteer. Tell them what you need, and ask if they want to do the work. Don't push them into something they don't want to try, but don't assume they'll turn you down.

"No one will go door-to-door for money."

"No one will work morning rush hour bus stops in the rain."

"No one will poster at 5 a.m."

"No one will hand out your literature in *that* neighborhood."

In my experience, these statements are almost always wrong. I am astonished and gratified to find that someone is ready to face the toughest task. Sometimes they take it on simply because they are very good at it. Other times, they don't know if they can succeed, but they very much want to take on a difficult challenge. Don't deprive them of the wonderful experience of making a difference in your campaign. And don't deprive yourself of the help you need.

People will do amazing things for your campaign if you tell them why it's important, and you ask for their help.

THE BOTTOM LINE

Treasure your volunteers. Treat your top people with the same respect you accord your $1,000 donors. Some of them, like your house-party hosts, will actually raise just as much or more for you. But all of your volunteer leaders who make substantial commitments of any kind will have a comparable impact on your campaign and on your chance of success.

David Fleischer is the coordinator of candidate and campaign manager training for the Gay and Lesbian Victory Fund Candidate Training Institutes. For the past ten years he has managed campaigns and trained candidates and managers. He co-created the first pilot project to provide intensive, nonpartisan candidate training in New York State, the LaGuardia Public Life Training Center.

The Winning Difference
Jackie Goldberg

GOTV – Get Out the Vote! These four little words can mean the difference between victory and defeat, especially for openly gay and lesbian candidates. For example, Rochester (NY) City Councilmember Tim Mains won his first election by a mere 11 votes; former Boston City Councilmember David Scondras lost his seat by 61 votes. In my 1993 race for Los Angeles City Council, an aggressive GOTV effort was the key element in my successful campaign. 25,000 votes were cast, and I won by only 681.

GOTV efforts are essential to almost every campaign, large or small. Anyone running for office, or managing a run for office, will need to research different GOTV methods, especially those that have been effective in your particular race in the past, and form a GOTV strategy based on this information. Because the basic concept of GOTV is outlined in numerous books and articles, I will focus here on my successful GOTV experience, and how it made the winning difference for me.

To win your race you must lay the groundwork for your GOTV effort long before election day. The first step I recommend taking is voter identification. We targeted people in the district who we thought would be supportive, and then went door-to-door to their homes and called them on the phone to describe my views and ask them if they would vote for someone with those views. Because my district is largely low- and middle-income, and my platform reflected their needs and interests, we got a positive response from a large number of the voters.

After voter identification, we separated the people we talked to into three categories: supportive, undecided and unsupportive. The people who were identified as undecided and supportive began to receive our mailings. Our mailings were targeted based on voter demographics — we had a women's piece, a Democratic piece, a lesbian and gay piece, a Republican piece, a senior piece, a Latino piece, etc. We prioritized precincts based on the level of support and voter turnout. The precincts with the best response were the first precincts we covered on foot and on the phone.

We then recruited hundreds of volunteers to go to the priority precincts and talk to people one on one to persuade the undecideds and firm up the yeses. We spoke to about 15,000 people on the phone or at their door. We thus increased our "target universe" to about 13,000 people, all of whom told us that they would vote for Jackie Goldberg for City Council. We continued to send mailings and to make periodic phone calls because by then the "hit" pieces against me had begun. These mailings attacked my record on the school board and said that I was too "global" in the things I cared about. Though the opposition's mailers did not attack me directly for being a lesbian, my opponent's phoners and canvassers focused on my "lifestyle" and told people that their candidate was the only one in the race who was married. The key to countering these attacks was face-to-face contact between my diverse volunteer base and the voters. Our volunteers spoke from their hearts to thousands of voters about why they were spending hours of their free time working to get me elected.

The weekend before election day our GOTV effort went into high gear. We had 200 people out the last Saturday in spite of an unseasonable rain storm. We went back to all of our yeses to remind them to vote on Tuesday. We called everyone again Sunday and Monday nights to make sure they were planning to vote and knew where their polling place was.

On Tuesday, about 100 volunteers came to the office at 4:00 a.m. to hang "doorhangers." These brightly colored little leaflets had my name, my endorsers names and the voter's polling place listed on them, and were made to hang on their doorknobs. They were the first things the voters saw on their way to work. After a brief break for coffee and bagels, GOTV volunteers were dispatched to twelve phone banks all around the district. While phoners reminded my supporters to vote, dozens of teams went to polling places to see who had actually voted. We crossed the names of people who had voted off our lists and sent that information to the phone banks so that we could focus our attention on those who needed it most. This ongoing updating of information was essential to making the most of our people power. All day long, we walked to thousands of homes, urging people to get out and vote. We told people who were tired of hearing from us that freedom was only a ballot away! After 5:00 p.m., we turned the heat up and literally pulled people out of their homes to get them to go vote. We drove people to the polls, watched their kids and stirred their soup while they were gone – in short, we did whatever it took to get **our** voters out to the polls. It was an extremely well-organized, 16-hour effort.

And it paid off.

We truly believe that the repeated contact and the gaining of people's trust were what made it an even race up to election day, and that on election day, it was our GOTV efforts that made the winning difference. With more than 350 GOTV volunteers on election day, each person only had to get one or two extra voters each to make up the 681 vote margin. Early identification and persuasion, then getting your voters out are critical in races against incumbents or where there is an open seat, especially if you are a gay or lesbian candidate.

It made the difference for me. Now I sit as the elected representative of the 13th Council District for the City of Los Angeles. If you want a place at the table, as gays and lesbians deserve, then Get Out the Vote!

───────────────────────────────────────

When she won her 1993 election, Jackie Goldberg became the first openly lesbian or gay person to serve on the Los Angeles City Council. Ten years earlier, in 1983, Goldberg was elected to the Los Angeles Board of Education. Reelected in 1987, she served as its president from July 1989, through June 1991. During her tenure, Goldberg served on the Community Affairs Committee, the Educational Development Committee, and as chair of the Committee of Whole and the Budget Committee. Goldberg developed the Project 10 counseling program for gay and lesbian high school students, which has since become a model for schools across the country.

The Rules of the Game

Tammy Baldwin and Linda Willsey

A LTHOUGH no campaigns and no candidates are the same, what most winners have in common is that they followed a few basic rules. In a crowded field that includes several good candidates, like Tammy Baldwin's 1992 Democratic primary race for the Wisconsin State Assembly, following these rules can make the difference between winning and coming in second. Here's our advice:

Begin early

Campaigns take a lot of time, preparation and hard work. It's difficult to make up for lost time if one of your opponents has been laying the groundwork for his/her campaign months before you even start to think about running. Most elected officials begin exploring a career in politics years before they announce their candidacy for a specific office. To get started, the potential candidate should assess his/her strengths and weaknesses and ask him/herself the following questions:

▼   What have I done that qualifies me for public office and prepares me for the rigors of a campaign?

▼   Who do I know, and what organizations can I count on to support my candidacy?

▼   Do I have the background, the experience, the roots in my community, to be an authentic representative for the voters in the political jurisdiction where I seek election?

▼   Can I afford, personally and professionally, to take a leave of absence from my job and my family obligations to be a serious candidate?

Once you determine that it's the right time for you to run for a particular office, get a reaction from other people. Start floating the possibility of your candidacy with friends, community leaders and other movers and shakers. Find out who else is thinking about running, and don't be afraid to meet with other rumored candidates. The Baldwin Committee's early efforts — which began nearly two years before the election - were critical in discouraging other women and other gays and lesbians from entering the Democratic primary.

Assemble a campaign committee

A candidate who tries to run her own campaign will lose. Every candidate needs to count on other people who have the experience and expertise to identify issues, schedule fundraising events, help with hiring decisions, develop a campaign plan and keep the volunteers fired up. That's what a campaign committee should do. The candidate must be free of administrative details so that she can concentrate on meeting voters, asking people for money, talking to the media, sounding intelligent at debates and being friendly and approachable at all times.

Because the Baldwin Committee was at times too large to function effectively, we recommend a core committee of no more than ten people, at least half of whom have hands-on experience with political campaigns. A chair or co-chairs should be named by the candidate; they should have the authority and willingness to resolve conflicts without involving the candidate.

Most campaigns hire professional, full-time staff. Here's a rule of thumb that was practiced by the Baldwin Committee: If the office the candidate is seeking pays a full-time salary, hire at least one full-time staff person. If your budget permits it, contract with additional consultants for computer services (for donor records and voter files), fundraising assistance, media services and supervision of the campaign committee (specifically, the chair or co-chairs, not the candidate). Hiring the partner or other family members of the candidate is not recommended.

Establish a fundraising program

Money can't buy you love, but it sure makes it easier to run a campaign. And the best place to get money is from the people who love you. Every campaign needs seed money to get started, and this usually comes from the candidate, family members and close friends. Don't be afraid to ask for generous checks, preferably as a contribution but also as a loan if necessary.

Make sure you have filed the necessary paperwork in your state or community to establish a political committee. Learn all the rules about who can give you money and what the maximum contribution levels are for your race. Designate one person on your campaign committee who will oversee data entry of contributions and timely filing of financial disclosure reports. (Your official campaign treasurer may or may not be the person who does this work; it is more important that the treasurer be a well-known and trusted pillar of the community and that the person handling the numbers be responsible, detail-oriented and good with figures.)

Once the early money is secured, it's time to build. How much is determined by what your campaign needs to build an organization and communicate your message to voters. You should develop two budgets: one for a bare bones voter contact and Get-Out-the-Vote (GOTV) campaign, the other for a campaign that includes a major media buy and additional targeted mailings.

The candidate and the campaign committee should collect appropriate lists of potential donors, maintain them on a computer, and assess giving levels of the individuals on the lists. Obvious list acquisitions for gay and lesbian candidates are the donor lists of other gay and lesbian elected officials and organizations. If you can't obtain organization lists directly, be creative. As a last resort, annual reports usually list names; volunteers will have to look up addresses and phone numbers.

It's the candidate's job to pick up the phone and ask supporters for large contributions. To make this job easier, a staff person or consultant should (1) prepare call slips containing the names and phone numbers of potential donors and identifying a contribution goal; (2) schedule *daily* calling times for the candidate; and (3) base the candidate at a location with at least two phone lines. The candidate then takes the stack of call slips and starts making calls. A staff person handles all incoming calls from potential donors and generates pledge letters. A staffer or a volunteer − not the candidate − follows up on unfulfilled pledges.

One of the easiest ways to raise large contributions is to "sell" sponsorships for an upcoming event. For example, the Baldwin Committee planned a high donor reception on the eve of the official kickoff of the campaign. Its goal was to recruit 50 sponsors at $100 each, which netted $5,000. The names looked impressive on the invitation, the campaign committee made sure the political pundits knew the sponsors gave generously, and it helped boost the turnout of the event. Roughly 100 invitees either came to the fundraiser or mailed in a check. They gave an average of $25 each, which raised another $2,500.

This event helped establish Tammy Baldwin as a serious contender and helped raise nearly $15,000 in a six-week period. The effort did not go unnoticed by her chief opponent, the early frontrunner and member of Madison's liberal political establishment, who reportedly said: "I didn't expect Tammy to raise so much money."

Don't forget your gay and lesbian supporters

The most important piece of the Baldwin fundraising program was without a doubt the gay and lesbian community from Wisconsin and nationwide through the Gay and Lesbian Victory Fund donor network. Many gays and lesbians of modest financial means regularly wrote checks for $100 or more. Though the main word of advice and caution that you will receive will be to avoid being pigeonholed as a single-issue candidate, this does not mean that you should neglect your strongest supporters. These people need to be respected and even catered to at times; they are the base of your financial, volunteer and endorsement support. Without them, quite simply, there may not be a campaign at all.

Develop a message

Message development is more than just a slogan to put on campaign literature. Your message tells voters who you are and convinces them that you are an authentic representative of them and their concerns. People tend to vote for someone they feel good about, so it's more important to tell a story during the course of the campaign than to pontificate about the issues. Don't be afraid to show some emotion.

A message, of course, has some relation to the issues that you care about. But the challenge in Tammy's primary, where all four candidates had similar positions on most issues, was to play to the natural progressive tendencies of the voters and show them that she had something unique to offer. We also had to counter the impressive resumé of her chief opponent – who was older, more experienced in local politics, and had garnered the endorsements of major liberal Democratic leaders and organizations – by highlighting Tammy's strengths.

Throughout the primary campaign, we hammered away at a message that urged voters to "Take a stand for change." This message, which dovetailed nicely with the national message that Democrats stood for change, promoted Tammy's strengths (female, courage to run openly as a lesbian, independent and articulate member of the County Board, a new voice and a new perspective for the legislature) and cast a shadow over her chief opponent's resumé (a member of the local political "machine" who represented "politics as usual"). The fact that women candidates were being hyped as agents for change certainly gave additional credence to our message.

You also need to pay attention to the package that delivers the message. Hire professional photographers to make you look good in studio shots and action shots. Make sure the writing for your direct mail and literature is snappy and clear. Voters should be able to learn your message and your priorities in a 10-second scan of your literature; use pictures to tell the story. All your literature should pass the "drop test" – your name, photo and message should be prominent on whichever side faces up.

Make a plan (and stick to it)

Once you settle on a message, develop a plan for getting it out to the voters and *stick to that plan*. A campaign without a plan will end up reacting to its opponent(s) and will spend resources inefficiently. This plan determines which campaign events take place when, where and by whom. Your goal is to make sure that every likely voter has at least seven contacts with the campaign, whether it is a personal visit by the candidate, literature that is mailed or left at the door, a radio ad, a neighbor's yard sign or a phone call. Do what you know you can afford to do first and add the extras later.

The cornerstone of Tammy's voter contact plan was a database of all registered voters in the district. For the primary, the campaign concentrated on a subset of voters who voted regularly in the primary elections. These likely voters became the focus of campaign activities in all wards except student and transient areas, which we concentrated on in the final three weeks of the campaign. With the database, we were able to select and generate mailing labels for a wide or narrow set of likely voter households and mail campaign literature at the lowest possible cost. We also used it to generate walking lists of likely voters for our door-to-door efforts. Every sophisticated campaign should invest in a good computer and voter file.

The best way for a candidate to make an impression on a voter is through a personal contact. Either the candidate or a volunteer should knock on the door of every likely voter and leave a campaign brochure; schedule the candidate to visit areas with voters who tend to vote in high numbers for the candidate's party. Ideally, the campaign mails or drops a follow-up postcard to voters who talked with the candidate. In transient areas, rely on volunteers to distribute literature to every household where there is reason to believe that the residents will vote for the candidate. Wisconsin has election-day registration, but in states where individuals must register to vote a month or more in advance of an election, consider organizing voter registration drives prior to the deadline.

Direct mail

At the very least, a direct mail campaign should provide three contacts to all likely voters. The direct mail component of the Baldwin campaign provided four contacts: an introductory piece that told voters about Tammy, her family, and the values she learned growing up in Madison; a newspaper tabloid/issues profile with the definitive campaign photo of Tammy; a simple but direct appeal that recapped the Baldwin message of change and contained the photos of the 20 men and one woman who had represented downtown Madison since 1903; and finally, an oversized GOTV postcard that listed more than 500 Baldwin supporters.

Most campaigns should also send targeted letters to key constituencies (for example, gays and lesbians, women political activists, environmentalists) and "Dear Neighbor" appeals. Well-known leaders in the targeted mailing areas are well suited to write solicitation letters for contributions, volunteers, etc.

Build an organization

Volunteers are the backbone of any legislative campaign. They prepare the mailings, update the database, distribute literature door to door, and staff the phone banks. You can't have too many volunteers, but first you need a volunteer coordinator who likes chaos, has a good sense of humor, will make sure the work gets done right and on time, and can cajole just about anyone into working on the campaign.

The volunteer coordinator will spend most of her or his time on the phone recruiting volunteers for one of the most important volunteer projects: the phone bank. After the first literature has been dropped at the doors and the direct mail is starting to arrive, a good campaign will check the pulse of the electorate with a voter identification phone bank. The phone bank provides another contact with a voter and attempts to identify who the voter is likely to support. Most voters remain undecided until the final weeks of a campaign; however, your solid supporters – and the supporters of your opponents – identify themselves early. All information about voter preferences must be neatly recorded on the phone lists and, if possible, in the computer voter file.

Unless you use a professional telemarketer, your campaign will need to set up or rent a location with at least five phone lines, assemble ward lists of voters with phone numbers, and prepare scripts for volunteers. Phoning is most productive in the evening, Sunday through Thursday. A good voter identification phone bank is essential to run a GOTV effort. This effort requires a massive number of volunteers in the final days of the campaign, when volunteers will mail GOTV reminder postcards to every known supporter *and* call them the Sunday or Monday before the election *and* knock on the doors of supporters on election day. For elections where voter turnout is low, campaigns should consider using poll watchers on election day to track when their supporters actually show up to vote.

If it benefits a candidate to boost voter turnout, a campaign should consider a blanket literature drop to all households just before the election. In a district with many students and young adults, it was in Tammy's best interest – as the candidate promising a new generation of leadership – to boost the turnout of that population.

Furthermore, a poll of a randomly selected sample of likely voters conducted by the volunteer phone bank revealed that Tammy was running a close second two weeks before the election. She needed the student vote to win.

On the final weekend before Tammy's primary, campaign volunteers went to every household in the district and distributed a door hanger that reminded people to vote, told them how to register at the polls and gave them the location of the ward's polling place. Volunteers also knocked on doors in student wards from morning until the polls closed on election day. Tammy won every student ward by an overwhelming margin.

Radio advertising

Radio ads can be an effective, relatively inexpensive way to reinforce your message and to reach a larger pool of voters. It is critical to pay for a professional studio and voice talent to produce the ads, to have crisp copy that catches the listener's attention and to work with a media buyer you trust. Your media buyer can recommend other consultants and advise you on how much money you need to reach your targeted audience.

Try to reserve your radio time at least one month before the election, even if you're not sure you will have enough money. You can always cancel your reserved time, but if you wait until the end of the campaign, you won't be able to place your ads where they will have the greatest impact. If you don't have adequate funding, don't waste your money on just a few spots that will never penetrate the market; spend it on something else. Finally, be creative. Politicians tend to run incredibly boring ads on the air – take a chance and jump out of the clutter.

---

*Elected in 1992 as the first openly lesbian state assemblymember in Wisconsin, **Tammy Baldwin** has a long history of political involvement, including service on the Dane County Board of Supervisors. As an attorney, Baldwin's private practice emphasized civil rights, workers rights, tenants rights and family law, and represented many women, gays and lesbians, and people living with AIDS. Her political affiliations include the Rainbow Coalition, the National Women's Political Caucus, the National Organization of Women, the American Civil Liberties Union, the National Network of*

Lesbian and Gay Officials, the Gay and Lesbian Victory Fund and the Democratic Party.

Linda Willsey is a political activist and campaign consultant in Madison, Wisconsin. She has an unblemished record of electing progressive women to the Wisconsin Legislature and specializes in come-from-behind primary victories and general election campaigns in swing districts. Willsey was the campaign consultant for Baldwin's 1992 primary campaign and also played a key role in the election of another Victory Fund candidate, Madison (WI) Judge Shelley Gaylord. Currently employed as a lobbyist on reproductive health issues, Willsey looks forward to working with Baldwin in the future when she seeks higher office.

Running for Public Office
Sherry Harris

FOR lesbians and gay men, the process of running for office is essentially no different than running as a nongay person. The key to winning your campaign is your ability to develop a winning strategy and carry it out. Here are some pointers for doing just that.

Pick a race *you* believe *you* can win. Never run for office just for the sake of building name familiarity. You must put forward a 100-percent effort. You can only do that if you believe you can win. Weigh all the factors: Is this an incumbent's seat or an open seat? Who else will be in the race? Do you know people who will donate money to you immediately? Seek advice from people who circulate in the political arena but make your own decision. Remember, when women ask the question "Should I run?" the answer they usually get is "no." The same is true for lesbians and gay men. Don't wait for a blessing if your gut tells you the time is right.

Hire a professional team, run a professional campaign and limit your overhead expenses. Don't try to run your campaign out of your basement using your family members for campaign managers. Hire a professional political consultant or a campaign manager with a good track record to develop your campaign plan and strategy and to oversee your operations. Find a volunteer to be your treasurer. Hire additional staff as necessary, but not immediately; don't drain your finances too early. If you choose *not* to hire help, at least seek professional advice on developing a campaign strategy.

Start with a strong core group and build a base of support. You need a dedicated core group of five to ten people (more if you can get them) who will volunteer from the beginning to work days, nights and weekends to see that you win. You need people with computer skills, those with contacts in the community, and folks who have the ability to bring other resources into the campaign.

Decide *in advance* how you are going to deal with subtle and overt prejudice, racism, homophobia and sexism. Treat your sexual orientation as you would any other personal characteristic about yourself. Develop a strategy on how to deal with voters' and your opponent's possible responses to your sexual orientation, including attempts to portray being gay as a negative characteristic. Anticipate questions and actions, formulate responses and make the responses part of your overall campaign strategy.

The obstacles you will face as a candidate will not be unlike the obstacles you may have faced all your life as a member of a group that is discriminated against. People may ignore you, discount you, make sexist, racist or homophobic remarks to you, label you, exclude you and use other excuses not to support you. The worst that can happen is that you can be attacked just for being who you are. Don't let the bigots get you down. Decide based on your own value system how you may want to respond to these situations and make your response part of your campaign plan. Don't compromise your principles, and always maintain a positive public image. Make an effort to give even your detractors a reason to consider your candidacy that goes beyond their prejudice. Have a support system of friends with whom you can share your experiences and who can help you get through difficult situations.

Know the issues before you run and prioritize those with which the voters are most concerned.

One of the biggest obstacles minorities, women, and gay candidates face is stereotyping. People will try to label you as a single-issue candidate. Develop a campaign platform that shows that you are concerned with a cross-section of issues and a resumé that reflects a diversity of experiences, thus demonstrating your ability to embrace a wide variety of issues. You will be a more credible candidate if your resumé reflects active involvement in areas beyond those that people may perceive as affecting your personal agenda.

As the candidate, your job is to raise money, make campaign appearances, gather endorsements and keep up your campaign team's morale. Don't try to manage your campaign and get involved in the intricate day-to-day decisions. Be involved in your campaign from an overseer's perspective and make only key decisions such as approving your campaign plan, strategy, literature and media decisions. You must be the candidate, not the manager, so stay focused on the candidate's job.

Don't be afraid to ask people for money. If you believe in yourself, you'll be benefitting the public by winning and having the opportunity to serve. You are not a charity, donations to your candidacy are a worthy exchange of money for service.

Exercise, eat well, drink lots of water, get up early, keep yourself healthy and carefully plan the use of your time. If the candidate falls apart, so does the campaign. You must push yourself harder than you ever have. Maintaining good health will give you the strength and sharpness to be a successful candidate. Making the best use of your time is essential. Plan each week, then review how you did and make improvements or modifications for the next week.

Develop and refine your skills as a public speaker and a fundraiser. Even if you have had prior experience in public speaking, speaking as a candidate is different. You must learn to speak in "sound bites" and get your point across in short, concise sentences. This takes practice. There are many books that help; you can also schedule sessions with a professional speech coach.

Your appearance must be impeccable at all times. You must look the part for what you are asking people to elect you to. Having a good appearance will prevent people from writing you off before you've even had the chance to speak to them because you don't look like a public official.

Develop a profile of constituency support for all the minority groups you are a part of (this includes being gay also). A show of support from the minority groups you are a part of is an essential part of your campaign strategy. Sometimes, this show of support is more important to the nonminority people than it is for the minority groups themselves. It's a form of validation to which only minority candidates are subjected.

Elected to the Seattle City Council in 1991, Sherry Harris is the first openly lesbian, African-American officeholder in the United States. Harris serves as chair of the Council's Housing, Health, Human Services and Education Committee and as a member of the Transportation Committee and the Utilities and Environment Committee. In the 10 years prior to her election, Harris was elected to and served on five city boards and commissions. A trained engineer, Harris has long been active in civic and community affairs, focusing her work on transportation, environmental and human rights issues.

One Step Ahead
Gary Miller

THREE key aspects to running a winning campaign are advance planning, targeting, and precinct walking. **Advance planning** is crucial. When I decided to run for school board, I literally started two years ahead of the election — organizing, strategizing, and getting to know the school district, the voters and the key players. You should plan on at least this amount of time also.

Early in this two-year cycle, you can start building positive name recognition in your district. Walking precincts for another candidate in your area is a good way to accomplish this. For instance, if you plan to run for school board in 1996, walk precincts now for a candidate for city council or state legislature who represents the same area that your school board does. If possible, choose a candidate who is well known and popular – perhaps even a candidate with only token opposition. The point here is not necessarily to work for the candidate, but to get your name and face out to the voters so they will remember you when you visit them again during your campaign.

As you are walking for this other candidate, send a follow-up letter to some of the people you meet saying, for example, "It was a pleasure meeting you when I was out walking our neighborhood ("our neighborhood" implies that you are one of "them") for Mary Smith, candidate for city council. If you have any questions about her campaign, call ---." The letter should be on your letterhead. If your handwriting is good, it should be handwritten. If your handwriting is as bad as mine, typewritten is okay, but add a short handwritten note such as "I plan to vote for Mary Smith by absentee ballot." Perhaps you can arrange something with the candidate to get him/her to write to the voter after you have walked. For example, "One of your neighbors, Gary Miller, was out walking door to door last week. He had the opportunity to meet with you about my campaign for City Council, etc." The goal is to get your name out as often as possible.

Targeting helps you zero in on the people who are most likely to vote for you, which allows you to make the most efficient use of your limited campaign resources, including your time. To target voters, you'll need to use voter registration rolls and voting records. These records contain invaluable information such as which precincts within your jurisdiction are the most consistently Democratic/Republican; which districts have the highest percentage of voter turnout; which precincts voted for candidates similar to you in the recent past; and which people vote in primary, off-year and special elections.

Before you begin your own **precinct walking**, you need to print campaign brochures to give to each voter. Make sure that your brochure includes a phone number where voters can call for more information. If you decide to have campaign pieces and letterhead printed at a union print shop, make sure they put a union "bug" on the piece.

When it is time for you to start walking, you need to get as much personal contact with your voters as possible. Door to door is best. Make sure you make eye contact. Physical contact is also good; a firm handshake, of course, and if you can, a light touch to the person's shoulder or upper arm. Obviously this needs to be done carefully, but I do believe that people respond favorably and subconsciously to touch.

You will obviously want to make verbal contact. People like to hear their own names, so use their first names when possible. However, if you are using voter registration lists, be careful. Most people use their formal name for registering. The trick here is to use the name that is listed, for example John, but then when corrected "Oh, you mean Jack," make a note and from then on always refer to Jack, never to John. Also, keep in mind that some people do not like being called by their first name by strangers. Pay attention to body language.

Keep your verbal pitch short, simple, and to the point. "My name is Gary Miller and I am running for Robla School Board. I want more classrooms (not schools; you want to make your pitch as local as possible) for our children." (Again, "our children" implies you are one of them.) To keep track of whether the voter is with you or not, end your time together with the question, "Can I count on your support on election day?" Use a scale like the following to record the voter's answer.

1 – Strongly Supports You
"Hey, right on, you're the one" type of response. These are your constituents – gays, feminists, friends, etc. Be especially nice to them. Ask if they want a yard sign, want to volunteer, contribute money, etc.

2 – Mild Yes
The voter said "yes," but did he/she say it just to get rid of you? These people need more contact so you can upgrade them to ones.

3 – Undecided
What will turn these voters on? You'll want to spend the most time with these folks and turn them into ones or twos.

4 – Lean No
"Well, I like your opponent" type of answer.

5 – No Way
Homophobes and people who don't agree with your stand on the issues. Don't bother the fours or fives again. If you don't remind them, maybe they'll forget to vote.

Closer to election day you will want to make sure your supporters (ones and twos) get to the polls. Perhaps you can encourage them to vote by mail, if this is allowed in your area. The sooner you get those votes in, the better. Continue to work on the threes. What is going to excite them to vote for you?

As you go door to door, take note of bumper stickers on the person's car and stickers on the door and windows. These often indicate some personal belief such as "We are pro-choice" or "Member of NRA." Try to focus your remarks accordingly. If you don't agree with the bumper stickers, avoid discussing that issue, but still keep notes. Also, if the voter(s) have children or animals, try to jot down the names and use them later in your follow-up letter. Leave a brochure with every targeted voter. If the voter is not home when you knock, leave your brochure with a personal note like "Sorry I missed you... if you have any questions, give me a call." Just as you did when you were walking for another candidate, you will want to follow up your visit with a letter: "It was nice talking to you the other day while I was out walking in our neighborhood on behalf of my campaign for school board."

I hope these suggestions will be of assistance to you in your run for public office. Feel free to call me if you have any questions.

A member and past president of the Robla School Board, Gary Miller was elected as Sacramento's first openly gay or lesbian public official in 1987. Miller's accomplishments on the school board include passage of an anti-discrimination policy that includes sexual orientation, a mandate that states that information on AIDS and Hepatitis B must be provided to staff on an annual basis, development of a policy to accommodate employees with AIDS or HIV, institution of an AIDS curriculum for elementary school children and implementation of domestic partner language in the teacher's contract. He has been involved with the Democratic Party and the Sacramento County Human Rights Commission and served as a delegate to the 1992 Democratic National Convention.

Winning an Election:
One Candidate's Story
Will Fitzpatrick

NINETEEN ninety-two was an unusual election year for Rhode Island. There were three times the usual number of candidates running for General Assembly seats as there were in 1990. This increase can be directly attributed to the public's general sense of outrage at the powers-that-be and the status quo. Among some of the pre-election scandals:

▼   More than one third of the state was directly (and all of the state was indirectly) affected by the closing of 40 credit unions and other financial institutions when the insurer known as RISDIC failed. RISDIC collapsed after it bailed out a failed bank when the president of the bank stole $15 million.

▼   The mayor of a major city was indicted, convicted and imprisoned for running an extortion ring in city hall.

▼   An associate justice was jailed for taking bribes.

I was one of 1,400 candidates vying for 150 seats in the State General Assembly – 100 in the House of Representatives, 50 in the Senate. It was an uphill battle because I was challenging a 15-year incumbent who had a lot going for him. He was chairman of the influential Senate Health, Education and Welfare Committee. He was quite wealthy and had built up a loyal constituency over the years. His followers were mostly conservative and anti-choice, and supported his annual "no" vote on the sexual orientation anti-discrimination act.

The principal reason I challenged the incumbent was because I felt that he was not effectively representing the 20,000 people in Senate District 11. Evidence of this could be found in the fact that he did not return phone calls or letters. I had called and written him many times over the course of four years and not once did I get a response. Many others in the community had been similarly ignored.

The first challenge I had when I became a candidate was getting people to take me seriously. I sought endorsements from local groups, including labor unions, Vote-Choice, the Rhode Island Alliance for Lesbian and Gay Civil Rights, Vote Environment and others. One of the greatest difficulties in running for office is raising money, and in my case, it was especially hard because I was challenging a 15-year incumbent. Initially, most of my campaign money came from friends. I held a fundraiser that was targeted at gay, lesbian and pro-choice groups. I also went into debt. The majority of the money raised was spent on printing, postage, and refreshments for volunteers. Because my campaign was a grassroots effort and relied heavily on volunteers, it was very important to thank them repeatedly and to provide them with food and beverages at every turn.

I consulted with several political experts and they told me that there were three ways to win an election: (1) walk the district, (2) walk the district and (3) walk the district. As a Democrat challenging a Democrat, I targeted voters who had voted in the 1992 spring Presidential primary and the 1990 Democratic primary for members of the General Assembly. Volunteers researched these voters and highlighted them on voter lists that were arranged by street within the district. I visited 90 percent of these homes and spoke to about half of the people. The other half was either not at home or would not answer the door. I left personal notes on a campaign brochure at each of these households.

When walking the district, I'd introduce myself to the voters, hand them my campaign brochure, and find out what they thought was the most important issue in terms of what they felt was wrong or could be improved with state government. Did I get an earful! I kept good notes and used these in writing my follow-up letters. This showed the people I visited that I really listened to their concerns. If I could give one piece of advice to potential candidates it would be to get as much personal contact with likely voters as possible. Nothing will motivate a voter to vote for a candidate more than eye-to-eye contact.

Another important aspect of the campaign was literature drops. We divided the district up into 40 sections and had 40 volunteers distribute literature to each household four times during the campaign. This was a two- to three-hour commitment for each volunteer. We also had phone banks. Likely Democratic primary voters were called and on the first go-round were surveyed to see how many had heard of my candidacy. Then we did persuasion calls. If people were not interested in speaking to a volunteer, we were polite and left them alone. We also did community things like a candidate's night at each of the senior centers in the district. We brought coffee, lemonade, lots of homemade cookies (baked by volunteers) and ice cream.

Each voter contacted, either by phone or in person, was rated as:

1. Strongly supporting me
2. Leaning towards me
3. No preference
4. Leaning toward my opponent
5. Strongly supporting my opponent

When primary day came around, we called all the ones, twos, and threes and reminded them to vote. This Get-Out-the-Vote (GOTV) effort began at 9:00 a.m. and ended at 8:00 p.m., an hour before the polls closed.We repeated our GOTV efforts on election day.

We used bumper stickers and lawn signs to build name recognition. Lawn signs were strategically located along major routes throughout the district. I talked to people along these streets and was aggressive in soliciting spots for lawn sign placement. We asked all identified supporters if they would allow a lawn sign in their yard. Besides helping with name recognition and visibility, the ubiquitous lawn signs added credibility to my campaign.

Beginning about 12 weeks before the election, we sent out weekly press releases. News release content consisted of platform issues and endorsements. About four weeks before the election, the number of news releases increased to one every other day. Print, television and radio media were targeted. Visibility on election day was also very important. We had cars parked near the polls with lawn signs. We also had people stand at the polls with signs who smiled at voters and encouraged them to vote for me.

Being an openly gay candidate was worrisome to me because I did not want to make my personal life a campaign issue. The press left it alone even though it was generally known that I was gay. My opponents did make it a public issue. Lawn signs along major thoroughfares were defaced with the word "GAY." My opponent announced my sexual orientation at public meetings and outside the polls on primary day. He also distributed literature indicating I was supported by lesbian and gay groups. His tactics backfired. My hard work and the hard work of my supporters paid off. I won every machine in every ward in my Senate district, and won the election with 62 percent of the vote.

Because of the emphasis my opponent placed on my sexual orientation, I felt that I could not take my seat and be an effective legislator until I had faced the issue head on. I came out publicly after the November election and made the front page of the statewide daily, *The Providence Journal*. It was an anxiety-ridden step to take but, in retrospect, it was the most fulfilling thing I have ever done in my life. With the support of my partner of a decade, David Anderson, I faced my demons of the past and overcame them. I became the first openly gay elected official in the history of the state. The reaction of the public, both inside and outside the district, was overwhelmingly positive. Hate calls and letters were outnumbered 20 to 1 by calls and letters of support and encouragement.

I like to quote lesbian author Dorothy Allison, who inspired me at an OutWrite conference a few years ago when she said "we can only truly help ourselves when we tell the truth about our lives." It is important that openly gay, lesbian, and bisexual people take our place at the table and speak out for ourselves. I think that my presence in the Rhode Island State Senate this year had something to do with the passage of the sexual orientation/anti-discrimination act by a margin of 30-17. This was an unprecedented margin in the nine-year history of the bill.

Recently, the first African-American female United States Senator inspired other senators to switch their votes when she gave an impassioned speech about the significance of the confederate flag and its ties to the horrors of slavery. Only African-Americans can really speak about African-American issues from the heart. Only gay, lesbian and bisexual people can speak about our issues from the heart. It is important to have our people in all elected offices to tell it like it is for us.

Elected in 1992 to the Rhode Island State Senate, Will Fitzpatrick has been involved in community causes since he immigrated to the United States from Ireland in 1982. With a broadly based career in computer programming and systems analysis, Fitzpatrick has also been involved with the Digital Equipment Corporation Users Group, Edgewood Neighborhood Association, Irish Business Institute, Literacy Volunteers of America and the Rhode Island Alliance for Lesbian and Gay Civil Rights.

Running for School Board
Jeff Horton

THE children and young people of today need advocates. The heterosexuals who run our country have plunged our children and young people deeper into poverty, malnutrition, homelessness, abuse and neglect than at any time in this century. The time is ripe for our community to step forward on behalf of these children, and running for the school board is one way to do that.

We gay men and lesbians must get more involved in the lives of children. If we are already involved with children, either as parents or in our careers, we must do so as openly gay men and women. As an openly gay school board member in Los Angeles, I have assumed two areas of responsibility with respect to our community. On the one hand, I am striving to make the institutions and practices of public education more responsive to the needs of gay and lesbian students and school employees, and more aware of the need for all students and employees to be taught the truth about sexual orientation. This is an obvious and urgent need, and it shouldn't take a gay school board member to pursue these reforms.

On the other hand – and this has been an unexpected responsibility – I feel a strong need to persuade our community, my gay and lesbian brothers and sisters and the organizations they participate in, to pay more attention to children and youth and the institutions that serve them, especially the schools. In my view, the right to participate in the perpetuation of the human race through helping to raise the next generation is a basic human right that homophobia has attempted to deny us.

Denied the right and opportunity to be parents, many gay men and lesbians have already entered fields such as teaching, child care and social work, which do serve the needs of children. All too often, however, they feel they must be deeply closeted to avoid the accusations, innuendos and, in many cases, dismissals that might come with being openly gay. The entire gay and lesbian community must support the rights of these brothers and sisters to be open about their sexual orientation, and one effective way to do this is to show political support for their efforts to meet the needs of children and youth.

I urge gay men and lesbians, especially those of us who are teachers or parents, to consider getting involved in school politics, whether it's in the unions, in parent and community organizations or on the school board. Proud, openly lesbian and gay educators and parents make great school board members, and with the right political work they can build on this experience and run for higher office.

The best route to school board electoral success for gay men and lesbians is through the teachers union or the PTA. Both organizations provide access to a broad base of people with proven commitment not only to children but to activism on behalf of children. This is the raw material that can be fashioned into an aggressive and successful electoral campaign.

One obvious point of entry for this activism is on behalf of lesbian and gay youth, a group that has been cruelly neglected and is at grave risk in many ways. To become effective potential candidates for school boards, however, we must be passionate advocates for all children and young people. If we are, it will be noticed and remembered.

Although gay and lesbian school board members will unavoidably spend the vast majority of their time on matters of concern to all students, they can push for such policies as counseling programs on sexual orientation (such as Project 10 in Los Angeles) and recognition of gay and lesbian issues in school curriculums (such as New York City's Rainbow Curriculum). In addition to the potential involvement in policy matters decided by school boards, consider the impact on the children and youth in the schools of having an openly lesbian or gay school board member. The gay and lesbian youth will certainly hold their heads a little higher to see such a role model, and non-gay youth (and adults) will be forced to revise their stereotypes of us.

Finally, let me remind everyone that a seat on the school board is often viewed as a beginning step to a longer political career. It may well be followed by a seat on the city council, the state legislature, or even a federal office. Whatever your intentions in running, one thing's for sure: Once you've been on a school board, you will forever be an advocate for children.

And so I call upon our lesbian and gay community to kick aside the barriers of homophobia that keep us from participating in the great human project of raising the next generation. I call upon all gay men and lesbians to become involved in the lives of children and young people in whatever way we can. If this happens, I know we can look forward to a whole batch of openly gay and lesbian school board members in the near future. I sure could use the company.

A member of the Los Angeles Board of Education since April 1991, Jeff Horton became Los Angeles' first openly gay elected official in municipal government when he came out publicly in October 1991. As a board member, Horton has authored successful motions to establish the Gay and Lesbian Education Commission — the first of its kind in the country — and to declare June Gay and Lesbian Pride Month. Horton, cofounder of the Gay and Lesbian Caucus of the National Education Association, also presided over the first official school board hearings on the needs of gay and lesbian students.

Stand Up for Office

Tom Ammiano

I ran for a seat on the Board of Education here in San Francisco three times, and lost the first two; obviously, my first word of advice to prospective candidates would be **tenacity**. All three of my campaigns had some similarities: I ran as an educator — someone who has a lifelong involvement in education; I knew that the issues reached out to a variety of communities; I never downplayed my gayness; and I kept my name recognition high. Each campaign increased my positive name recognition and the base of support for my next race.

It is unfortunate that most people do not scrutinize the actions of their board of education. As a teacher, however, I already knew our board, warts and all, and was not shy about criticizing them, especially when it came to the welfare of the kids. My observation of the board made me even more aware of the difference between electing our "friends" and electing our own. Some of the incumbents had won their seats with gay support, money and votes, but were actually very cavalier when it came to lesbian and gay issues. For instance, one of our "friends" on the school board said that the lesbian/gay speakers bureau was advocating homosexuality and tried to sabotage the school program. When it came time for the board to vote on the Boy Scout issue [whether or not the San Francisco public schools would continue to allow the anti-gay Boy Scouts of America to use its facilities], yet another "friend" feigned a sudden illness and left the meeting. Some gay leaders at the time preferred to overlook these homophobic attitudes rather than rock the boat.

In 1980 I took my first shot at this citywide election. Openly gay, I was known for starting a gay teachers' group and for working with Harvey Milk to fight the anti-gay-teacher Briggs initiative in the late 1970s. (Ironically, although the gay democratic clubs were generally supportive, I had to convince them that, while straight "friends" were important, one of their own could make a significant

difference. We've come quite a way since then, but have still far-
ther to go in overcoming our internalized homophobia.)

My first campaign was against four strong incumbents. Personally, it was grueling. I started a year ahead of time because
there was so much ground work to do. I spent untold hours raising
money, establishing a platform, and building credibility. The early
start and hard work really paid off – I garnered enough endorsements and money to make people think. Even though I didn't win,
I placed very well and was encouraged to run again.

Running for office requires a lot of sacrifice and takes a high
toll on your personal life. Lovers, friends, family and co-workers
need to be clear about the amount of time it takes and the emotional
roller coaster a campaign can be. I am fortunate that my lover is
also a teacher and shares my commitment to the public schools.
Teaching first-grade takes a lot of energy, but he still gave 150
percent to my campaign. And there's nothing like running for office to let you know who your true friends are. They're the ones
who remain with you no matter what the consequence. Finding
good campaign staff should be a top priority. You can't do everything yourself (this will be hard for control queens, I know) so
you've got to find people you can trust. Having campaign management that respects your values is essential. Once, while I was proof-
ing my campaign literature, I noticed that references to my founding the Gay and Lesbian Speakers Bureau were "accidently" omit-
ted by a well-intentioned staffer. I insisted that the information be
included despite the complaints of how much it would cost to rewrite the copy. Remember, it's you who are the candidate, not the
consultant.

Despite my good showing in the first race for school board, I
decided "to hell with electoral politics!" and started a second career
as a stand-up comic instead. (This is not as disparate as it may
seem. Comedy and politics have a lot in common: both require
quick thinking, a sense of humor, an understanding of the crowd,
and knowing when to get off the stage.) In 1988, while still teaching and performing, I couldn't sit back any longer. The issues,
including district elections for the board, a school named after Harvey
Milk, AIDS/HIV education, support programs for lesbian and gay
students, were too important, too close to home. I was also fed up
with school board members who, while still taking our money, had

not internalized our issues. I decided to run again.

This time I launched an unorthodox campaign. Seeking no endorsements and raising no money, I used my comedy act and media savvy to confront the issues. I held a series of events that raised money for other causes (AIDS, the library, etc.). I had one event using my comic friends and another just for kids. Both received good media coverage, improved my name recognition and built bridges in the community.

My 57,000 votes in that election astounded many and dictated a serious stab in the next go-round. In 1990, the grass-roots campaign that was built on my previous two races resulted in the dumping of three incumbents and my coming in first at the polls. I now serve as president of the board, and I can assure you that there is no hemming and hawing around our issues.

Tom Ammiano, longtime special education teacher and community organizer, made history as the first openly gay teacher in San Francisco in 1975, as the first openly gay comedian to appear in the San Francisco Comedy Competition in 1984 and as the first openly gay man to be elected to the San Francisco School Board (to which he has been elected president) in 1990. A widely respected educator and activist, Ammiano's involvement led to the City of San Francisco's decision to prevent the Boy Scouts of America from using public school facilities, to condom availability in the public schools and to the first lesbian/gay support services for public school students.

Running in a Small Town
Irene Rabinowitz

ALTHOUGH running for political office as an openly gay or lesbian candidate in Provincetown, Massachusetts, may be unlike the experience anywhere else in the United States, the skills and strategy involved are applicable to campaigning in small towns all over the United States. For starters, the quality of your background research can make or break your campaign. Always find out as much as you can about the community and the government and political scene *before* you decide to run. That way there'll be no surprises halfway through your campaign.

A little background on our unique form of local municipal government may be helpful in understanding the dynamics of Provincetown politics. In the Commonwealth of Massachusetts, towns with fewer than 10,000 residents (Provincetown has a year-round population of approximately 3,600) have a Board of Selectmen (yes, select*men*!), as their chief elected officials. The term selectmen is a holdover from colonial days when members of the community were "selected" to represent the citizenry. (There are other options available. Some communities, although fewer and fewer, have a three-member full-time board that is responsible for day-to-day operations of the municipality.)

Provincetown has a five-member part-time board that sets policy and oversees the town manager, whom it appoints. Meetings are public, in accordance with the Massachusetts Open Meeting Law, and boards of selectmen are traditionally the lightning rods of the community. Budgets, zoning, general by-laws, capital expenses, and land purchases are voted upon in an annual meeting. Tourists sometimes attend the town meeting just because it's the best show in town! Terms on the board are three years long, elections are nonpartisan, and election day is just about a month after the end of the annual town meeting, so campaigns are short and intense. When

I ran for the board in 1990, it was to fill a seat vacated with one year left before the term expired.

Prior involvement in local politics is practically a necessity if you're planning to run in a small town. This includes getting appointments, working for your political party, serving on committees, etc. One of my greatest advantages as a candidate was that I had served on the town's Finance Committee, which makes recommendations to the town meeting on the operating, capital, and school budgets. During my two appointed terms on this committee, I developed a reputation for being fiscally conservative, but willing to work with the town employees to find fiscally viable solutions to problems. Because of my service on this committee, I was also knowledgeable about the municipal budget and inner workings of each department, and had made important contacts and allies within the system.

Getting as much campaign experience as you can before you run is another plus. I had gained previous political experience in New York City during the 1970s when I worked on field operations in several campaigns, both citywide and in local legislative races. That experience paid off in planning my campaign in Provincetown. I knew, for example, that it was absolutely essential for me to become familiar with key citizens who were involved in areas of the community with which I had little experience. For example, although Provincetown's fishing industry has been in decline for several years due to overfishing and environmental problems, the fishing fleet is influential in the "native" population (I'm considered a "washashore" — someone who has moved here from somewhere else, whether gay or straight). Friday is the traditional day in port for Provincetown fishermen; that's when they make repairs on the boats, fix their nets, etc. I took advantage of this during the campaign by spending a portion of each Friday on the pier speaking to members of the fleet about their concerns. I also made an effort to spend time with senior citizens, a sometimes overlooked population in elections, both at the local council on aging and the municipally owned nursing home.

Although there are a substantial number of gay and lesbian residents in Provincetown, political alliances are not always drawn along sexual orientation lines. Gay and straight business owners often join together to support a candidate, as they did in our last election when a lesbian guesthouse owner was elected with strong support from the business community. Because of this, my employment as a case manager at the Provincetown AIDS Support Groups was not an advantage in my campaign. Because Provincetown has an extremely high per capita HIV rate and depends on tourism for its livelihood, there are those in the community who, though they may donate willingly to the AIDS Support Group, would prefer that AIDS not be focused on too highly during the tourist season.

During the campaign, I needed to prove that my interests were not limited to gay issues and AIDS, as was being charged by some of my opponents. Even though I'm openly lesbian and work for an AIDS organization, I was able to refute these charges by being knowledgeable about the issues and taking my message directly to the voters. *In a small town more than anywhere else, personal contact is the key to winning votes.* To be a successful candidate you must get out and meet voters, find a common ground for discussion, and show them the depth of your interest in matters that concern them.

In small towns, the best allies to have when running for office are those who have served previously and those who are presently sitting who have similar views. Endorsements can be very helpful in larger communities, but in small towns, word of mouth is the best way to get your message out. Again, voter contact, whether in person, by phone or by mail, is a key element in building positive name recognition. Other than on election day, I made all my own campaign phone calls to voters. (Obviously, if you are running for mayor of New York City you can't do this.) I followed up on all calls with a mailing and included personal notes on many of the flyers.

In both of my election efforts (I ran unopposed the following year for a three-year term, but still needed to get people out to vote), people who did not know me posed questions regarding my personal life. This was complicated sometimes because my ex-husband lives in Provincetown. If someone asked me my marital status, I said that I was divorced from my husband and currently in a relationship with a wonderful woman, whom I identified. If you have decided to be "out" during a political campaign, I believe it will come back to haunt you if you are not "out" about your relationship as well. My partner attended campaign fundraising events with me, and has attended many official events with me since I have been on the board.

Obviously, some of the obstacles that gay candidates face did not apply to my candidacy because of the nature of the community in which I ran; Provincetown has a large year-round gay and lesbian population. But no matter where you run, for those who believe that gay and lesbian candidates will only care about specifically gay and lesbian issues, an educational process will have to be part of the campaign. It's very necessary to remain focused on the issues when speaking with voters who express concern about voting for someone who is gay. Point out to voters, if you find it necessary to do so, that gay environmentally sound choices are no different than heterosexual environmentally sound choices, that solid economic development policies are not based on sexual orientation, and so on. Again, nothing beats personal contact with the voters to reassure them and assuage their fears.

In 1990, the first year that I ran for the board of selectmen, there were two gay men and another lesbian running, as well as three other candidates. Our board now has two lesbian members, the first time more than one gay person has served concurrently. As we become more visible and effective as political forces within our own communities, we add validity to our political stature, both locally and nationally. With this increased clout, and with support from progressive straight people, we are on the way to full and equal civil rights protections.

Irene Rabinowitz was elected to finish a partial term on the Provincetown Board of Selectmen in 1990. She was then reelected to a full term in 1991 and became chair of the board in 1992. Concurrently, she is a case manager for the Provincetown AIDS Support Group, a member of the Provincetown Democratic Town Committee and the Health Project Advisory Task Force, and an advisory boardmember of Helping Our Women. Prior to her election, Rabinowitz was a columnist, a counselor at an ex-offender program and a freelance editor.

Running in a Rural District
Dale McCormick

WHEN I first raised the idea of my running for the state legislature to a straight poll friend of mine, he responded, "Well, I think you could be elected from a district in Portland, but not in rural Maine." That was a little discouraging, because I didn't want to move. I chose to ignore the advice.

I kept floating the balloon to other friends, and got better responses. One friend, thrilled at the possible match up between me and a 10-year incumbent who was the point man for the right wing, noted "There certainly would be a clear choice!" Another suggested that I wouldn't have any trouble raising money. Almost everyone got excited and thought I should run.

I was about as out as one can be. I was the first president of the Maine Lesbian/Gay Political Alliance (MLGPA) and had appeared on TV regularly. There is a great freedom to this. I was so out that I didn't have to try to be an openly lesbian candidate. I didn't have to worry about being discovered. In fact, this drove my opponent crazy. He gay-baited me from day one, and when that didn't work, he got mad that my literature didn't proclaim my sexual orientation. The newspaper had the last word on this. They editorialized: "Everyone knows Dale McCormick is a lesbian — has he been living under a rock?"

I mention all this because how you portray yourself is important, especially in a rural district. There usually aren't gay or lesbian neighborhoods in rural districts so special appeals to our community for votes is not a winning tactic. To be elected one must appeal to a broad spectrum of people. As President of MLGPA from 1984-88, I lobbied a lot on AIDS issues. This led me to get involved in the battle for universal health care. As I look back on it, I realize how much I have focused on health care reform, and am proud to have sponsored a single-payer bill, the Family Security Act.

My campaign committee figured that my opponent was going to target my sexuality as an issue in the campaign. Because there is no television station, bus, or subway to advertise on, I went door to door. We figured, to know me was to love me, and so I set about meeting 6,000 people before November 6. I campaigned on Beano nights and at football games. I got up at 4:00 a.m. to get to hunters' breakfasts. I tried to go to as many community suppers as possible, both for the food and to talk to people.

My favorite place to campaign is the town dump, or transfer station as they are called in the recycling age. On Saturday and Sunday everyone from town takes their garbage to the transfer station. Several volunteers and I would meet at the dump and set up a table of muffins, coffee, juice, campaign literature and voter registration cards. The volunteers would approach patrons with, "Would you like to talk to Dale McCormick while I unload your garbage?" We all wore canvas nail aprons (I'm a carpenter by trade) printed with "Build a better future for District 18" on them, and carried our literature in the pockets.

The political affiliation of my district is evenly divided between Democrats, Republicans, and nonregistered voters. There are 11 towns and one city of 6,000 people. It is so rural that I've found that the best mode of transportation for going door to door is a bicycle. Like most lesbians, I name my vehicles. My truck is named Jaime and my bike is Tony. During the campaign I went door to door every night after work. I'd put Tony in the back of Jaime and set off. When I got to the town where I was going door to door that day, I'd take Tony out and ride from house to house. People love it. They think the fact that I'm riding a bicycle means I'm conservative with money and don't like wasting gas. All true.

Because of the gay-baiting my opponent was doing, and all the letters to the editor about Sodom and Gomorrah and Leviticus, my name was in the paper quite a bit. It got so that as I rode up the driveway on Tony, people would come to the door and say, "You must be Dale McCormick, come in, come in!" People were very nice. I'd say that five out of the 6,000 people that I met going door to door said, "shoo." (Actually, one lady really *did* say that while flapping her apron at me!)

Mostly, it was heartwarming how nice people were. After weeks of letters to the editor about me being the embodiment of

Satan, and "an insult to womanhood because I had not endured the pain and agony of childbirth," one elderly Republican lady said to me, "You have a rather nasty opponent, don't you?" That's what all his gay-baiting came down to for her. The next week another woman was telling me about how the elderly in her town couldn't afford to pay the property taxes for the schools. In the midst of a tirade on taxes she inserted, "And I don't care a hoot who you live with."

All in all, running for office really did a lot for my internalized homophobia. I highly recommend it.

Elected to the Maine State Senate as an openly lesbian candidate in November 1990, Dale McCormick is now serving her second term in the legislature. In the senate she is chair of the Banking and Insurance Committee and is the primary sponsor of a major universal health care bill. In addition to her current political position, McCormick served as a delegate to the 1984 and 1988 Democratic National Conventions and is a member of the Monmouth Planning Board. In the legislature she has worked to obtain civil rights for lesbians and gays, to prevent hate violence, to protect the environment, to create AIDS policies and to reform health care.

Out in the Heartland
Bill Crews

S OUNDS like you'd make a good mayor," was the comment from the city council member. The remark came during a neighborhood picnic that first August after my partner Steve and I had moved to Melbourne, Iowa. The councilman and I were just visiting, getting to know each other, talking about our respective jobs. My response to his suggestion was that I liked to be involved in things, but having just moved to town, I wasn't sure it would be appropriate to be mayor. (The previous mayor was moving for a job transfer and had resigned, creating the vacancy we were discussing.)

Then, in September, as I was measuring the windows for new blinds, the councilman called and asked again if I wanted to be mayor. The city council was having its regular monthly meeting and was ready to appoint me. Apparently no one else wanted to do it. I asked them to give me an hour to finish with the lady from Sears, and then I would come over and talk with them about it.

Well, to make a long story short, my ego wouldn't let me turn them down even though I hardly knew any of my constituents.

My appointment was in 1984 at the beginning of a four-year term; because of this they held a special election for mayor during the 1985 municipal elections in which I was officially elected as mayor. I have since been reelected in 1987 and 1991. I have never had any opposition. In 1985, all 57 people who took the time to cast a ballot voted for me. In 1987 and 1991, I received the votes of all but one of the residents who voted.

Melbourne is a small community of about 700 people. It is composed primarily of families who commute both to work and to school, and of retired farm couples who have moved to town while their children live and work on the family farm. We have little retail activity, mainly farm supply and grain elevator businesses, and a good bank, formerly locally owned but now part of a stronger bank in a nearby farming community. Our commuters travel for work to Marshalltown, Des Moines, Ames and Newton, while the schools are in State Center, about eight miles away.

The city's annual budget is approximately $250,000. This includes our water supply and sewer utility, road maintenance, fire protection, parks, and library. We maintain a swimming pool and a recreation center that serves as the facility for community events such as soup or pancake supper fundraisers and local community clubs like the Lions and the 50-plus Club.

Since I have been mayor, the city has rebuilt streets, constructed a city maintenance facility, worked to improve the reliability and quality of our public water supply system and constructed a new fire station. In the past two years we have been able to lower our property tax levy. Our current major project is working to expand our library.

Steve and I have always been rather open about our relationship, but until 1993 we never publicly referred to ourselves as "gay." Our neighbors had come to realize that our living together was more than just two guys sharing a house. We have always interacted with our neighbors, gone to community fundraising suppers together and participated in other community events.

Our decision to "come out" at the Gay and Lesbian Victory Fund luncheon in conjunction with the 1993 March on Washington (MOW) did not really have much to do with our community, but was a result of the experience of my having run in the 1992 Republican primary for state senator and our desire for the MOW to have an impact on the people of Iowa.

Since high school, I have always wanted to be an elected official. Following in my father's footsteps, I was very active in Republican Party politics. Because of my dad's activism for social justice, I, too, was concerned about race relations and poverty, the war in Vietnam and the environment. With the lowering of the voting age in 1972, I was sure elected office was my calling. I planned to be a U.S. Senator by the time I was 33.

Two things happened however. First, Jim Leach, a man whom I supported and believe is one of the finest congressmen this county has had, won my congressional seat two years before I was old enough to run. Second, at that time I started realizing that I was gay. I was in law school at the University of Iowa and the two occurrences seemed to complement each other. My goal of elected office seemed to be put out of reach by circumstances beyond my control. Fine, I thought, I can still influence public policy without being an elected official. But though I *did* influence it through my jobs with The Nature Conservancy and as Marshall County Zoning Administrator, in the years that followed I could not shake the desire to lead and to be the one casting the vote. Though I was elected mayor in 1984, when the opportunity arose to run for the state senate – the position I had originally wanted – I could not pass it up.

To prepare for my run, in 1990 I resigned from my position as state director for The Nature Conservancy and took my current position as the Marshall County Zoning Administrator (both of which I held concurrently with my mayorship) to get to know people in the senate district in which I was likely to run. The senator, upon whose resignation rested my decision to run, didn't decide to retire until shortly before the precinct caucuses. In fact, he had given me the impression in the fall of 1991 that he would run again. (Lesson number one: Don't wait for others to make your decisions for you.)

For all the experience I had working on campaigns, and for all my desire to be a state senator, I was not fully prepared to make the run for senate in 1992. One of my biggest concerns was how to address my sexual orientation in my campaign. My final strategy was not to be "out." I would not lie, but I would not answer the question; instead I would respond with some comment about how one's private life was not pertinent to the campaign. However, after my experience, I no longer believe that this strategy works.

Early in the campaign, the local union president asked me point blank if I was gay. I mistakenly thought he would appreciate my candor, so I answered the question honestly. Then, later on, I had a phone call from a local leader of the anti-choice forces who asked me if I was gay. I decided to stick with my strategy this time, and gave the "not pertinent to the qualifications" answer. He told me that he assumed that that meant that I was gay and started quoting from the Bible. By not answering the question, it is assumed that you are, in fact, gay, whether you are or not. From this I learned that no matter how unpopular it is for you to be openly gay, when you avoid such direct questions, people not only assume you are gay, but also see you as a liar.

I devised this unsuccessful strategy for several reasons, not the least of which is that it is still not considered an asset to run as an openly lesbian or gay candidate. But a more important reason was that Steve and I were not quite ready to come out. We thought or hoped that we could still get by without a public acknowledgment and, therefore, avoid all the anticipated grief.

The campaign ended on primary election night with me coming up 56 votes short. I would not necessarily say that being gay was the reasons I didn't have enough votes; for 56 votes, I should have been able to knock on a few more doors and turn out a few more votes. The most important way that being gay affected my race is that Steve and I learned about the need to confront who you are head on. I think more than anything we learned that it is not possible to do this half way. Various incidents brought home the need to educate others and stand up for who we are.

Some of the incidents were particularly painful. Steve was my yard-sign coordinator. Two people, with whom he had worked for years and whom he had considered friends, had good high-traffic locations and initially agreed to let us put up our large signs. However, after the signs were in place, these people got phone calls telling them we were gay. They then called to say we had to remove the signs because they could not be seen as "promoting our lifestyle." I am sure many other gay people have experineced such prejudiuce, and hope that it energized them, as it did us, to stand up more forcefully.

We were also strengthened by the support we did receive. There were many Democrats who were "Republicans for a Day." So many, in fact, that the moderate Democratic candidate for county supervisor lost the primary to a reactionary "no-taxes-is-good-government" candidate. And by the way, the Republican primary winner was trounced in the general election.

After the primary, I became involved in the campaign for passage of the Equal Rights Amendment to the Iowa Constitution. Supporting the ERA was, of course, the right thing to do, plus it gave me a reason to say "no" to helping other Republican candidates. As co-chair of our countywide campaign effort, I expanded my contacts and visibility among voters who care about equality. This helped both Steve and me to overcome the disappointment of the primary. That the ERA was defeated primarily because of the Radical Right's campaign of lies, fear and hate also showed us the need to continue our struggle for justice.

In October of 1992, I had the opportunity to be in Washington, DC, the same weekend as the Names Project Quilt. The presence of so many gay and lesbian people moved me greatly. I knew I had to get Steve to the 1993 March on Washington for Gay/Lesbian/Bi/Transgender Equal Rights (MOW). I wanted him to experience the solidarity of so many of us together.

As we prepared for the MOW, I wanted to increase people's awareness of this historic event. Publicly coming out was an idea that appeared to have merit so I decided to write an op-ed piece in which I'd come out. I had met the editorial page editor of the *Des Moines Register* in February after he wrote a column urging people to ski Wyoming instead of Colorado (because of the anti-gay sentiment supported there by the November 1992 elections). After I wrote my op-ed piece, I called him and he was very interested in publishing it.

The piece ran on the front page of the Sunday *Register*'s Opinion section on Sunday, April 25, the day of the March. On Monday, I was the lead story in the *Register*'s front page coverage of Iowans at the March. On Tuesday, Steve and I came home to discover that our house had been vandalized. Three sides of the house had been spray-painted with anti-gay epithets like "No Faggots," "Melbourne Hates Gays," "Get Out" and "Queers Arn't Welcomed" (complete with the misspelling). Additional phrases used the "F" word and presumed sexual practices. A window had been broken in our family room and a fire extinguisher discharged, covering everything with a fine chemical powder.

Our reaction was mixed. Although we were extremely upset by the extent of the damage, we realized that it could have been much worse. Other gay men and lesbians have suffered much more than we have; many have lost their lives.

The support was almost immediate. There were numerous messages of support on our answering machine. One friend who had read a short reference to the vandalism in the Marshalltown paper drove down to check on us because she could not get through on the phone. Neighbors had already notified the sheriff's office. A city employee had boarded up the broken window before it rained that Tuesday afternoon, saving us from much more damage and cleanup. The next day, several friends came to help clean the inside of the house. The steel siding on the outside is being replaced as I write this. The insurance people have also been very supportive.

Iowa does have a Hate Crimes Law that includes sexual-orientation-related crimes. Rich Eychaner, a Des Moines businessman and longtime friend, established a reward fund to help find the criminals. The insurance company hired a private investigator who worked with the sheriff's office, but no suspects have been identified. Most vandalism in the area is solved because the perpetrators brag about doing it. The resulting publicity over our hate crime, with its universal condemnation of the vandals, apparently drove them back into their hole.

The local press was quick to pick up on the incident. "Gay Mayor's House Vandalized" was the headline on the front page of Wednesday's *Register*, with a picture of the anti-gay graffiti on our house taking up two-thirds of the top half of the paper. My "fifteen minutes of fame" had begun.

On Wednesday, six television stations representing the three major networks from the two largest media markets in Iowa showed up to interview me. It was the lead story on the six o'clock newscast for all six stations and was picked up by the national morning news shows the next day. Print media coverage has ranged from the *New York Times* to *USA Today*. Countless other papers picked up an Associated Press story and photo. The *Washington Post* did a feature article on me. *TIME* Magazine and *The New Yorker* also mentioned me in stories.

The importance of the coverage was that it proved one of the points of my coming-out op-ed piece, which was that there is a lot of hate and that I came out to put a face on Gay America. People need to know that we *are* everywhere and that they must stop and think about gay people they know before letting their prejudices kick in.

The town's overall reaction was initially very supportive. No one supported the vandalism, though some weren't sure I didn't ask for it. As the media circus continued however, some grew tired of the attention, especially because it was so favorable to me. The primary negative comment was that people were being harassed about being from the town with the gay mayor. I responded that they should realize that this harassment is what gay people experience all the time. On the other hand, one neighbor told me that when he was asked if he knew me, he would tell the person "yes" and that I was his neighbor and that I was "a hell of a nice guy." "That usually shut them up," he said.

Upon reflection, my coming-out experience has been very positive. Yes, we suffered through the vandalism and continue to wonder about reoccurrences, but it helped bring home the message of the presence of hate. Our response to this hate crime has been viewed very positively locally. I have always stressed that the town was not behind the vandalism and that the town for the most part has remained very supportive.

The passing of time and the floods of the summer of 1993 shifted the focus of the town away from my media blitz and onto keeping people dry and keeping water and sewage out of basements. Should I decide to run for reelection in 1995, my fate will be decided not based on my sexual orientation, but on whether or not I have done enough to get rid of junk cars, to solve the rusty water problem, to improve the storm-water drainage situation so another wet summer won't flood people's basements with sewage, and to help expand the size of our library.

The advice I would give to others running for local office are rather straight [sic] forward. Focus on providing quality, cost-effective public services. Be organized ahead of time, know who your supporters are and gain their commitment. Have a record of accomplishments that indicates that you know how to get things done in a consensus-building environment. These are the foundations of successful local politics – for all candidates, gay and straight.

I intend to remain committed and active in our cause for social justice and equal rights protection. I hope to keep my options open for further attempts at other elected offices. I will run as who I am: a proud, openly gay man who understands the love of Jesus, the needs of a democratic government and the meaning of the phrase "Liberty and justice for all."

Bill Crews, mayor of Melbourne, Iowa, came out as an openly gay elected official at the Victory Fund's "Recognizing Our Own" brunch held during the March on Washington for Gay/Lesbian/Bisexual/Transgender Equal Rights weekend in April 1993. He has been mayor for nine years, prior to which he was a practicing attorney, state director for the Nature Conservancy and administrative assistant for Natural Resources for former Iowa Governor Robert D. Ray. In addition to serving as mayor, Crews is Marshall County Zoning Administrator, advisor to the County Board of Supervisors and vice-chair of the Iowa Board of Physician Assistant Examiners.

Running with Limited Resources
Ken Yeager

A friend of mine ran for city council several years ago. For reasons associated with his lack of campaign experience and inability to raise money and recruit volunteers, his campaign faltered early. He did poorly on election day. Much later, I asked him how he took his defeat. His answer was one of the best political lines I've heard, "I was so bitter afterwards that I didn't have sex for a year." Now that's bitter.

Gay men and lesbians need to be elected to all levels of government – federal, state, city and local – but the fact is that most gay people won't be running for high-profile seats like mayor or state assembly. Rather, they will run in low-profile races in cities that have never before elected an openly gay person. This doesn't mean the stakes aren't as high – they are. It just means that the resources are limited.

One consequence of running a campaign with limited resources is that there is not enough money to hire a campaign consulting firm or a full-time manager. This means that you must either know about campaigns or know where to get the information directly. If you expect people to come to your rescue, your campaign – like my friend's – will never leave the starting gate.

Given that what might be considered low-profile in one city might be high-profile in another, the following is a list of campaign activities of which candidates in low-profile races need a basic understanding if they expect to run a viable campaign. You need to excel in all areas, but the list provides a "reality check" that will help you decide if this is the year you should run.

▼ **Money** is the name of the game. A high name identification is essential for winning public office, and increasing name ID, whether through the mail, in paid media or on the airwaves, is costly. It does no good to have a message if it is never delivered to the voters. Simply put, an effective campaign cannot be run without money.

One way to get a handle on whether fundraising goals can be reached is to figure out how many donors are necessary at certain levels. Let's say your budget is $10,000. Estimate that 100 people must give $25, 50 people must give $50, and 50 people must give $100. Put names of people after these dollar amounts and begin making phone calls. If you can't determine who will give the money, chances are fundraising will not go well.

▼ **In-kind Contributions** are almost as good as money, which is saying quite a lot. Oftentimes, individuals and businesses that are reluctant to write checks are willing to donate goods and services at a reduced rate or for free. This is called an in-kind contribution because the campaign is benefitting from not having to pay for a service or product.

There is a wide range of in-kind contributions that you should pursue. A major one is discounted or free consulting services. Others include free office space, reduced rates for creative work and printing, and discounts on office supplies. Pizza, chips and soft drinks for volunteers can be very costly over the course of a campaign, so don't overlook the possibility of getting free food and beverages, especially from gay bars and restaurants.

In-kind contributions must be reported just like monetary contributions. Be sure to get a receipt from the business indicating the market value of the product or service, and include that amount in the report.

▼ **Endorsements** by elected officials and community leaders are crucial in any race, but even more so in low-profile ones where voters have not heard of the candidates. If there is no political party designation on the ballot (which is true in many local races, especially in Western states), the main way for a voter to determine a candidate's politics is to see who endorses him or her. Early endorsements are especially critical because they help establish a candidate's credibility.

You should assess how many big-name endorsements you can get and determine whether you can personally contact community leaders or if you must go through an intermediary, or worse, send a letter. If you don't know the person well enough to phone, the odds decrease that you'll get an endorsement because politicians aren't likely to endorse people they don't know.

▼ **Volunteers** are essential, especially in low-financed campaigns. But, if you think that friends, ex-lovers and potential lovers have nothing else to do but work on your campaign, think again. If your campaign strategy calls for the use of volunteers, you need to assess if you can get four or five people a night, six times a week, for three or four months. Make a list of the people who might volunteer, then call them. It is not a good sign if you hears a lot of hemming and hawing.

▼ **Qualifications.** Good credentials in the gay community might qualify people for some things, but being elected to public office probably isn't one of them. All voters want reassurances that the candidates they support are credible and have knowledge about mainstream issues. They look carefully at a candidate's experience and qualifications, especially academic degrees, business titles, and community work. A list of five or more solid qualifications in a candidate's brochure looks impressive. If the list is too short, perhaps it would be wise to hold off running and get appointed in several governmental committees first.

▼ **A non-gay label.** People will vote for someone who is gay, but not for someone they think represents only gay interests. That's why it is important not to be classified as a gay candidate. Candidates should look in the mirror and say, "I'm the one who...." You must fill in the blank before voters or the opponent do. If not, the "gay" candidate label will stick.

In my campaign, I decided that I should own the title of the "educator" candidate. Because I was running for college board, we emphasized my Ph.D. in education and my faculty job at San Jose State. Even though I have been involved in gay politics for years, it was my educator image that was reinforced in my literature. As a result, when I was walking precincts people didn't say, "You're the gay candidate." but "You're the professor at San Jose State."

▼ **Issues.** Candidates aren't expected to be aware of all the issues at the beginning of the campaign, but it is essential that they know people to whom they can turn for assistance. You need to know people from various ethnic, racial, political, business and social groups who can assist you in responding to questionnaires and preparing for candidate forums. This help will increase the odds of your winning endorsements and forming coalitions with other minority groups.

▼ **Campaign literature.** Production of direct mail should

not be left to amateurs; if it is, it will look amateurish, and voters don't want to be represented by amateurs. A high-quality piece will look like it was easy to do, even though no one will notice its production value. A low quality piece will also look like it was easy to do; however, no one will notice its message.

Each mail piece should have one overall message or purpose, with three sub-areas to help make the message clear. The most common copy error is trying to tell too many different things. The rule is: one mail piece, one message.

Many components go into a quality mail piece: Photographs that capture the essence of the candidate, effective writing, a creative design and a good layout. One reason why direct mail consultants are so expensive is because of all the hours involved from conception to final copy. To help keep costs down, candidates need to be familiar with aspects of direct mail or know people who will provide their services at reasonable rates.

▼ **Graphics.** Good, crisp graphics will send a message that a candidate is competent and experienced. That is why it is important to have a professional look to the campaign. If possible, ask several graphic artists to come up with potential logos. Look them over and discuss the pros and cons of each design. Make sure that this process is started early so there is enough time to make the right decision, since logos can't be changed in mid-campaign.

▼ **Voter lists.** It makes little economic sense to mail to every voter in the district since only about 60 percent or fewer go to the polls in general elections. The percentage is much smaller for cities with non-concurrent elections. A vendor who works with voter files can determine which voters should receive the candidate's mail by using a variety of criteria: Voter history, age, political party, gender, etc. These are strategic decisions, and candidates must work with someone they trust. Good targeting is even more important in low-budget campaigns because money cannot be wasted on people who don't vote.

▼ **Printing.** As seasoned candidates know, as goes the printing, so goes the campaign. A candidate can have the best looking, best written literature in the world, but if it can't be printed in time, then no one will see it. Printing schedules fill up fast during campaign season, so it is important to establish a good relationship with several printers by taking work to them prior to the campaign.

▼ **Postage**. To save postage costs, it is important to learn the latest postal regulations, including what is considered oversize, how large to make the label area, and where to put the address return and indicia. Knowing this information ahead of time will prevent candidates from hearing bad news at the post office when they show up with thousands of pieces of literature ready to be mailed three days before the election.

▼ **Issues.** Candidates aren't expected to be aware of all the issues at the beginning of the campaign, but it is essential that you know people you can turn to for assistance. Without their help, candidates are unprepared and ill-informed. It is important that candidates know people from various ethnic, racial, political, and social groups so they can assist in responding to their questionnaires. This will increase the odds of winning endorsements and forming coalitions, something that gay and lesbian candidates must do.

▼ **Campaign Coordinator.** A candidate should be meeting voters, not spending time with volunteers. Even if there is no money to pay a staff person, you need to find someone who can coordinate activities and be responsible for volunteer efforts. This person must be very good with people, because nothing will sidetrack a campaign faster than unhappy, sniping volunteers.

▼ **Treasurer.** States and most cities have laws governing campaign financing and reporting. Missing a filing deadline or filling out the reports incorrectly can create unnecessary bad press and may result in fines, even when errors were unintentional and innocent. If you don't know how to complete the reports, you need to find someone who does.

▼ **Computer programmer.** A good database can make or break a campaign. It is important that you have someone who will create a database, continuously input new names and update donor records, send thank-you letters and generate mailing lists. If you are computer illiterate, it is all the more important that a computer genius be found.

▼ **Campaign headquarters.** Renting a campaign headquarters can be very expensive, so candidates on a low budget need to find an alternative. One option is to find a business owner who will donate the space. A second is to share space with some organization at no charge. A third is to run the campaign out of someone's house or garage. Any of the three are better than watching the money go down the drain in the form of rent checks.

▼ **Flexible work hours.** There are never enough hours in day to do the work required in a political campaign. That's why it is critical that candidates have a flexible work schedule. If the boss requires you to be at your desk from nine to five, then it will be difficult to run campaign-related errands, attend meetings, and make countless phone calls. Remember, in low-budget campaigns there is usually no paid staff, so the person doing most of the work is the candidate. If the candidate doesn't have time for campaigning, then there isn't much of a campaign.

This assessment is not meant to discourage you from running, because it is essential that more gays and lesbians run for office. Its purpose is to avoid having you jump into a campaign without forethought, only to raise false hopes for yourself and the gay and lesbian community.

If you're thinking of running for office but don't know enough about campaigns, there are some options. The first (and best) option is to volunteer on someone else's campaign to learn how it is done. A second option is to enroll in a candidate training program, such as the Gay and Lesbian Victory Fund Candidate Training Institute or Emily's List Candidate Training School. Another option (and one I do not often recommend) is to enter the race in order to gain experience, knowing that you are laying the groundwork for a second run. Nothing is wrong with this as long the candidate doesn't lose sight of this objective.

Candidates need to realistically assess their chances. If you think there is a good chance you can win, you should run. Sometimes, however, it pays to be patient and run later when everything is in place. If nothing else, this strategy might cut down on post-election bitterness and prevent candidates from having to go without sex for a year.

Ken Yeager teaches in the political science department of San Jose University and is a co-founder of the Bay Area Municipal Elections Committee (BAYMEC), a gay and lesbian political action committee. In November 1992, he ran in a field of six candidates for the San Jose/Evergreen Community College Board and won with 49.5 percent of the vote, making him the first openly gay elected official in San Jose and Santa Clara County.

How to Survive Once Elected
John Heilman

Y OU'VE just gone through a grueling campaign. You've spent months raising money, walking precincts and debating your opponents. On election night, all your hard work pays off: You're victorious! You thank your supporters and friends and celebrate for a few days. Now the really hard work begins.

As you assume your new role as an openly gay or lesbian elected official, you may need some suggestions to guide you. Looking back on my years of service, here are the ten suggestions I wish someone had given me when I started my career as an elected official.

1. Now that you are an elected official, you must do what's right for your community.

As a candidate, you undoubtedly sought the support of various constituencies and organizations. As an elected official, however, you owe an allegiance to the entire community. This requires you to do what is best for the community as a whole, not just those who supported you. Moreover, you must safeguard the interests of those who will be in the community in the future, not just those who are currently in your district.

This obligation is a heavy one. You have to get the facts and listen to input from a variety of sources. Ultimately, however, the burden is on you to do what's right for the community even when it does not seem politically advantageous. In the long run, you will be better served and respected, even by those who disagree with you, if your decisions are always motivated by your sincere effort to do the right thing for your community.

2. Don't lose sight of your goals.

Assuming that something other than an ego-driven desire for attention has motivated you to run for office, you want to accomplish something in your office, for example, improve public safety or increase funding for AIDS services. Whatever your motivation for running, make sure you do not lose sight of what your goals are. Write down your goals and set aside a regular time on a monthly basis to review them.

As an elected official, you will be faced with a myriad of issues, some generated by your staff and the public, others generated by your colleagues. While you can't avoid these issues, you can decide how much time you want to devote to each of them. Try to ensure that you are controlling at least part of the agenda and that some of your priorities are being advanced.

Don't feel that you have to do everything alone. Seek out sympathetic colleagues and staff members. Use your power as an elected official to bring together an ad hoc working group to advance your priorities.

3. The election is over so put it behind you.

During the campaign, you probably took some pot shots from people. Some otherwise intelligent people backed your opponent. People who should have contributed to your campaign didn't come through for you.

You need to get over these snubs for several reasons. First, although it's always tempting to be vindictive, it doesn't sit well with the public. As an elected official, the public holds you to a higher standard of conduct. If only for the sake of appearances, resist the temptation to punish your enemies. Not only will you promote a positive image for yourself, you'll be a more effective leader. You need the assistance and good will of as many people as possible to accomplish your goals. This is especially true with respect to your colleagues. If you're still harboring ill will toward your colleagues, you won't be able to enlist their support for your initiatives.

4. Cultivate a good relationship with your staff.

Staff members can make you look really good or really bad, usually depending on how you treat them. If you treat your staff with respect, you'll be accorded the same professionalism.How do you show respect for staff members? Get their opinions and advice before you embark on some policy initiative. Even when you disagree with a staff member's opinions, take the time to discuss his/her concerns and learn from his/her expertise.

Occasionally you will have to reprimand a staff member. When that problem arises, discuss the matter privately. Attacking a staffer in public will undermine the morale of the entire office. In addition, public rebukes will make staff members reluctant to give you forthright advice on difficult or controversial issues.

If you have the opportunity to participate in the selection of staff, make your selection based on the merits of the individual. You will be pressured for jobs by friends and political supporters, but don't succumb. In the long run, you will be best served by having the most qualified staff.

5. Don't get caught up in the trappings of power.

As an elected official, you will receive a lot of attention. You will be invited as an honored guest to dinners and events. People will recognize you in public places. Before you let the adulation and attention go to your head, remember the golden rule of elected politics: *you're replaceable.* And, if you begin to believe your own PR, you will probably be replaced sooner than later. Keep your sense of self and your sense of humor. Don't pretend you are someone other than who you are. As you already know by being openly gay or lesbian, if you aren't honest about yourself, you can't be effective. If you are honest about who you are, the public will accept you even with all your quirks.

6. *Always* respect your colleagues.

Your colleagues got where they did the same way you did, by running and winning an election. Even when you disagree, they are entitled to your respect. No matter how much you disagree, there will always be some issue upon which you agree or some situation where you face the public's wrath together.

If you resort to public name-calling with your colleagues, even when they deserve it, in the public's eye you will be just as guilty as your colleagues.

7. Take responsibility.

You were elected to address difficult questions, so don't avoid them. If your community faces a difficult decision, try to educate the public about the choices you face. Obtain the best information you can and share it with the public. Ultimately, however, you must make the decision and take the responsibility for your decision. If you duck the tough decisions, your community will be poorly served and ultimately you will lose the respect of your constituents.

8. Don't risk your career over something stupid.

No matter how supportive your community, remember that as an openly gay or lesbian elected official, you have enemies who are waiting to pounce on you the moment you give them some ammunition. It took you years to get where you are, but you can be dragged down in a day. Be careful about what you say in public and make sure you avoid even the appearance of impropriety. Why risk your career and your reputation over something involving questionable judgment or ethics?

9. Don't try to please everyone.

Your job involves making decisions. Usually there will be people on both sides of every issue, and invariably someone or some group will be angry with you for your opinion when it does not concur with theirs. Do your best to communicate your decision and explain your motivation, but don't make yourself crazy trying to please everyone. If you attempt to do so, you will ultimately sacrifice your values and appear indecisive and ineffective.

10. Take care of yourself.

Once you're elected, everyone will want a piece of you. Openly gay or lesbian elected officials face special scrutiny and pressure from both the mainstream and the gay community. You need to develop a network of support that will be there for you when times get rough. Schedule time to exercise and to spend with your friends and family. Take time to get out of town, refocus your energy and regain your perspective.

As a potential candidate, it may be daunting to hear that *getting* elected is the easy part, but once the election is over, all the work you had only *talked* during your campaign about doing, must now be done. And to fulfill your pledge to serve *and* any other motivation you may have — to serve the people *or* to get reelected to future terms or other offices — the work must be done well, with integrity and for the good of your constituents, *even those who didn't vote for you.* Throughout your campaign you focused on gaining the support of as many interest groups as possible, and now that you're in office you cannot lose sight of your broad base of support and turn instead to focus on the groups which reflect your more personal goals and interests. As well, you must attempt to bring this same broadmindedness to your work with your staff and colleagues. Alienating these people will only serve to make you less effective and more susceptible to attacks from in- and outside your office. Remember: you are only one person, one who was elected to serve others, not yourself.

Elected to the West Hollywood City Council in 1984, and as mayor in 1985, John Heilman has been reelected to the council and as mayor twice since, in 1986 and 1990. In addition to his efforts on the council to limit excessive development and protect tenants' rights, Heilman has focused on civil rights issues as a volunteer and board member for such groups as the American Civil Liberties Union and the Local Government Commission, and as an active member in the Harvey Milk Gay and Lesbian Democratic Club, the National Organization for Women, the National League of Cities and the Southern California Association of Governments. Heilman also teaches law at Whittier College School of Law.

Morality and Politics:
Lessons of a Lesbian Elected Official
Angie Fa

IN the past year I have learned some interesting lessons about the dilemmas and promises that face a lesbian serving as an elected official. I never expected to face these issues of morality and politics when I first jumped into the race for elected office.

I made the last-minute decision to run for San Francisco School Board at midnight. My nominating papers were due at 5:00 p.m. that day, and we had 17 hours to gather 20 key supporting signatures and write a statement, which would appear in the citywide Voter's Handbook. Little did I realize that I would soon become the first lesbian of color to win election in San Francisco *and* that I would be the top vote getter in the school board race, with the second highest number of votes for any citywide candidate for any local office and the highest number of votes per campaign dollar spent.

In some ways my campaign was easy compared to my time in office, which has been challenging, because my background is in community organizing. Through my work in the labor movement, and the lesbian/gay/bisexual movement, in support of people of color, women's civil rights, peace, solidarity, Central America and tenants groups, it was easier for me to build a campaign very quickly. As one friend once told me, no good organizing that you've done is ever lost.

There have been times when it has been a challenge to switch roles from that of a community organizer to that of an elected official. In the past year I've learned some valuable lessons.

Taking the heat

The first lesson I learned as an elected official is that if your first priority is your next election to higher office, or reelection, you make one set of decisions, and if your first priority is the communities to which you feel accountable, you make another set of decisions.

You face special challenges when you are an elected official representing the interests of specific communities and constituencies. Cesar Chavez, Dolores Huerta, and the United Farm Workers call the elected officials they help put into office "Servants of the People." I was elected not on my own individual merits as an educator, but because I could represent the interests of the lesbian, gay and bisexual community, people of color, labor and progressive communities. And the fact that I owe my election to those communities means that I behave in a certain way, I put the interests of those communities before the interests of my political donors, or the interests of my political career.

Once any elected official is in office, there is pressure not to rock the boat on any given board or body. There is a sense that certain issues are likely to divide elected officials and cause embarassment, or that certain issues don't have the votes necessary to win. Other elected officials who might be our allies on civil rights or labor issues might be bad, ignorant or insensitive on issues of concern to our queer community.

The pressure is certainly on when the boards or bodies are in public session, but things can become even more problematic behind closed doors in private sessions. In these settings, when there is no outside pressure, it may become even more challenging to stand firm on issues of importance to you and your constituency. I've started to learn that by taking the right principled stand you eventually come out on top. It may take a matter of days, weeks or years, but doing the right thing usually turns out to be the best thing in the long run. When you trade off political expediency for the wrong vote, you pay for it in the end.

At times it may seem easier just to raise uncomfortable items for discussion, rather than to force votes on these issues. But the only way communities can hold elected officials accountable is if there is a record of an actual vote.

We do need to elect more members of the lesbian, gay, bisexual and transgender community to public office. But we must choose representatives who will put the interests of our communities before their own careers. We also need to challenge any elected official, whatever their sexual orientation, gender or party affiliation, who joins with straight male Republicans or Democrats in attacking the rights of immigrant communities or the rights of working people, because if the rights of other communities are attacked, our rights may be attacked next.

Limited power

The second lesson I learned is that even after you get elected, you don't always have the power. I've talked privately with other local legislators running cities, counties and states who feel the same way.

Once you're elected, sometimes the only thing that you can try to do is set some policy and find some resources for huge institutions with tremendous human needs. There are often real limits in the power that elected officials have to persuade large dinosaurs to turn around in one direction or another. I've learned that one answer is to look for creative or structural solutions instead of just accepting the status quo reality of limitations. There are two ways to get through a term in office. You can either vote "yes" or "no" on every motion or bill that comes your way, or you can look for ways of shaping the course of what the legislation says, or what the budget is.

Learning to set priorities

The last lesson I've learned is about trying to set priorities. Lesbian, gay, bisexual and transgender elected officials face the challenge of watching out for our gay community plus trying to watch out for the needs of our entire constituency, queer and straight. It's not an easy job and serving in elected office can take a real toll on your personal and work life. In many areas, the phone calls, letters and requests for your time will be endless. The big challenge is to figure out where you might be able to make real contributions and where you will need to say "no."

For the small but growing number of queer elected officials who also come from communities of color, there will be added demands on your time because not just one but two communities will be asking for your help and inviting you to meetings, events and functions. As much as you want to, you may not always be able to say "yes." As more of us are elected to office, it will be easier to share the work and divide the responsibilities in the years to come.

Angie Fa serves on the San Francisco School Board and was the first lesbian or gay of color elected to San Francisco public office. She is past president of the Harvey Milk Lesbian, Gay, Bisexual Democratic Club, serves as the chair of Asian-American Studies at City College of San Francisco and as an organizer with the Hotel Employees and Restaurant Union.

Winning Appointments
Morris Kight

THE Gay and Lesbian Victory Fund provides political experience, resources and encouragement to lesbians and gay men who seek to serve society as openly gay elected *and appointed* officials. And with good reason. Appointed offices often carry as much (or more) political clout as elected ones of similar levels or purposes, and local gay and lesbian communities should actively seek to recommend its qualified members to appointed boards and committees. The Victory Fund expressed its support for appointed officials in its ardent 1993 campaign to get open gays and lesbians appointed to the Clinton administration. With the help and leadership of dedicated political gurus and Victory Fund board members Andrew E. Barrer and David Mixner, and the cooperation of other national gay and lesbian groups, it formed Coalition '93. The Coalition's sole purpose was to ascertain the appointment of open gays and lesbians to the Clinton Administration. As the longest-seated and first openly gay or lesbian appointed official in the country, I applaud our community's efforts in the historic Presidential appointments of 26 openly gay and lesbian people, and encourage gays and lesbians everywhere to seek to appointed positions. The following is the story of my gay activist career, one in which I have worked consistently and with dedication for gay and lesbian equal rights. I hope that through my example more and more gays and lesbians will seek appointments. Even if your ultimate goal is elective office, appointments are political springboards, a chance to gain experience and name recognition, and to give something back to your community.

In February, 1972, a conference to discuss, debate and define a gay political agenda was held in Chicago by the Gay Activists Alliance of New York (GAA). GAA, an offshoot of the Gay Liberation Front (GLF) of New York, which was founded in late 1969, chose to take a limited political and activist agenda that focused solely on specific narrowly defined gay issues. People came from all across the country to attend, and late in the conference a few of us were appointed to a committee to write the first-ever Gay and Lesbian Rights Platform; I was honored to be selected as the committee chair.

The preamble to the Platform read: "The Gay and Lesbian political community should aggressively support the candidacy of qualified members of our community for public office, and should, with equal vigor, seek the appointment of Gay/Lesbian People to Commissions, Boards, Task Forces, Joint Power Groups, and other appointive bodies of government." As the longest-seated openly gay appointed official in the country — Commissioner on Human Relations for the County of Los Angeles since 1979 — I obviously feel strongly about the importance of both the election and the appointment of openly gay and lesbian people to public office. The mandate of the Human Relations Commission, on which I continue to serve, is to work to reduce, and hopefully eliminate, acts of hostility, discrimination and violence stemming from "race, religion, national origin, ethnicity, gender, marital status." In 1976, three years before I was appointed to the commission, I appeared before it and successfully urged that its mission be expanded to include "sexual orientation." In the 15 years that I have served, I have consistently brought lesbian/gay issues to the commission at the same time as I have focused on the other items on my agenda: racism, feminist issues, the environment, poverty, justice and inclusive health issues.

One example of my work on lesbian/gay issues is a day-long hearing called "The State of Affairs for the Lesbian/Gay Community." We also held a hearing jointly with the County Commission on AIDS, on "The Impact of AIDS on the Minority Community." Both of these resulted in extensive reports to the Board of Supervisors (by whom the commissioners are appointed). Our next hearing will be on "The Lesbian/Gay Young/Youth Community." All of these are the first of their kind in terms of subject matter.

I urge the lesbian/gay community to seek out administrative and political appointments. Becoming appointed is both different and similar to becoming elected. Although the campaign is more informal and you are not focused on winning votes from the public, you do need to make the same kinds of decisions about why you want to run and to which position you would like to be appointed, and you have to avoid the same danger of being seen as a single-issue politician. You also must seek the endorsement of people and businesses in your community, just like candidates running for elective office; rather than winning votes, you must call upon them to support you with letters and phone calls to the official or to members of the board or committee to which you desire appointment.

Becoming an appointed official is often how elected officials take their first step into public life. Appointments give you many of the attributes you need to get elected: political and legislative experience, name recognition within the political and public spectrums and the credibility of someone who has a list of legislative accomplishments to back up other relevant educational and work experience. The credibility you gain by already having experienced the bureaucratic system in your district cannot be underestimated. As an appointed official you have very likely handled the same sorts of issues and responsibilities as do elected officials. You have the power to control legislation and attitudes within the reach of your appointed office. And perhaps most importantly, you educate large numbers of people on what gays and lesbians are like, defeating false, negative stereotypes, and serving as a positive role model for gay and lesbian youth and closeted adults who may be struggling with their sexual identity because of these stereotypes.

The following are ten guidelines which give a general idea of the steps necessary to become an appointed official:

1. **Make the personal decision to run. Think about why you want to serve in public office, about how it will affect your personal life, about the privacy you will give up by serving as an openly gay official, about whether or not you want to be constantly in the public eye, in the media, etc.**

2. **Decide which area you would like to work in. What issues, areas of the community are really important to you? On what can you imagine spending vast amounts of time working? And where do you think your efforts, talents, skills, education and experience will be utilized to their greatest advantage?**

3. **Once you've chosen a body of government for which**

you would like to work, call its offices and get a list of the appointed positions (*e.g.*, commissions, committees, task forces, etc.).

4. Find out when, where and how often they meet, then attend one or more meetings to see which you feel would best accommodate your interests and your skills. Once you've chosen a position, write the assembled committee or commission and let them know your interest and why you think you deserve the position.

5. Once you've chosen the specific seat you would like to hold, *bury your humility.* Humility is almost always a positive trait, but it won't get you far in public life. Assumedly you've chosen an office that you are certain you would like to hold, and one about which you have conviction that you are the best person for the job. Show that strength of conviction to the people considering appointing you.

6. Humility buried, get people, other elected or appointed officials, business and community leaders, friends, etc. to write letters in support of you to the board/person making the decision about your appointment.

7. Develop your agenda. What do you want to work on in this position? Usually this will be included in your decision about the position for which you choose to run, but you must still narrow it down so you can speak to the people who are making the decision about your appointment with specific points about the changes you would like to see made and how you think you can help make them.

8. Adopt a generalist/universalist attitude. Though you don't want to seem too open-ended, if your only objective is to work on lesbian/gay issues, stop right there. Though this will be, and rightly so, one of your main concerns, you will be ineffective as an appointed official, if you even get that far, if you are seen as being a single-issue person.

9. Once appointed, be an agent of change. Progressive-minded people, which most lesbians and gay men are, are the kinds of people who make things happen in the face of adversity, simply because adversity has often been part of their daily lives.

10. And finally, be part of the solution. Certainly, gaining an appointed seat and working for positive change for the lesbian/gay community and other important issues on your agenda makes you part of the solution to the struggles our community faces. But to be truly effective as a public official, you must learn to work with the system, and the colleagues, you are given. I feel fortunate enough to work with people whom I respect, and have sought open communication with them because I believe they are socially concerned human beings. Whether or not you are as fortunate, if you cannot be a team player, you should not be part of a board or body of governors. Generally speaking, if you respect what your colleagues say, they will do the same for you, and your differences will complement each other. It is natural to seek out like-minded and supportive people to build a community of interest, but be careful not to become part of a clique. Much more is to be gained by group action.

Los Angeles County Commissioner on Human Relations **Morris Kight**, *the longest-seated openly gay appointee in the history of the United States, has held his appointed seat since 1979. Throughout his career as a gay rights activist/politician/environmentalist/humanist Kight has become well-known for the many organizations he has founded, including the 1960s Dow Action Committee to protest the military's manufacturing of napalm, herbicides and defoliants; the Gay Liberation Front in 1969; Christopher Street West; the Gay and Lesbian Community Services Center in Los Angeles, the largest and oldest gay and lesbian service organization in the world; Van Ness Recovery House, the first such organization for gays and lesbians with substance abuse problems; the No on the Briggs Initiative Committee, 1977-78; Asian/Pacific Lesbian/Gays; and the Morris Kight/McCadden Place Collection, in 1984, the largest-known collection of gay and lesbian Asian art; and Stonewall 25, an international celebration of lesbian/gay pride. His most recent work has focused on the needs of elderly lesbians and gay men.*

Campaign Professionals

Abacus Associates
Janet Grenzke
52 School Street
Hatfield, MA 01038
Phone: 413-247-9430
Fax: 413-247-5813
Services: Strategic research, polling, focus groups

AB Data Ltd.
Jerry Benjamin
8050 North Port Washington Road
Milwaukee, WI 53217
Phone: 800-558-6908
Fax: 414-352-3994
Services: Mail consulting, fundraising, list management, direct mail computer services

ACT UP/Queer Richmond
Bernard Artabazon
207 1/2 East Leigh
Richmond, VA 23219
Phone: 804-643-7004
Services: Consulting, petitions, campaign management, direct action

The Advance Group
Andrew Grossman
30 East 29th Street
New York, New York 10016
Phone: 212-679-4570
Fax: 212-684-0074
Services: Campaign consulting and event planning, field and canvass organization

Afriat Blackstone Consulting
Steven Afriat
6430 Sunset Boulevard, Suite 1501
Hollywood, CA 90028
Phone: 213-856-7070
Fax: 213-856-9581
Services: Governmental relations, campaign management, fundraising

Ambrosino and Muir
945 Front Street, Suite 106
San Francisco, CA 94111
Phone: 415-781-0579
Fax: 415-434-3229
Services: Consulting and direct mail

American Data Management
Doug Winslow
1920 Old Middlefield Way
Mountain View, CA 94043
Phone: 800-829-5800
Fax: 415-968-9870
Services: Direct mail, list management

American Mandate
John Rossner
1760 Terrace Drive
Belmont, CA 94002
Phone: 415-598-0425
Fax: 415-593-7760
Services: Strategic planning, direct mail

Angle Media
Todd Cunningham
2200 North Lamar Street, Suite 208
Dallas, TX 75202
Phone: 214-953-0010
Fax: 214-953-0012
Services: Mailhouse, list management, printing

Arcadia Press, Inc.
Thomas Leavitt
One Bert Drive
West Bridgewater, MA 02379
Phone: 508-559-9896
Fax: 508-559-0044
Services: Commercial printing

Aristotle Industries
Shawn Harmon
205 Pennsylvania Avenue SE
Washington, DC 20003-1164
Phone: 202-543-8345
Fax: 202-543-6407
Services: Voter lists, contributor lists, FEC-approved software

Austin Sheinkopf Ltd.
John Silvant
379 West Broadway, Suite 305
New York, NY 10012
Phone: 212-941-6630
Fax: 212-941-6634
Services: Media consulting and public relations for Democratic candidates

Avenel Associates, Inc.
Earl Bender
1201 Connecticut Avenue NW
Washington, DC 20036
Phone: 202-328-0199
Fax: 202-452-4175
Services: Campaign consultants

David Axelrod and Associates
David Axelrod
730 North Franklin Street, Suite 404
Chicago, IL 60610-3526
Phone: 312-664-7500
Fax: 312-664-0174
Services: Media consulting

Bass and Howes
Marie Bass, Joanne Howes
1601 Connecticut Avenue NW
Suite 801
Washington, DC 20009
Phone: 202-328-2200
Fax: 202-667-0462
Services: Fundraising

Belden and Russonello Research and Communications
Nancy Belden
1250 I Street NW, Suite 460
Washington, DC 20005
Phone: 202-789-2400
Fax: 202-789-0022
Services: Professional polls and focus groups, strategic planning

Bennett, Petts and Associates
Anna Bennett, David Petts
1875 Connecticut Avenue NW
Suite 630
Washington, DC 20009
Phone: 202-332-1100
Fax: 202-223-5240
Services: Polling and strategic consulting for Democratic candidates

Ruth Bernstein
9168-B Regents Road
La Jolla, CA 92037
Phone: 619-558-9180
Services: Campaign management

Birleffi-Kopf Productions
Bobbie Birleffi, Beverly Kopf
2126 Cahuenga
Los Angeles, CA 90068
Phone: 213-962-9678
Fax: 213-466-4420
Services: Media press kits,
political profiles

Bonnie Lytle Photography
Bonnie Lytle
10220 Yuma Court
Manassas, VA 22110
Phone: 703-369-2586
Services: Full-service photography

Campaign Connection
Cathy Allen
1809 Seventh Avenue, Suite 1610
Seattle, WA 98101
Phone: 206-443-1990
Fax: 206-382-1338
Services: Consulting

The Campaign Design Group
Joel Bradshaw, Lisa Lyon
727 Fifteenth Street NW, 11th Floor
Washington, DC 20005
Phone: 202-393-0404
Fax: 202-347-4308
Services: Consulting, campaign
management

The Campaign Group
*Neil Oxman, Doc Sweitzer, Bill
Wachob*
720 East Zia Road
Santa Fe, NM 87505
Phone: 215-732-8200
Fax: 215-790-9969
Services: Media consulting, direct
mail consulting

Campaign Performance Group
Jim Crounse, Rich Schlackman
901 North Pitt Street, Suite 300
Alexandria, VA 22314
Phone: 703-519-7400
Fax: 703-519-7414

Carville and Begala
John Shakow
329 Maryland Avenue NE
Washington, DC 20002
Phone: 202-543-1196
Fax: 202-822-9088
Services: Consulting

Cerrell Associates Inc.
Joseph Cerrell
320 North Larchmont Boulevard
Second Floor
Los Angeles, CA 90004
Phone: 213-466-3445
Fax: 213-466-8653
Services: Public relations, media

Changing America Inc.
Mal Warwick
2550 Ninth Street, Suite 103
Berkeley, CA 94710
Phone: 510-843-8888
Fax: 510-843-0142
Services: Direct mail, fundraising

Clarenbach Consulting Group
David Clarenbach
454 Sidney Street
Madison, WI 53703
Phone: 608-251-2528
Services: Consulting, campaign
management, strategy, fundraising

Dennis Collins
67 Pierce Street, Number 4
San Francisco, CA 94117
Phone: 415-861-1690
Services: Consulting

Communications Services
Libby Post
4 Central Avenue
Albany, NY 12210
Phone: 518-463-3522
Fax: 518-426-3961
Services: Printing, direct mail

Communikatz, Inc.
Ric Katz
4500 Biscayne Boulevard, Suite 325
Miami, FL 33137
Phone: 305-573-4455
Fax: 305-573-4466
Services: Graphic design and
production, media buying, audio and
video production, public opinion
research, news media relations

Paul Cooper
1320 Rhode Island Avenue NW
Suite 450
Washington, DC 20005
Phone: 202-462-7068
Fax: 202-462-7068
Services: Media, research and
persuasion mail, fundraising, written
materials and trouble shooting

Cooper and Secrest
Alan Secrest
228 South Washington Street
Suite 330
Alexandria, VA 22314
Phone: 703-683-7990
Fax: 703-739-0079
Services: Polling

Coyle/Gould and Company
Ed Coyle, Diane Gould
1511 K Street NW, Suite 723
Washington, DC 20005
Phone: 202-628-4331
Fax: 202-628-3090
Services: Fundraising

Dan Carol and Company
Dan Carol, Agustin Paculdar
7003 Carroll Avenue, Suite 200
Takoma Park, MD 20912
Phone: 301-270-5693
Fax: 301-270-5696
Services: Research

Creative Campaigns
Linda Davis
230 G Street NE
Washington, DC 20002
Phone: 202-543-9070
Fax: 202-544-0863
Services: Fundraising

Decision Research
Bob Meadow, Heidi von Szeliski
11400 West Olympic Boulevard
Second Floor
Los Angeles, CA 90064
Phone: 310-914-0124
Fax: 310-445-8800
Services: Polling, survey
research, targeting

Desktop Campaigns
Andrea Shirley
2504 Wyeth Court
Louisville, KY 40220
Phone: 502-456-5981

Direct Approach
Karen Bowie, Nancy Clack
6860 Commercial Drive, Suite 100
Springfield, VA 22151
Phone: 703-642-1313
Fax: 703-642-8505
Services: Direct mail, targeting
analysis, voter identification and
persuasion, GOTV, data entry, in-
house lettershop, printing and
production

Doak, Shrum, Harris, Carrier, and Devine
Robert Shrum
1000 Wilson Boulevard, Suite 2401
Arlington, VA 22209
Phone: 703-522-8910
Fax: 703-522-2649

Donnelly/Colt
Clay Colt
Post Office Box 188
Hampton, CT 06247
Phone: 203-455-9621
Fax: 800-553-0006
Services: Campaign advertising materials: buttons, bumperstickers, posters, brochures, imprinted items

EDK Associates
Ethel Klein
235 West 48th Street
New York, NY 10036
Phone: 212-582-4504
Fax: 212-265-9348
Services: Message development, polling, focus groups, in-depth interviews

Harryette Ehrhardt
5731 Swiss Avenue
Dallas, TX 75214
Phone: 214-826-1231
Fax: 214-826-2763

Eidolon Communications
John Graves, Dennis Lonergan
156 Fifth Avenue, Suite 707
New York, NY 10010
Phone: 212-633-0404
Fax: 212-989-7777
Services: Direct mail, graphics, printing

Election Victories
Susan Hibbard
594 Broadway, Room 403
New York, NY 10012
Phone: 212-343-0255
Fax: 212-343-2876
Services: Political and campaign consulting

Erickson and Company
Tom Erickson
216 Seventh Street SE
Washington, DC 20003
Phone: 202-544-2994
Fax: 202-546-5470
Services: Fundraising

Evans/McDonough Company
Alex Evans
1600 Shattuck Avenue, Suite 224A
Berkeley, CA 94709
Phone: 510-549-6900
Fax: 510-649-7642
Services: Polling, market research, consulting, data processing, interviewing, mail studies

Evans/McDonough Company
Don McDonough
111 Queen Anne Avenue North
Suite 500
Seattle, WA 98109
Phone: 206-282-2454
Fax: 206-285-2644
Services: Polling, market research, strategic consulting, data processing, telephone and door-to-door interviewing, mail studies

Fairbank, Maslin, Maullin and Associates
John Fairbank, Richard Maullin, Paul Maslin
2401 Colorado Avenue, Suite 180
Santa Monica, CA 90404
Phone: 310-828-1183
Fax: 310-453-6562
Services: Polling

The Feldman Group, Inc.
Diane Feldman
1001 Connecticut Avenue NW
Suite 1016
Washington, DC 20036
Phone: 202-467-4200
Fax: 202-467-4201
Services: Polling

Fenn, King and Murphy Communications
Peter Fenn
1043 Cecil Place NW
Washington, DC 20006
Phone: 202-337-6995
Fax: 202-337-6997
Services: Media consulting

David Fleischer
803 President Street
Brooklyn, NY 11215
Phone: 718-230-9865
Fax: 718-230-9819
Services: Campaign management

Foreman and Heidepriem
Carol Tucker Foreman
1155 21st Street NW, Suite 1000
Washington, DC 20036
Phone: 202-822-8060
Fax: 202-822-9088
Services: General campaign consulting

John Franzen Multimedia
John Franzen
610 C Street NE
Washington, DC 20002
Phone: 202-543-4430
Services: Media campaigns for Democratic candidates, advertising

Fraoli Jost Associates
Steven Jost, Michael Fraoli
555 New Jersey Avenue NW
Suite 201
Washington, DC 20001
Phone: 202-347-3042
Fax: 202-347-3046
Services: Campaign consulting, fundraising, political strategies

Garin Hart Strategic Research
Geoff Garin, Fred Yang
1724 Connecticut Avenue NW
Washington, DC 20009
Phone: 202-234-5570
Fax: 202-232-8134
Services: Polling

Gay and Lesbian Victory Fund
William Waybourn
1012 14th Street NW, Suite 707
Washington, DC 20005
Phone: 202-842-8679
Fax: 202-289-3863
Services: Political action committee for gay and lesbian candidates, technical support for campaigns, candidate training

General Campaign Management
Richard Silver
824 Winslow Street, Apartment 214
Redwood, CA 94063
Phone: 415-368-7112
Services: Campaign management

Geto and de Milly, Inc.
Ethan Geto, Michele de Milly
130 East 40th Street, 16th floor
New York, NY 10016
Phone: 212-686-4551
Fax: 212-213-6850
Services: Public relations: lobbying/
public policy, consulting

Gold Communications Company
David Gold
San Jacinto Center
98 San Jacinto Boulevard
Number 160
Austin, TX 78701
Phone: 512-478-1676
Fax: 512-480-9315
Services: Fundraising, voter
persuasion, direct mail

Great Lakes Communications
Jerry Benjamin
4057 North Wilson Drive
Shorewood, WI 53211
Phone: 414-963-2800
Fax: 414-963-2803
Services: Telemarketing, fund-
raising, grassroots campaigns,
lobbying, survey projects

Greenberg Research, Inc.
Stan Greenberg, Al Quinlin
515 Second Street NE
Washington, DC 20002
Phone: 202-547-5200
Fax: 202-544-7020
Services: Polling

Greer, Margolis, Mitchell and Burns
Frank Greer
2626 Pennsylvania Avenue, Suite 301
Washington, DC 20037
Phone: 202-338-8700
Fax: 202-337-0864
Services: Media consulting

Grunwald, Eskew and Donilon
Sarah Callahan
1250 24th Street NW, Suite 260
Washington, DC 20037
Phone: 202-973-9400
Fax: 202-973-9408
Services: Media consulting

Herzog Swayze, Inc.
Kathy Swayze
2000 P Street NW, Suite 305
Washington, DC 20036
Phone: 202-872-1205
Fax: 202-872-1511
Services: Fundraising, telemarketing

Hickman/Brown Research
Carrie Werts
1350 Connecticut Avenue, Suite 206
Washington, DC 20036
Phone: 202-659-4000
Fax: 202-659-1832
Services: Polling

Hill and Knowlton, Inc.
Tom Latimer
1360 Peachtree Street
Atlanta, GA 30309
Phone: 404-249-8550
Fax: 404-249-8560
Services: Public relations

Hot Source Media, Inc.
Michael Vaughan, Susan Joslin
1916 Wilson Boulevard, Suite 304
Arlington, VA 22201
Phone: 703-527-5992
Fax: 703-527-6290
Services: Video production, 2D
and 3D graphics, on-line and off-
line editing

John M. Houston
1 Beekman Street #303
New York, NY 10038
Phone: 212-587-1015
Services: Message development,
media consulting

Huff Printing and Copying
Andrea Sharkey
1100 17th Street NW
Washington, DC 20036
Phone: 202-833-2000
Fax: 202-452-1307
Services: Printing, copying,
campaign materials

Human Rights Campaign Fund
Eric Rosenthal
1012 14th Street NW, Suite 607
Washington, DC 20005
Phone: 202-628-4160
Fax: 202-347-5323
Services: Fundraising, strategy

Hunter and Associates
Susan Hunter
6129 Leesburg Pike, Suite 712
Falls Church, VA 22041
Phone: 703-820-8497
Fax: 703-578-3455
Services: Fundraising

Interchange International, Inc.
Lillie Brock, Mary Ann Salerno
150 South Washington Street
Suite 204
Falls Church, VA 22046-2921
Phone: 703-533-7400
Fax: 703-533-7403
Services: Presentation develop-
ment and delivery skills

Ernie Jones and Associates
1893 Fairpointe Trace
Stone Mountain, GA 30088
Phone: 404-808-4304
Services: Public relations, lobbying

Joe Kaplan
JFK Station
Post Office Box 9205
Boston, MA 02114-0042
Phone: 617-961-2099
Services: Freelance writer

Kennedy Signs
Ricky Mandella, Sr.
Post Office Drawer "O"
Roseland, LA 70456
Phone: 800-535-5680
Fax: 504-748-6246
Services: Signs

Laser Communication
Gary Vigran
931 East 86th Street, Suite 111
Indianapolis, IN 46240
Phone: 317-259-4700
Fax: 317-475-0521

Laser Image Inc.
Barbara Morris, Chele Butler
1525 Stemmons Freeway
Dallas, TX 75207
Phone: 214-744-1313
Fax: 214-744-5343
Services: Direct mail, advertis-
ing, laser printing, list services

Roger Lee and Carol Beddo, Inc.
Roger Lee, Carol Beddo
101 Park Center Plaza, Suite 1100
San Jose, CA 95113
Phone: 408-280-5900
Fax: 408-280-7887
Services: Direct mail, campaign
management and consulting,
fundraising, media management

J.H. Leitner, Inc.
John H. Leitner
166 2nd Avenue
New York, NY 10003
Phone: 212-475-8995
Fax: 212-674-1889
Services: Media, direct mail

MacWilliams, Cosgrove, Snider Strategy and Communications
Matthew McWilliams, Tom Cosgrove
Steve Snider
6 Grant Avenue
Takoma Park, MD 20912
Phone: 301-891-2230
Fax: 301-891-2207
Services: Media consulting

Martin and Glantz
Gina Glantz
100 Shoreline Highway, Suite 140B
Mill Valley, CA 94941
Phone: 415-331-1970
Fax: 415-331-3252
Services: Grassroots organizing, strategy, research, ballot initiative, campaign management

Marttila and Kiley, Inc.
Tom Kiley, John Marttila
84 State Street, Third Floor
Boston, MA 02109
Phone: 617-523-1525
Fax: 617-589-0787
Services: Polling

Mellman, Lazarus, Lake, Inc.
Mark Mellman, Celinda Lake
1054 31st Street NW, Suite 530
Washington, DC 20007
Phone: 202-625-0370
Fax: 202-625-0371
Services: Campaign research and strategy, polling

MG Associates
Marilyn Gordon
4319 Oak Lawn, Suite C
Dallas, TX 75219
Phone: 214-520-9205
Fax: 214-520-9206
Services: Strategy, direct mail, media, fundraising, canvassing

M and R Strategic Services
Michael Cover
1725 K Street Street, Suite 1209
Washington, DC 20006
Phone: 202-223-9541
Fax: 202-223-9579
Services: Campaign management

Nagel, Sossen and Associates
Robert Nagel, Nina Sossen
2011 Atwood Avenue
Madison, WI 53704
Phone: 608-249-0243
Fax: 608-249-0243
Services: Fundraising, graphic design, targeting, research, direct mail

National Women's Political Caucus
Mary Beth Lambert
1275 K Street NW, Suite 750
Washington, DC 20005-4051
Phone: 202-898-1100
Fax: 202-898-0458
Services: Grassroots organization for women candidates

The November Group
Martin Davis
1188 20th Street NW, Suite 650
Washington, DC 20036
Phone: 202-466-2700
Fax: 202-466-2244
Services: Direct mail for Democratic candidates

On Target Solutions
182 Colly Way
North Lauderdale, FL 33068
Phone: 305-975-6797
Fax: 305-975-6811
Services: Fundraising, direct
mail, strategy, consulting

Osanka Communications
Jeff Osanka, Ph.D.
1742 Skyline Blvd
Eugene, OR 97403
Phone: 503-345-0931
Services: Specializing in Republican candidates and opposition to
Radical Right referenda, media,
research and polling

Dick Pabich
2804 Piedmont Avenue
Berkeley, CA 94705
Phone: 510-649-0254
Fax: 510-704-0942
Services: Campaign management

Penn and Schoen Associates
Mark Penn, Doug Schoen
245 East 92nd Street
New York, NY 10128
Phone: 212-534-4000
Fax:: 212-360-7423
Services: Polling

Photography by Michael Murphy
12 NE 19 Court, Number 106A
Fort Lauderdale, FL 33305
Phone: 205-565-8666
Services: Public relations and
event photography

Politics, Inc.
Leslie Israel, Ann Lewis
1920 L Street NW, Suite 700
Washington, DC 20036
Phone: 202-331-7654
Fax: 202-659-5559
Services: Media consulting

Positive Communications
Christine Jahnke
120 Maryland Avenue NE
Washington, DC 20002
Phone: 202-547-1244
Services: Consulting, public speaking

Prime New York
Stuart Osnow
1560 Broadway, Suite 711
New York, NY 10036-1525
Phone: 212-730-0833
Fax: 212-302-8807
Services: Voter lists and labels

Promotional Strategies
Lois Marbach
64-64 229th Street
Bayside, NY 11364
Phone: 718-229-4201
Fax: 718-279-2456
Services: Consulting, prime
voters, issue and literature
development, direct mail

Ridder/Braden
Rick Ridder, Kris Bess
1701 Wynkoop, Suite 239
Denver, CO 80202
Phone: 303-893-2001
Fax: 303-893-3948
Services: Consulting, public
relations, voter contact, research,
media

Robert Kaplan Company
Robert Kaplan
12021 Wilshire Boulevard, Suite 542
Los Angeles, CA 90025
Phone: 310-451-8919
Fax: 310-451-2189
Services: Direct mail, telemarketing,
fundraising

Beth Schapiro and Associates
Beth Schapiro
134 Peachtree Street NW, Suite 315
Atlanta, GA 30303
Phone: 404-584-5215
Fax: 404-581-0058
Services: Strategic research,
focus groups, polling

Kimberly Scott and Associates
Kim Scott
219 Pennsylvania Avenue SE
Washington, DC 20003
Phone: 202-543-5008
Fax: 202-543-5009
Services: Political consulting and
fundraising for Democratic candidates

Seder/Laguens, Inc.
Dawn Laguens
2853 Ontario Road NW, Suite 402
Washington, DC 20009
Phone: 202-232-0300
Fax: 202-232-8682
Services: Media consulting and
production services

Sheehan Associates
Deborah McGraw
1901 L Street NW, Suite 400
Washington, DC 20036
Phone: 202-452-9440
Fax: 202-833-2471
Services: Media training

Sheingold Associates
Larry Sheingold
Margaret Gladstein
501 Santa Ynez Way
Sacramento, CA 95816
Phone: 916-452-9704
Fax: 916-452-9861

Shorr and Associates, Inc.
Saul Shorr
1831 Chestnut Street, Suite 602
Philadelphia, PA 19103
Phone: 215-567-4080
Fax: 215-567-6494
Services: Media consulting

**Skadden, Arps, Slate, Meagher
and Flom**
Ken Gross
1440 New York Avenue NW
Washington, DC 20005
Phone: 202-371-7956
Fax: 202-393-5760
Services: Campaign finance, ethics
and conflict-of-interest law advice

Skelton, Grover, and Associates
Barbara Grover
6305 Yucca Street, Number 304
Los Angeles, CA 90028
Phone: 213-465-3773
Fax: 213-465-1731
Services: Consulting, campaign
management

Springer Associates
Maggie Springer, Suzie Brewster
1201 Pennsylvania Avenue NW
Suite 500
Washington, DC 20004
Phone: 202-626-6842
Fax: 202-626-6211
Services: Fundraising consulting

The Sondermann Group
Darcy Grieve
312 East Seventh Avenue
Denver, CO 80203
Phone: 303-832-4422
Fax: 303-832-0035
Services: Media relations, candidate/
ballot issues, direct mail, video/press

Squier-Knapp-Ochs Communications
Robert Squier, Bill Knapp, Tom Ochs
511 Second Street NE
Washington, DC 20002
Phone: 202-547-4970
Fax: 202-543-6911
Services: Media consulting

Staton/Hughes
Mary Hughes
530 Howard Street, Suite 200
San Francisco, CA 94105
Phone: 415-495-4910
Fax: 415-495-5733
Services: Strategy, communications, research, direct mail

The Strategy and Campaign Management Group
John Whitehurst
2269 Chestnut Street, Suite 391
San Francisco, CA 94123
Phone: 415-921-5394
Fax: 415-921-0329
Services: Political consulting

Strother/Duffy/ Strother, LTD.
Jim Duffy
717 D Street NW
Washington, DC 20004
Phone: 202-626-5650
Fax: 202-639-8974
Services: Media consulting

Struble/Totten Communications
Tom Opel, John Donovan
700 Seventh Street SE
Washington, DC 20003
Phone: 202-544-2300
Fax: 202-547-2804
Services: Media consulting

Syndicated Graphics
Sal Sapia
82-27 164th Street
Jamaica, NY11432
Phone: 718-380-2790
Fax: 718-380-1251
Services: Political printing and
typesetting, union label

Syscom Services, Inc.
Thomas Coddington
1010 Wayne Avenue, Number 520
Silver Spring, MD 20910
Phone: 800-888-3292
Fax: 301-650-9139
Services: Fax broadcasting

TeleMark
Don Powell
8600 SW Salish Lane
Wilsonville, OR 97070
Phone: 800-777-4817
Fax: 503-682-0403
Services: Telephone persuasion

Terris and Jaye
Eric Jaye
381 Bush Street, Eighth Floor
San Francisco, CA 94104
Phone: 415-291-0679
Fax: 415-291-0724
Services: Political media and
strategy for Democratic candidates

Thalia Zepatos
Liz Kaufman
1524 SE Ash
Portland, OR 97214
Phone: 503-236-7704
Services: Campaign consulting

Townsend, Hermocillo,
Raimundo and Usher
David Townsend
1717 I Street Suite B
Sacramento, CA 95814
Phone: 916-444-5701
Fax: 916-444-0382
Services: Strategy, statewide
campaigns, public relations

Voter Contact Services
Jack Kane
4500 SW Kruse Way, Suite 215
Lake Oswego, OR 97035
Phone: 503-635-5859
Fax: 503-635-5651
Services: Labels and voter lists

Mal Warwick and Associates
Bill Rehm
2550 Ninth Street, Suite 103
Berkeley, CA 94710
Phone: 510-843-8888
Fax: 510-843-0142
Services: Issue advocacy and
electoral politics, direct mail,
fundraising

White Communications
Will Robinson
130 West 88th Street
New York, NY 10024
Phone: 212-580-1052
Fax: 212-877-2167
Services: Political consulting,
media relations

Winning Directions
Anthony J. Fazio
1366 San Mateo Avenue
South San Francisco, CA 94080
Phone: 415-875-4000
Fax: 415-875-1015
Services: Direct mail, targeting,
voter data

Winner, Wagner and Francis
Les Francis
1000 Potomac Street NW, Suite 401
Washington, DC 20007
Phone: 202-333-2533
Fax: 202-342-0763
Services: General campaign
consulting

Jim Wise Associates
Jim Wise, Sharon Hodgdon
104 North West Street
Alexandria, VA 22314
Phone: 703-548-6295
Fax: 703-548-8520
Services: Fundraising consultants

Bob Witeck
1914 N Johnson Street
Arlington, VA 22207
Phone: 703-351-6150
Services: Media relations,
grassroots, crisis communications,
political strategy

Women's Campaign Fund
Amy Simon
120 Maryland Avenue NE
Washington, DC 20002
Phone: 202-544-4484
Services: Financial contribution,
technical assistance, leadership and
media training

Z Printing
H. Suk Kim
15873 Commerce Court
Upper Marlboro, MD 20772
Phone: 301-249-1900
Fax: 301-249-2150
Services: Printing

ZYNYX Marketing Communications
David Nixon
1901 North Fort Myer Drive
Suite 1104
Arlington, VA 22209
Phone: 703-358-0012
Fax: 703-358-9328
Services: Public relations, crisis management, target marketing, radio services, advertising

Zimmerman and Markman
Bill Zimmerman, Pacy Markman
1250 Sixth Street, Number 202
Santa Monica, CA 90401
Phone: 310-451-2522
Fax: 310-451-7494
Services: Political consulting, media, advertising

Gay and Lesbian Elected and Appointed Officials

Judy Abdo
Mayor of Santa Monica
1685 Main Street
Santa Monica, CA 90401

Roberta Achtenberg
Assistant Secretary for Fair Housing
U.S. Department of Housing
and Urban Development
451 Seventh Street SW, Room 5100
Washington, DC 20410

Lisa Albrecht
Civil Rights Commissioner
4721 14th Avenue South
Minneapolis, MN 55407

Tom Ammiano
President San Francisco School Board
135 Van Ness Avenue
San Francisco, CA 94110

Cal Anderson
Washington House of Representatives
Post Office Box 40685
Olympia, WA 98504-0685

Virginia Apuzzo
First Deputy Commissioner
New York State Division of
Housing and Community
38-40 State Street
Albany, NY 12207

Larry Bagneris, Jr.
Advisory Commission on Human Relations
1407 Decatur Street
New Orleans, LA 70116

Tammy Baldwin
Wisconsin State Assembly
Post Office Box 8952
Madison, WI 53708

Andrew E. Barrer
Senior Advisor
Office of the National AIDS Policy
Coordinator
Executive Office of the President
750 Seventeenth Street NW, Suite
1060
Washington, DC 20503

Keith Boykin
Special Assistant to the President
The White House
1600 Pennsylvania Avenue NW
Washington, DC 20500

Tom Brougham
Peralta Community College Board
1725 Berkeley Way, Number B
Berkeley, CA 94703

Steven A. Camara
Fall River City Councilor
199 Purchase Street
Fall River, MA 02720-3222

William M. Chambers
Morristown Town Clerk
110 South Street
Morristown, NJ 07960

Karen Clark
Minnesota House of Representatives
2633 18th Avenue South
Minneapolis, MN 55407

Lisa Cohen
Executive Assistant
Special Counsel to the Attorney General
100 West Randolph Street, Suite 12-199
Chicago, IL 60601

Tim Cole
Civil Rights Commissioner
3801 26th Street East
Minneapolis, MN 55406-1857

Bill Crews
Mayor
Post Office Box 1994
Melbourne, IA 50162

David Cruise
Director of Intergovernmental Relations
U.S. Department of Commerce
14th Street and Constitution Avenue NW
Washington, DC 20230

Romulo Diaz, Jr.
Deputy Assistant Secretary for
International Affairs
U.S. Department of Energy
Room 7B-164
1000 Independence Avenue SW
Washington, DC 20585

Dennis de Leon
Human Rights Commissioner
337 West 14th Street
New York, NY 10014

Thomas K. Duane
New York City Council
275 Seventh Avenue, 12th Floor
New York, NY 10001

Helen Dunlap
Deputy Assistant Secretary for Multi-
Family Housing Programs
U.S. Department of Housing and
Urban Development, Room 5100
451 Seventh Street SW
Washington, DC 20410

Robert Ebersole
Lexington Treasurer
41 Morton Street, Number 24
Jamaica Plain, MA 02130

George Eighmey
Oregon House of Representatives
1423 SE Hawthorne Boulevard
Portland, OR 97214

Angie Fa
San Francisco Board of Education
135 Van Ness Avenue
San Francisco, CA 94102

Susan Farnsworth
Maine House of Representatives
222 Water Street
Hallowell, ME 04347

Todd Fernandez
Assistant Secretary
Executive Officer of Consumer Affairs
1 Ashburton Place, Room 1411
Boston, MA 02108

John Fiore
Wilton Manors City Council
2450 NE 15th Avenue, Number 210
Wilton Manors, FL 33305

Jay Fisette
Fiscal Affairs Advisory Committee
Arlington County Board
2100 Clarendon Boulevard, Suite 300
Arlington, VA 22201

Will Fitzpatrick
Rhode Island State Senate
187 Narragansett Street
Cranston, RI 02905-4109

Martha Fitzwater
Texas Funeral Service Commission
3308 Broadway Suite 300
San Antonio, TX 78209

Tom Fleury
Vermont State Assembly
12 Avenue A
Burlington, VT 05401

Barney Frank
U.S. House of Representatives
2404 Rayburn House Office Building
Washington, DC 20515-2104

Roslyn Garfield
Provincetown Town Moderator
City Hall
260 Commercial Street
Provincetown, MA 02657

Shelley Gaylord
Municipal Judge
210 Martin Luther King, Jr., Boulevard
Madison, WI 53710

Robert Gentry
Laguna Beach City Council
1475 Pacific Avenue
Laguna Beach, CA 92651

David Gernant
Multnomah County District Court
1021 SW Fourth Avenue
Portland, OR 97204

Deborah J. Glick
New York State Assembly
853 Broadway, Suite 2120
New York, NY 10003

Jackie Goldberg
Los Angeles City Council
City Hall, Room 240
Los Angeles, CA 90012

Ricardo A. Gonzalez
Madison Common Council
504 Wisconsin Avenue, Number 1
Madison, WI 53703

Sarah Goodfriend
Public Utility Commission
7800 Shoal Creek Boulevard
Austin, TX 78757

Richard Gordon
San Mateo County Board of Education
101 Twin Dolphin Drive
Redwood City, CA 94065-1064

Edward Grandis
National Capital Planning Commission
1735 20th Street NW
Washington, DC 20009

Vernita Gray
Lesbian and Gay Victim-Witness Coordinator
Cook County State Attorney
2650 South California Street
First Floor
Chicago, IL 60608

Kenneth P. Hahn
Los Angeles County Assessor
500 West Temple Street, Room 320
Los Angeles, CA 90012

Edward Harrington
Controller
City Hall, Room 109
San Francisco, CA 94102

Gregory Harris
Chief of Staff
City Hall, Room 209
121 North LaSalle Street
Chicago, IL 60602

Jill Harris
New York City School Board, District 15
Legal Aid Society
175 Remsen Street
Brooklyn, NY 11201

Sherry Harris
Seattle City Council
600 Fourth Avenue
Seattle, WA 98104

Bob Hattoy
*Assistant Deputy Secretary and White
House Liaison*
U.S. Department of the Interior
1849 C Street NW, Room 5100
Washington, DC 20240-5100

Sheila Healy
Office of Lesbian and Gay Concerns
Executive Chambers of the Governor
Albany, NY 12224

Thomas Hehir
*Director of the Office of Special
Education Programs*
Department of Education
400 Maryland Avenue SW
Washington, DC 20202

John Heilman
West Hollywood City Council
8611 Santa Monica Boulevard
West Hollywood, CA 90069-4109

Emma Hixson
Department of Civil Rights
239 City Hall
Minneapolis, MN 55415

Mike Hodgson
Commissioner of Human Relations
1248 West Ardmore Avenue
Chicago, IL 60660

Nancy Hoff
Goshen Board of Selectmen
Post Office Box 109
Goshen, MA 01032

Jeff Horton
Los Angeles Board of Education
Post Office Box 3307
Los Angeles, CA 90051

Andy Humm
New York Human Rights Commission
445 West 23rd Street, Number 4-F
New York, NY 10011

Nan Hunter
Deputy General Counsel
U.S. Department of Health and
Human Services, Room 707F
330 Independence Avenue SW
Washington, DC 20201

Susan Hyde
Hartford City Council
52 Lincoln Street
Hartford, CT 06106

Babo Janssen
*Delaware State Advisory Commission
on Civil Rights*
39 Baltimore Avenue
Rehoboth Beach, DE 19971

Mitchell Katine
Texas Real Estate Commission
6671 Southwest Freeway, Suite 303
Houston, TX 77074-2209

Michael Keeley
Deputy Mayor for Civil Services
Office of the Mayor
200 North Spring Street
Los Angeles, CA 90012

Christine Kehoe
San Diego City Council
2515 Meade Avenue
San Diego, CA

Morris Kight
Commission on Human Relations
1148 Hall of Records
320 West Temple Street
Los Angeles, CA 90012

Stephen M. Lachs
Los Angeles Superior Court
111 North Hill Street
Los Angeles, CA 90012

Susan Leal
San Francisco Board of Supervisors
4115 26th Street
San Francisco, CA 94131

Bruce Lehman
Assistant Secretary of Commerce and
Commissioner of Patents and
Trademarks
U.S. Department of Commerce
Patents and Trademarks Office
14th Street and Constitution Avenue NW
Washington, DC 20231

Linda T. Leslie
Village Trustee
Post Office Box 511
Douglas, MI 49406

Mark Loveless
Community Representative of the
Pulaski School Board
2130 West McLean, Apartment 1
Chicago, IL 60647

Phyllis Lyon
San Francisco Human Rights Commission
651 Duncan Street
San Francisco, CA 94131

Tim O. Mains
Rochester City Council
413 Broadway
Rochester, NY 14607

David Martin
Assistant to the Assistant Secretary for
Legislative and Intergovernmental Affairs
U.S. Department of Commerce,
Room 5422
14th Street and Constitution Avenue NW
Washington, DC 20230

Art Mattox
Police Commissioner
Los Angeles Police Department
150 North Los Angeles Street
Number 150
Los Angeles, CA 90012

Glen Maxey
Texas House of Representatives
Post Office Box 2910
Austin, TX 78768

Vincent McCarthy
Chairman
Massachusetts Housing Partnership Fund
35 Riverview Road
Boston, MA 02135

Dale McCormick
Maine State Senate
RFD 1 Box 697
Monmouth, ME 04259

Craig McDaniel
Dallas City Council
Post Office Box 140944
Dallas, TX 75214-0944

Lawrence J. McKeon
Liaison to the Gay Community
City of Chicago
510 North Pestigo Court, Suite 608
Chicago, IL 60611

Scott Andrew Mendel
Hate Crimes Project Coordinator
Cook County State Attorney's Office
309 Richard J. Daley Center
Chicago, IL 60602

Ben Merrill
Special Assistant
White House Office of AIDS Policy
The White House
1600 Pennsylvania Avenue NW
Washington, DC 20500

Greg Mertz
Special Assistant
Office of Solid Waste
and Emergency Response
U.S. Environmental Protection Agency
401 M Street SW OS-100
Washington, DC 20460

Ellen A. Meyers
Liaison for Lesbian and Gay Issues
Cook County State Attorney's Office
406 Daley Center
Chicago, IL 60602

Carole Migden
San Francisco Board of Supervisors
City Hall, Room 235
San Francisco, CA 94102

Gary Miller
Robla School Board
363 Berthoud Street
Sacramento, CA 95838-1699

Tony Miller
Chief Deputy Secretary of State
1230 J Street
Sacramento, CA 95814

Mike Monosmith
Deputy Press Secretary
Mayor of Los Angeles
200 North Spring Street, Number 305
Los Angeles, CA 90012

Laura Moore
St. Louis Civil Rights Commission
10 North Tucker, 1 Mezzanine North
Civil Courts Building
St. Louis, MO 63101

Michael Morand
New Haven Board of Alders
Post Office Box 6537
New Haven, CT 06520

Howard Moses
*Deputy Assistant Secretary for Special
Education and Rehabilitative Services*
Department of Education
400 Maryland Avenue SW
Washington, DC 20202

Brandon Neese
Deputy County Clerk
118 North Clark Street, Room 434
Chicago, IL 60602

Michael Nelson
Carrboro Board of Aldermen
501 West Poplar Avenue
Carrboro, NC 27510

Zoon Nguyen
Special Assistant to the Assistant Secretary
U.S. Department of Housing and
Urban Development
451 Seventh Street S, Room 5100
Washington, DC 20410

Patrick Nolen
*Special Assistant to the Undersecretary
of Commerce*
International Trade Administration
Washington, DC 20230

Antonio Pagan
New York City Council
City Hall
New York, NY 10007

Jay Pagano
Neighborhood Advisory Committee 2B
1526 Connecticut Avenue NW
Washington, DC 20009

Joe Pais
Key West City Commission
Post Office Box 4381
Key West, FL 33041-4381

Annise Parker
Citizens Review Committee
Houston Police Department
609 Welch Street
Houston, TX 77006

Bob Pearce
Village Commissioner
28-V Fernwood Drive
Bolingbrook, IL 60440

David Peterson
*Confidential Assistant to the General
Counsel*
U.S. Department of Commerce
14th Street and Constitution Avenue NW
Room 5870
Washington, DC 20230

Miriam Pickus
Director of Human Rights
Compliance
510 North Peshtigo Court, Room 607
Chicago, IL 60611

Mark Pocan
Dane County Board of Supervisors
One East Gilman, Number 206
Madison, WI 53703

Julian Potter
Special Assistant to the Interagency
Council on the Homeless
U.S. Department of Housing and
Urban Development
800 4th Street SW, Apartment 417
Washington, DC 20024

Irene Rabinowitz
Board of Selectmen
7 Washington Avenue
Provincetown, MA 02657

Larry Ray
Neighborhood Advisory Committee
1825 T Street NW, Suite 404
Washington, DC 20009

Kenneth Reeves
Mayor of Cumbridge
City Hall
Cambridge, MA 02139

R. Paul Richard
Deputy Staff Secretary
The White House
1600 Pennsylvania Avenue NW
Washington, DC 20500

G. Keith Richardson
Housing Court Liaison
Clerk of the Circuit Court
Daley Center, Room 601
Chicago, IL 60602

Tom Roberts
Santa Barbara City Council
Post Office Box 91808
Santa Barbara, CA 93190

Marty Rouse
Director of the Office for the Lesbian
and Gay Community
52 Chambers Street, Room 311
New York, NY 10007

Bill Scott
Board of Directors
Texas Department of Health
3415 Graustark
Houston, TX 77006

Vivian Shapiro
New York City Human Rights
Commission
147 West 79th Street
New York, NY 10024

Gail Shibley
Oregon House of Representatives
Post Office Box 6805
Portland, OR 97310

Debra Silber
Civilian Complaint Review Board
305 Broadway, Suite 1201
New York, NY 10007

Richard Silver
Chief Clerk
San Mateo County
824 Winslow Street, Apartment 214
Redwood, CA 94063

Kevin M. Smith
Governor's Chief of Staff
360 State House
Boston, MA 02133

Richard Socarides
White House Liaison
U.S. Department of Labor
200 Constitution Avenue NW
Room S-1004
Washington, DC 20210

Abbey Soven
Los Angeles Superior Court
111 North Hill Street

Allan Spear
Minnesota State Senate
27 State Capitol
St. Paul, MN 55155

Cynthia Spires
Special Assistant
Office of the Secretary
U.S. Department of Housing and
Urban Development
451 Seventh Street SW, Room 5100
Washington, DC 20410

Keith C. St. John
Albany Common Council
116 Philip Street
Albany, NY 12202-1727

Liz Stefanics
New Mexico State Assembly
Post Office Box 1301
Santa Fe, NM 87504-1301

Gerry Studds
U.S. House of Representatives
237 Cannon House Office Building
Washington, DC 20515-2110

Wallace Swan
Board of Estimate and Taxation
Towers, A-420
15 South 1st Street
Minneapolis, MN 55401

Robert Sykora
Civil Rights Commissioner
332 Minnesota Street, Suite E1324
St. Paul, MN 55101-1314

Ron Tindle
Aldermanic Aide
City Hall, Room 209, Office 27
121 North Lasalle
Chicago, IL 60602

Katherine Triantifillou
Cambridge City Council
City Hall
Cambridge, MA 02139

David Tseng
*Special Assistant to the Assistant
Secretary of Labor*
Pension and Welfare Benefits
Administration, Room N-5677
200 Constitution Avenue NW
Washington, DC 20210

Gerald E. Ulrich
Mayor of Bunceton
City Hall
Post Office Box 200
Bunceton, MO 65237

James Vaughn
Mayoral Aide
Office of the Mayor
200 North Spring Street
Los Angeles, CA 90012

Carlos Velez
Director of the AIDS Prevention Cluster
White House Office of AIDS Policy
The White House
1600 Pennsylvania Avenue NW
Washington, DC 20500

Braulio Veloz
Community Action Advisory Board
230 West Craig Place
San Antonio, TX 78212-3421

Richard Wagner
Dane County Board of Supervisors
739 Jenifer Street
Madison, WI 53703

Steve Wakefield
City Board of Health
1948 West Evergreen
Chicago, IL 60622

Brian Wheeler
*Special Assistant to the Assistant
Secretary*
Department of Commerce
14th Street and Constitution Avenue NW
Room 3422
Washington, DC 20230

Chris Wilson
Oakland Park City Council
Post Office Box 70187
Oakland Park, FL 33307

Janice Wilson
Multnomah County District Court
1021 SW Fourth Avenue
Portland, OR 97204

Tim Wolfred
San Francisco Community College
Governing Board
975 Duncan Street
San Francisco, CA 94131

Cynthia Wooten
Oregon House of Representatives
State House of Representatives
State Capitol
Salem, OR 97310

Ken Yeager
San Jose Community College Trustee
1925 Cleveland Avenue
San Jose, CA 95126

Victor Zonana
Deputy Secretary for Public Affairs
U.S. Department of Health and Human
Services, Room 638 E
200 Independence Avenue SW
Washington, DC 20201

Political Organizations

ALABAMA
Gulf Alliance for Equality
1102 Ginion Circle
Mobile, AL 36605

ALASKA
Alaskans for Civil Rights
Post Office Box 201348
Anchorage, AK 99520
Phone: 907-258-3439

ARIZONA
Arizona Human Rights Fund
Post Office Box 26
Phoenix, AZ 85001-0026

Lambda Democratic Caucus
Debra Broner
Post Office Box 3501
Tucson, AZ 85722
Phone: 602-791-7000

ARKANSAS
Arkansas Women's Political Caucus
Post Office Box 2494
Little Rock, AR 72203

Gay and Lesbian Action Delegation
Post Office Box 2897
Fayetteville, AR 72702

CALIFORNIA
Alice B. Toklas Democratic Club
Matthew Rothschild
Post Office Box 422698
San Francisco, CA 94142-2698
Phone: 415-621-3296

Bay Area Municipal Elections Committee
Post Office Box 90070
San Jose, CA 95109
Phone: 408-297-1024

California Capital PAC
Linda Bivner
1008 10th Street, Suite 255
Sacramento, CA 95814

Lesbian and Gay Caucus of the California Democratic Party
Robert Barnes
c/o 910A Steiner Street
San Francisco, CA 94117
Phone: 415-864-6118

East Bay Lesbian and Gay Democratic Club
Post Office Box 443
Berkeley, CA 94701

Gay and Lesbian Action Alliance
Post Office Box 7293
Santa Cruz, CA 95061

International Gay and Lesbian
Human Rights Commission
Jorge Cortinez
520 Castro Street
San Francisco, CA 94114
Phone: 415-255-8680

Lambda Democratic Club
Post Office Box 14454
Long Beach, CA 90803

Lesbian Agenda for Action
3543 18th Street, Number 32
San Francisco, CA 94110

Long Beach Lambda
Democratic Club
Post Office Box 14454
Long Beach, CA 90803

Radical Women
National Office
Nancy Reiko-Kato
523-A Valencia Street
San Francisco, CA 94110
Phone: 415-864-1278

River City Democratic Club
Michael Boyd
Post Office Box 161958
Sacramento, CA 95816
Phone: 916-448-2383

San Diego Democratic Club
Post Office Box 80193
San Diego, CA 92138

Stonewall Democratic Club
Al Rodriguez
Post Office Box 26367
Los Angeles, CA 90026
Phone: 213-969-1735

Stonewall Gay Democratic Club
150 Eureka Street
San Francisco, CA 94114

Uptown Democratic Club
Post Office Box 3113
San Diego, CA 92163
Phone: 619-286-5571

West Hollywood Democratic Club
Post Office Box 691005
West Hollywood, CA 90069
Phone: 213-343-1908

CONNECTICUT
Connecticut Coalition for
Lesbian and Gay Civil Rights
Charlotte Kinlock
Post Office Box 141025
Hartford, CT 06114

WASHINGTON, D.C.
Gay and Lesbian Activists Alliance
Jeff Courtier
1734 14th Street NW, Second Floor
Washington, DC 20009
Phone: 202-667-5139

Gay and Lesbian Victory Fund
William Waybourn
1012 14th Street NW, Suite 707
Washington, DC 20005
Phone: 202-842-8679

Gertrude Stein Democratic
Club
Post Office Box 21067
Washington, DC 20009
Phone: 202-232-5198

Human Rights Campaign Fund
1012 14th Street NW, Suite 607
Washington, DC 20005
Phone: 202-628-4160
Fax: 202-347-5323

Log Cabin Republicans
1012 14th Street NW, Suite 703
Washington, DC 20005
Phone: 202-347-5307

National Gay and Lesbian Task Force
1734 14th Street NW
Washington, DC 20009-4309
Phone: 202-332-6483

National Organization of Women
Alice Cohan
1000 16th Street NW, Suite 700
Washington, DC 20036
Phone: 202-331-0066
Fax: 202-785-8576

FLORIDA
Atlantic Coast Democratic Club
3273 Grove Road
Boynton Beach, FL 33435

Dade ActionPAC
Shari McCartney
Post Office Box 431151
Miami, FL 33243-1151
Phone: 305-757-6833

Dan Bradley Democratic Club
Alex Sanchez
Post Office Box 107
Coconut Grove, FL 33233
Phone: 305-446-2806

Dolphin Democratic Club
Post Office Box 4646
Fort Lauderdale, FL 33338-4646
Phone: 813-563-4879

Floridians Respecting Everyone's Equality
Post Office Box 20021
Tallahassee, FL 32316
Phone: 904-561-6336

Floridians United Against Discrimination
1409 Rodman Street
Hollywood, FL 33020
Phone: 904-656-7661

Rainbow Democratic Club
Post Office Box 532041
Orlando, FL 32853-2041
Phone: 407-236-9476

GEORGIA
GAPAC
Ed Stansell
Post Office Box 8420
Atlanta, GA 30306
Phone: 404-872-8095

Republicans for Individual Freedoms
Gary Bastien
Post Office Box 13162
Atlanta, GA 30324
Phone: 404-239-1679

HAWAII
Alliance for Equal Rights
Post Office Box 240423
Honolulu, HI 96837
Phone: 808-373-9000

Gay and Lesbian Education and Advocacy
Post Office Box 37083
Honolulu, HI 96837-0083
Phone: 808-526-3000

IDAHO
Idaho Voices for Human Rights
2027 Springbrook Lane
Boise, ID 83706
Phone: 208-336-7351

ILLINOIS
IMPACT
909 West Belmont, Suite 201
Chicago, IL 60657
Phone: 312-528-5868

IOWA
**Des Moines Gay and Lesbian
Democratic Club**
3500 Kingman Boulevard
Des Moines, IA 50311

LOUISIANA
**Louisiana Lesbian and Gay
Political Action Caucus**
Jim Wiltberger
Post Office Box 53075
New Orleans, LA 70153
Phone: 504-522-6629

Rainbow Coalition
Post Office Box 70811
New Orleans, LA 70172

**Louisiana Electorate of Gays and
Lesbians**
Post Office Box 70344
New Orleans, LA 70172

MAINE
Maine Civil Liberties Union
97A Exchange Street
Portland, ME 04104
Phone: 207-774-1200

**Maine Lesbian and
Gay Political Alliance**
Dave Garrity
174 Danforth Street
Portland, ME 04102

MARYLAND
Free State Justice Campaign
John Hannay
Post Office Box 13221
Baltimore, MD 21203
Phone: 410-837-7282

**Gay and Lesbian Interest
Consortium**
John Burlison
c/o 2101 Bucknell Terrace
Silver Spring, MD 20902
Phone: 301-220-4089

**Lesbian and Gay Democrats
of Montgomery County**
John Burlison
c/o 2101 Bucknell Terrace
Silver Spring, MD 20902
Phone: 301-946-0517

Prince Georgians for Equal Rights
Kevin Watkins
c/o 7024 Hanover Parkway
Number B2
Greenbelt, MD 20770
Phone: 301-982-4875

MASSACHUSETTS
Cambridge Lavender Alliance
Sue Hyde
Post Office Box 884
Cambridge, MA 02238
Phone: 617-354-7457

**Coalition for Lesbian
and Gay Civil Rights**
David Lafontaine
Post Office Box 611
Cambridge, MA 02238
Phone: 617-828-3039

Grass Roots Gay Rights Fund
Jeff Lane
533 Columbus Avenue, Number 11
Boston, MA 02118
Phone: 617-536-6395

Greater Boston Lesbian and Gay Political Alliance
Don Gorton
Post Office Box 65
Back Bay Annex
Boston, MA 02117
Phone: 617-338-GAYS

Massachusetts Gay and Lesbian Political Caucus
Arline Isaacson
Post Office Box 246
State House
Boston, MA 02133
Phone: 617-262-1565

MICHIGAN
Michigan Coalition for Human Dignity
Bob Egan
Post Office Box 27383
Lansing, MI 48909-7283
Phone: 517-887-2605

Michigan Coalition for Human Rights
Katherine Savoie
4800 Woodward Avenue
Detroit, MI 48201
Phone: 313-831-0258

Michigan Lesbian and Gay Democratic Caucus
Post Office Box 1708
Royal Oak, MI 48068

MINNESOTA
International Network of Lesbian and Gay Officials
Tim Cole
3801 26th Street East
Minneapolis, MN 55406-1857
Phone: 612-724-5581

Minnesota Independent Republican Club
2518 Blaisdell Avenue South
Minneapolis, MN 55404
Phone: 612-377-7778

Prairie Lesbian and Gay Community
Post Office Box 83
Moorhead, MN 56560

MONTANA
Pride Montana
Diane Sands
Post Office Box 775
Helena, MT 59624

MISSOURI
Action
Gay/Lesbian Human Rights Caucus
Debbie Law
Post Office Box 1926
St. Louis, MO 63118
Phone: 314-997-9897

Human Rights League for Lesbians and Gays
Post Office Box 92674
Milwaukee, WI 53202

Human Rights PAC
7230B Raytown Road
Raytown, MO 64135

Privacy Rights Education Project
Post Office Box 24106
St. Louis, MO 63130
Phone: 314-862-4900

Triangle Coalition
Jeff Passmore
A022 Brady Commons
University of Missouri
Columbia, MO 65211
Phone: 314-882-4427

NEBRASKA
Citizens for Equal Protection
Neva Cozine
Post Office Box 55548
Omaha, NE 68155

Coalition for Gay and Lesbian Civil Rights
Post Office Box 94882
Lincoln, NE 68509

NEW HAMPSHIRE
Citizens Alliance for Gay and Lesbian Rights
Post Office Box 816
Concord, NH 03302
Phone: 603-798-5187

NEW MEXICO
New Mexico Lesbian and Gay Political Alliance
Post Office Box 25191
Albuquerque, NM 87125

NEW YORK
Citizens for Equal Rights Fund PAC
Sharon Randall
Post Office Box 301
Upton, NY 11973
Phone: 516-399-3891

Coalition for Lesbian and Gay Rights
Eleanor Cooper
208 West 13th Street
New York, NY 10025
Phone: 212-627-1398

East End Gay Organization
Sandy Papp
Post Office Box 708
Bridgehampton, NY 11932-0077
Phone: 516-324-3699

Eleanor Roosevelt Democratic Club
Post Office Box 2180
Albany, NY 12220-2180

Empire State Pride Agenda
Dick Dadey
611 Broadway, Number 907A
New York, NY 10012
Phone: 212-673-5417

Gay and Lesbian Independent Democrats
Laura Morrison
208 West 13th Street
New York, NY 10025
Phone: 212-475-0271

Lambda Independent Democrats
Liz Schalet
309 5th Avenue, Number 434
Brooklyn, NY 11215
Phone: 718-361-3322

Queens Gays and Lesbians United
Ed Sedarbaum
Post Office Box 4669
Sunnyside, NY 11104
Phone: 718-463-2938

Rochester Lesbian and Gay Political Caucus
Bill Pritchard
179 Atlantic Avenue
Rochester, NY 14607-1255
Phone: 716-244-8640

Stonewall Democratic Club
Brice Peyre
Post Office Box 1750
Old Chelsea Station
New York, NY 10011
Phone: 212-969-8854

Voter Registration Project/Lesbian and Gay Community Center
208 West 13th Street
New York, NY 10011
Phone: 212-620-7310

NORTH CAROLINA
North Carolina Coalition for Gay and Lesbian Equality
Post Office Box 15533
Winston-Salem, NC 27113

North Carolina Pride PAC
Post Office Box 813
Carrboro, NC 27510
Phone: 919-968-8900

North Carolina Human Rights Fund
Post Office Box 10782
Raleigh, NC 27605

Orange Lesbian/Gay Association
Doug Ferguson
Post Office Box 307
Chapel Hill, NC 27514
Phone: 919-932-5817
Fax: 919-839-3066

OHIO
Bisexuals Engaging in Politics
Barbara Nicely
Post Office Box 594
Northfield, OH 44067
Phone: 216-467-6442

Citizens for Justice
1487 West 5th Avenue, Box 226
Columbus, OH 43212
Phone: 614-228-5878
Fax: 614-224-4708

Greater Cincinnati Gay and Lesbian Coalition
Post Office Box 19158
Cincinnati, OH 45219

Jerry Mayer Democratic Club
Lynn Greer
1227 Neil Avenue
Columbus, OH 43201
Phone: 614-294-3953

Out Voice
1487 West 5th Avenue, Box 226
Columbus, OH 43212
Phone: 614-228-5878
Fax: 614-224-4708

Stonewall Cincinnati
Kelly Malone
Post Office Box 954
Cincinnati, OH 45201
Phone: 513-541-8778

Stonewall Cleveland
Post Office Box 5936
Cleveland, OH 44101

Stonewall Union
Post Office Box 10814
Columbus, OH 43201-7814

Stonewall of Ohio PAC
B. Scott Sanchez
Post Office Box 10095
Columbus, OH 43201
Phone: 614-299-7764

OKLAHOMA

Simply Equal
Post Office Box 61305
Oklahoma City, OK 73146
Phone: 405-842-2922

**Tulsa Oklahomans for
Human Rights**
Post Office Box 52729
Tulsa, OK 74152
Phone: 918-743-GAYS

**Oklahoma Gay and Lesbian
Political Caucus**
Paul Thompson
Post Office Box 61186
Oklahoma City, OK 73146
Phone: 405-524-2131

OREGON

**Citizens United Against
Discrimination**
Kelly Weigel
380 East 40th Street, Number 107
Eugene, OR 97405
Phone: 503-485-1755

**Electronic Political Action
in the Gay Environment**
Post Office Box 19851
Portland, OR 97280-0851
Phone: 503-727-7243

**Gay and Lesbian United
Effort PAC**
Muril Demory
Post Office Box 2004
Newport, OR 97365
Phone: 503-265-3087

Lesbian and Gay Democratic Club
Robert Ralphs
Post Office Box 36
Sherwood, OR 97140
Phone: 503-625-5795

Lesbian and Gay Caucus
Oregon Democratic Party
1703 SW Montgomery Drive
Portland, OR 97201

Right to Privacy PAC
921 SW Morrison, Number 518
Portland, OR 97205
Phone: 503-228-5825

**Southern Oregon Lambda
Association**
Post Office Box 4387
Medford, OR 97501

Support Our Communities
Post Office Box 40625
Portland, OR 97240
Phone: 503-222-6151

PENNSYLVANIA

League of Gay and LesbianVoters
Chris Young
Penn West Office Building
909 West Street, Suite 150
Pittsburg, PA 15221
Phone: 412-243-8337

League of Gay and LesbianVoters
Post Office Box 3063
Erie, PA 16508
Phone: 814-456-9833

**Lesbian and Gay Pride of the
Delaware Valley**
Post Office Box 395
Philadelphia, PA 19105

**Pennsylvania Justice Campaign
for Lesbian and Gay Rights**
Patrick Wallen
Post Office Box 614
Harrisburg, PA 17108
Phone: 717-234-2250

**Philadelphia Equal
Rights Coalition**
4519 Osage
Philadelphia, PA 19143

**Philadelphia Lesbian
and Gay Task Force**
Rita Addessa
1616 Walnut Street, Suite 105
Philadelphia, PA 19103
Phone: 215-772-2000

Tri-PAC
414 South Craig Street, Number 282
Pittsburg, PA 15213

RHODE ISLAND
Network of Rhode Island
Post Office Box 1474
Pawtucket, RI 02862-1474

**Rhode Island Alliance for Gay
and Lesbian Civil Rights**
Post Office Box 5758
Weybosset Hill Station
Providence, RI 02903
Phone: 401-861-4686

SOUTH CAROLINA
**South Carolina Gay and Lesbian
Pride Movement, Inc.**
Post Office Box 12648
Columbia, SC 29211

**South Carolina Women's
Consortium**
Post Office Box 3099
Columbia, SC 29230

Voters United for Equality
Tim Fowler
Post Office Box 8381
Greenville, SC 29604
Phone: 803-235-5019

TENNESSEE
Memphis Gay Coalition
Post Office Box 3038
Memphis, TN 38173-0038

**Tennessee Gay and
Lesbian Alliance**
Post Office Box 41305
Nashville, TN 37204-1305

TEXAS
**Austin Lesbian and Gay
Political Caucus**
602 West Seventh Street
Austin, TX 78701
Phone: 512-474-0750

**Houston Gay and Lesbian
Political Caucus**
Terri Richardson
Post Office Box 66664
Houston, TX 77266
Phone: 713-521-1000

Lesbian and Gay Political
Coalition of Dallas
Paul Rogers
Post Office Box 224424
Dallas, TX 75222
Phone: 214-357-1660

Lesbian and Gay
Democrats of Texas
Post Office Box 190933
Dallas, TX 75219

Lesbian/Gay Rights
Lobby of Texas
Laurie Eiserloh
Post Office Box 2579
Austin, TX 78768-2579
Phone: 512-474-5475

Metroplex Republicans
Post Office Box 191033
Dallas, TX 75219-8033
Phone: 214-941-8114

Texas Republicans for
Equality and Privacy
Post Office Box 191033
Dallas, TX 75219-8033

UTAH
Gay and Lesbian
Utah Democrats
Post Office Box 11311
Salt Lake City, UT 84147
Phone: 801-461-5058
Toll-free: 800-864-0310

VERMONT
Northeast Vermonters for Gay
and Lesbian Rights
c/o Umbrella
1 Prospect Street
Saint Johnsbury, VT 05819
Phone: 802-748-8645

Vermont Coalition of Lesbians
and Gay Men
Post Office Box 1125
Montpelier, VT 05602

VIRGINIA
Virginia Partisan Gay and
Lesbian Democratic Club
Adam Ebbin
Post Office Box 20633
Alexandria, VA 22320
Phone: 703-548-2264

Virginia Political Action Network
Ken Stillson
2036 Peach Orchard, Number 21
Falls Church, VA 22043

Virginians for Justice
Janice Conard
Post Office Box 342
Capitol Station
Richmond, VA 23202
Phone: 804-643-4816

WASHINGTON
Seattle Municipal Elections
Committee for Gays, Lesbians
and Bisexuals
1202 East Pike, Number 901
Seattle, WA 98122-3934

Stonewall Committee for
Lesbian and Gay Rights
Chris Smith
6727 Seward Park Avenue South
Seattle, WA 98118
Phone: 206-722-0938

Washington Freedom Coalition
Post Office Box 7703
Olympia, WA 98507

WISCONSIN
Lambda Rights Network
Post Office Box 93252
Milwaukee, WI 53203

Lesbian Alliance Metro
Milwaukee
Post Office Box 93323
Milwaukee, WI 53203

Madison Community United
Jane Vanderbosch
14 East Mifflin
Madison, WI 53703
Phone: 608-255-8582

Gay and Lesbian
Visibility Alliance
Post Office Box 1403
Madison, WI 53701-1403

For more information about the political organizations listed here, please call the Victory Fund at (202) VICTORY.

If you were not listed in *Out for Office,* but would like to be included in the Victory Fund database and in future publications or lists, please complete the following information and mail to:

Out for Office
Gay and Lesbian Victory Fund
1012 14th Street NW, Suite 707
Washington, DC 20005

Name of political organization/openly gay or lesbian official/ campaign professional

Contact person

Mailing address

City   State   Zip

*Phone:*_____
*Fax:*_____

- ❑ *Consulting*
- ❑ *Direct Mail*
- ❑ *Polling*
- ❑ *Targeting*
- ❑ *Research*
- ❑ *Voter Identification*
- ❑ *Products and Services*
- ❑ *Advertising*
- ❑ *Media Relations*
- ❑ *Copywriting/Written Materials*
- ❑ *Finances/Fundraising*

- ❑ *Graphic Design*
- ❑ *Creative Services*
- ❑ *Communications*
- ❑ *Campaign Manager*
- ❑ *Public Relations/Publicity*
- ❑ *Printing/Copying*
- ❑ *Radio/Television*
- ❑ *Film/Video*
- ❑ *Photography*
- ❑ *Production Services*
- ❑ *Other*_____

JUST WHEN YOU THOUGHT ONE PERSON COULDN'T MAKE A DIFFERENCE:

▼ Seattle City Councilmember Sherry Harris has sponsored or cosponsored nine gay-positive ordinances and resolutions.

▼ Washington State Representative Cal Anderson introduced HB1443, a measure that would give gays and lesbians equal protection against discrimination. He is also the prime backer of another bill that would outlaw malicious harassment of gays and lesbians.

▼ Wisconsin State Assemblymember Tammy Baldwin is drafting a statewide domestic partnership bill.

▼ Oregon State Representative Gail Shibley sponsored three gay-positive bills this legislative session: one banning employment discrimination based on sexual orientation, one deleting the definition of sodomy as deviant sexual intercourse and the third calling on Congress to repeal the ban against gays and lesbians in the military.

▼ Texas State Representative Glen Maxey proposed a bill that would ban discrimination on the basis of sexual orientation.

▼ U.S. Congressman Gerry Studds, an original sponsor of the Lesbian and Gay Civil Rights Bill and the bill to rescind the Department of Defense's directive against gays and lesbians in the military, cosponsored the Comprehensive HIV Prevention Act.

▼ U.S. Congressman Barney Frank sponsored the provision that ended discrimination against gays and lesbians in America's immigration laws.

▼ Minnesota State Senator Allan Spear and Representative Karen Clark led the successful fight to extend protection to gays and lesbians under the state's Human Rights Act.

▼ State Senator Dale McCormick and State Representative Susan Farnsworth are spearheading a ninth attempt to pass a gay and lesbian civil rights bill in Maine.

FINANCIAL CLOUT FOR CANDIDATES WE CAN COUNT ON!

❏ I want to join the Victory Fund network today. Please send me detailed profiles of openly lesbian and gay candidates from across the country who need my support to win. I enclose:

❏ $100 ❏ $500 ❏ $1000 ❏ Other $ ___

❏ I want to support the Victory Fund and its programs to elect openly gay and lesbian candidates to office. I enclose:

❏ $25 ❏ $50 ❏ $75 ❏ Other $ ___

GAY AND LESBIAN **VICTORY FUND**

❏ Check enclosed
❏ MasterCard
❏ Visa
❏ Discover

NAME

ADDRESS

CITY, STATE, ZIP

PHONE

CREDIT CARD ACCT. #

EXP. DATE

SIGNATURE

Make checks payable to the Victory Fund and mail with this coupon to 1012 14th Street NW, Suite 707, Washington DC 20005. For more information call the Victory Fund at (202) VICTORY. Contributions are not tax-deductible.

YOU CAN MAKE A DIFFERENCE!
JOIN THE GAY AND LESBIAN VICTORY FUND

The Gay and Lesbian Victory Fund gratefully acknowledges the following individuals for their generous support.

Sponsors

George Harris and Jack Evans
Dallas, TX

Michael Smith
San Francisco, CA

Howard J. Cavalero
East Hampton, NY

Capitol City Brewing Company
Washington, DC

Carl Rosendorf
Weston, MA

David Franco
Washington, DC

Fentress Ott
San Diego, CA

Patrons

Edith Dee Cofrin
Atlanta, GA

David Geffen
Los Angeles, CA

Edward Gould
Encino, CA

Charles Holmes
San Francisco, CA

Jonathan Sheffer
New York, NY

In Memory of

Colin Higgins, Jerry E.Berg, Jim Proby and Steven Kozak

The Colin Higgins Foundation
San Francisco, CA

Underwriter

Ron Ansin
Harvard, MA

Underwriter

Terry Watanabe
Omaha, NE

Underwriter

Andrew E. Barrer
Washington, DC

Underwriter

Henry van Ameringen
New York, NY

Underwriter

Miller Brewing Company
Milwaukee, WI

In Memoriam

The Honorable
Harvey Milk
San Francisco Board of Supervisors

The Honorable
Ronald Squires
Vermont State Legislature

The Honorable
Bryan Coyle
Minneapolis City Council

The Honorable
Richard C. Failla
New York State Supreme Court

The Honorable
Rand Schrader
Los Angeles Municipal Court Judge